THE ROMANTIC RHETORIC
OF ACCUMULATION

The Romantic Rhetoric of Accumulation

◆

LENORA HANSON

STANFORD UNIVERSITY PRESS
Stanford, California

Stanford University Press
Stanford, California
© 2023 by Lenora Hanson. All rights reserved.

No part of this book may be reproduced or transmitted in any form or by any means, electronic or mechanical, including photocopying and recording, or in any information storage or retrieval system without the prior written permission of Stanford University Press. Printed in the United States of America on acid-free, archival-quality paper

Library of Congress Cataloging-in-Publication Data
Names: Hanson, Lenora, author.
Title: The Romantic rhetoric of accumulation / Lenora Hanson.
Description: Stanford, California : Stanford University Press, 2022. | Includes bibliographical references and index.
Identifiers: LCCN 2022022176 (print) | LCCN 2022022177 (ebook) | ISBN 9781503632714 (cloth) | ISBN 9781503633940 (paperback) | ISBN 9781503633957 (epub)
Subjects: LCSH: English literature—18th century—History and criticism. | Capitalism in literature. | Discourse analysis, Literary. | Romanticism—Great Britain.
Classification: LCC PR448.C34 H36 2022 (print) | LCC PR448.C34 (ebook) | DDC 820.9/3553—dc23/eng/20220727
LC record available at https://lccn.loc.gov/2022022176
LC ebook record available at https://lccn.loc.gov/2022022177

Cover design: George Kirkpatrick
Cover art: J. M. W. Turner, *Shade and Darkness—the Evening of the Deluge*, oil on canvas, 1843
Typeset by Elliott Beard in Arno Pro 11/15

Contents

	Acknowledgments	vii
	Introduction	1
	The Romantic Rhetoric of Accumulation	
1	**Apostrophe and Riot**	35
2	**Anachronism, Dreams, and Enclosure**	71
3	**Tautology, Witchcraft, and a Thingly Commons**	97
4	**Figure, Space, and Race between 1769 and 1985**	139
	Coda	183
	Rhetorical Reading toward a Global Romanticism	
	Notes	211
	Bibliography	255
	Index	271

Acknowledgments

THIS BOOK FEELS MORE LIKE the side effect of many conversations that roam across and far exceed any university or discipline, even if the latter often provided an occasion for conversational gathering. The conversations that morphed into this book emerged at labor union meetings that sometimes felt as if they'd never end and that now I often wish hadn't; in hallways and text messages after graduate seminars; through serendipitous encounters with other lovers of Romanticism, poetry, and philosophy who had responded to the Palestinian call for solidarity through an academic boycott of Israeli academic institutions; after poetry readings in Madison, Wisconsin, and New York City; on Skype calls—it wasn't Zoom back then—to organize meetings as university workers about survival and precarity that took the form of a counterconference; at gatherings of autonomously organized abolitionist libraries; through friendships that sparked after the contingency of conference panel meetings. That is to say, this book is not the effect of particularly direct conversations but rather an association of indirect, incomplete, afterward, and undisciplined social relations. I don't know if those whom I have in mind as interlocutors will see some trace of themselves here, and I certainly do not want to make them responsible for what follows. But I want to acknowledge them as resources without which I could not think.

I cannot imagine having found Romanticism to be a hospitable literary home without the work of Sara Guyer, Celeste Langan, Rei Terada, Anne Lise-François, and Amanda Jo Goldstein. In particular, Sara's work lured me into Romanticism with its beauty and rigor and gave me tools for reading that could be repurposed through wandering. And to Samantha Webb, thanks for starting me off on this path with so much faith.

At the University of Wisconsin–Madison, I learned how to think and write about literature in ways that prepared me to write this book. To Mario Ortiz-Robles, thanks for an education in insatiable curiosity and de Manian precision. To Theresa M. Kelley, thanks for inspiring my interest in Romantic science. Caroline Levine was an exemplary model of generative and engaged disagreement. Ernesto Livorni was a truly Romantic interlocutor, always prepared for a long walk, no matter the weather. Julia Dauer, Devin Garofalo, Anna Vitale, and Lewis Freedman made writing feel like an ongoing conversation.

My research was supported by a Mellon/ACLS fellowship and by the Jacob K. Javits Foundation; without that support this book would not exist. Michael Demson, Christopher Clason, and Brian Price gave me different spaces for beginning to work out new ideas about Romanticism that provided a much-needed transition point between my earlier work and this book. Thanks especially to Brian for the formative community that World Picture provided. At the University of Nebraska–Lincoln, I was introduced to many of the questions and problems with which this book struggles by Nicholas Spencer, Marco Abel, Aaron Hillyer, and Roland Végső.

Many thanks to Michael Hardt, Gigi Roggero, Anna Curcio, Chris Newfield, Elise Thorburn, Eli Meyerhoff, Max Haiven, Thea Sircar, and Zach Schwartz-Weinstein for creating and re-creating so many common spaces throughout my graduate studies, and particularly to Elsa Noterman: I am so grateful that you showed up across the street from the English Department to create new forms of kinship and study with and for me.

At NYU I've been routinely overwhelmed with the kindness and support of colleagues and friends far afield from Romanticism. Pacharee Sudhinaraset, Simón Trujillo, Nick Boggs, Juliet Fleming, Brandon Woolf, John Archer, Pat Crain, Patrick Deer, Paula McDowell, Liz McHenry, Jini Kim Watson, and Greg Vargo have made the English Department an incredible home.

In recent years, David Lloyd, Fred Moten, Laura Harris, Jordy Rosenberg, Mary Mullen, Eddie Connor, Michelle Castañeda, Pedro Cabello, and Silvio have offered exceptional kin- and comradeship. The ways I've thought about Romanticism in my time in New York have forever changed thanks to Maureen N. McLane, Joe Albernaz, and Matthew Sandler. Maureen, you've been more than a mentor—more like a prototype—in a poetics of living. Joe, thanks for oscillating with me between a love for the classroom and dreams of escaping the institutions that hold them. I am deeply indebted Frédéric Neyrat's indifference to measuring time, both in office hours and in life. To Laura Goldblatt and Bennett Carpenter, thanks for the survival strategy of your friendship and fellow-traveling in unprofessional activities. To Alex Wolfson, may we never know where your thoughts end and mine begin. To Sonya Postmentier, Dara Regaignon, and Paula Chakravarty, you continue to knit new patterns of solidarity to hold life together, both inside and outside the walls of the university. To Wendy Anne Lee, thanks for the uniquely unbounded enthusiasm that no other mortal I know possesses. Through Walter Johnston I found a gorgeously ungrounded Romanticism in which friendship flourishes; you are so deeply missed. To Elaine Freedgood for offering such a welcoming home in my first few years at NYU. To Marie Buck for more hours, thoughts, provocations, and poetry recommendations than I can recount. To Kay Gabriel, for reading me poems in the street. To Brian Whitener for the shelter of your home and the radical presence of your conversation. To Daniel Nemser and Amanda Armstrong for opening up entirely new ways of knowing to me. To Joshua Clover, thanks for the spontaneity of your unparalleled generosity, in words and actions. Paul Youngquist and Fran Botkin have shown me that criticality and joy can coexist—and travel. Rebecca Comay has continuously inspired and sustained my desire to reread texts I thought I knew, both through her writing and in our conversations. Darien Lamen has been an unending source of dialogue and dreaming. More recently, Mohommad

Sakhnini, Sarah Copsey Alsader, Donna Landry, and Sahar Darabeaa have been the spark for developing connections between Romanticisms of past and present and the Palestinian struggle. And not a single word of this book would have been written without the patient care of Romy Reading.

Thanks to Kate Singer, David Ruderman, Taylor Schey, Walter Johnston, Eric Lindstrom, Manu Chander, and David Collings for making NASSR a conference to look forward to each year. Carmen Faye-Matthes, Nathan Snaza, Julietta Singh, and again Walter Johnston invited me to conference panels at crucial points of this project.

I'm so grateful to have first come to Marx through labor struggles alongside Eleni Schirmer, Adrienne Pagac, Sigrid Peterson, Michael Billeaux, Katie Linstrom, Matt Moehr, Kevin Gibbons, Nancy Rydberg, Alex Hanna, and Colin Gillis.

I want to thank the graduate students in my Romanticism, Race, and the Life Sciences seminar and my Romantic Habits seminar, especially Alliya Dagman, Heba Jahama, Gabriella Johnson, Alex Ramos, Corey Risinger, Isaac Robertson, and Ryan Healey. To Guilherme Meyer and Colin Vanderburg, thanks for continually inspiring conversations, especially at the picket line. And thanks to Corey Risinger, again, for swooping in at the end of the project and providing so much excellent research support.

Finally, but certainly not last, my thanks and love to Ciarán Coyle, who has accompanied me in a practice of questioning, struggling, and differing in more ways than I could ever have expected.

THE ROMANTIC RHETORIC
OF ACCUMULATION

Introduction

The Romantic Rhetoric of Accumulation

Romanticism, Dispossessed

Dispossession is both a ubiquitous and a marginal term in our definitions of Romanticism. On the one hand, the historical process of enclosure appears consistently in introductory contextualizations of Romantic poetry, especially that of John Clare, where it tends to refer directly to the Enclosure Acts, through which five million acres of common fields were privatized between 1760 and 1810.[1] Enclosure here refers to a historical period in which an agrarian mode of production was finally dismantled, making possible the emergence of industrialized labor and commodity production. On the other hand, dispossession has been defined in ontological terms by deconstructive readers of Romanticism, for whom it names an alternative to the self-possessed and autonomous subject inaugurated by a deeply Wordsworthian orientation to a modern market and the extinction of other ways of being.[2] A critical enclosure has resulted from these quite distinctive approaches in which dispossession marks the successful subsumption of modernity by capital's "force of self-infinitizing, subjectifying, repetitive motion" under the dominance of industrialized capitalism.[3] As a result, rhetorical and poetic language become fixed as either a lost past or an ontology of difference cut off from material and historical conditions. The constitutive indeterminacy and openness prompted by figurative language is claimed always in oppositional or subversive relation to a modernity defined by the capitalist drives of development and homogenization.

This book proposes another relation across Romanticism, rhetorical reading, and capitalism through the entwinement of subsistence ways of living and the processes of dispossession that seek to destroy them. Dispossession here is not a purely temporal marker that inaugurates an essential opposition between rhetorical language and history but is, rather, the figural, which is to say, the logically contradictory, origins of capital accumulation that rely upon the reproduction of noncapitalist ways of living. Histories of dispossession cannot be separated from the figural means of subsistence with which they become enmeshed and which Romanticism helps us to see as deeply figural ways of living. They are, to borrow from the preeminent Romantic poet of enclosure, John Clare, "a thread's end in ravelled windings crossing."[4] Where Marxist and deconstructive readers alike have presumed a singular historical model for the development of capitalism, here I propose that dispossession is a historical process that cannot be accounted for by narratives of transition and the loss of "communal property . . . which lived under the cover of feudalism."[5] Instead, this project inhabits the figural knot of capitalism's simultaneous dependency upon and destruction of the noncapitalist ways in which people reproduce themselves and each other from one day to the next. In this association between figure and subsistence, which is also an association with dispossession and enclosure, it becomes impossible to treat the rhetorical or poetic as an always subversive resource or site of alterity, or capitalist modernity as a machine of sameness or homogeneity. With this project, I work to undo such binaries in favor of ways of life and language rooted in the impure solidarities required by the passage from one day to the next or the "unpalatable agreements and actions communities have to resort to in order to guarantee their members' survival."[6] If Romanticism is to remain useful for us today, it will be because its peculiarly rhetorical approach to history makes it easier to understand how capitalism has emerged since the late eighteenth century not purely through contradictions but through coincidences, simultaneities, apostrophes, anachronisms, and tautologies.

While often referred to as a meager or bare means of survival, subsistence ways of living also acquired manifold associations with noncapitalist habits, riots, unpaid labor, dreams, wanderings, inactivity, superstitions, and unregulated sensations in the Romantic period. It is these proliferating associations through which subsistence became racialized and gendered, by what Silvia Federici has called the "accumulations of differences," in which bodies were violently separated and hierarchized as productive or unproductive.[7] For Federici, the European enclosures of common lands are historically significant because they enabled the division of subsistence into the devalued labor of social reproduction and the productive labor of commodity production. Along with these divisive processes, I am interested in the simultaneous proliferation of subsistence, as noncapitalist ways of living and being, that emerges alongside capitalism. According to the *Oxford English Dictionary*, subsistence conjoins "senses relating to the basis or foundation of existence"; "continued existence, the state of remaining in effect or force"; "senses relating to the maintenance and support of life"; and only in "modern use," "often with reference to a bare or minimum level of existence."[8] Designating the very fact of existence and the "bare or minimum" subsistence suggests a paradoxical sense of necessity both as the condition for everything and almost nothing. Dispossession targets subsistence ways of living for destruction in order to reduce our "maintenance and support of life" to the bare minimum for which capital will pay. But we cannot grapple with the history of dispossession without a *rhetorical* reading of subsistence, in which "the basis or foundation of existence" is simultaneously an excess of the essential and the basis of use, a historically produced scarcity that continues to rely on the continuation of modes of reproduction superfluous to the market. As Clare once put it, enclosure is a "lawless law." I only want to add that this lawlessness derives not only from the self-positing claims that turn land into property but also from the wayward and unmeasured ways of living that are required for capitalism's ongoing emergence.[9]

In going back to figure in order to read a history of dispossession that continues in the present, I return to one of the most basic commitments of rhetorical reading—namely, to historical origins as a problem that sits outside a purely temporal and successive framework. According to Paul de Man, it is only through figures of *substitution* that a genetic account of the social can be given, and it is through reading these figures that we come to understand the simultaneously literal and figural, the historical and the metaphorical, production of such accounts.[10] While de Man's reading helps us to ironize bourgeois historical narratives staked in claims of universal equality, his reduction of figure to substitution remains stuck in a bourgeois imaginary of history through the relations of exchange and circulation. My concern here is to show the ways in which the violence of capital's origins requires attention to figures other than those of substitution, figures such as coincidence, apostrophe, anachronism, and tautology that are never far away from figure's affective dimensions in Romantic usage.

Such figures are quite visible in the abolitionist and revolutionary rhetoric of Robert Wedderburn, for whom "the earth cannot be justly the private property of individuals, because it was never manufactured by man."[11] Here Wedderburn speaks to that more familiar sense of dispossession, in which what was originally shared in common was stolen and enclosed as private property. But Wedderburn also reveals the other side of dispossession, rerouting developmentalist narratives of history, when he comments that subsistence ways of living afforded to slaves in the form of provision grounds made them freer and more strategically advanced than the workers of England. Dispossession here is not reducible only to the loss of land and home. It also names the simultaneous undoing of straightforward histories and the resources of struggle that were available to slaves rather than to European workers. Instead of a "linear causality," dispossession organizes global space and historical time through those terms we tend to consider as being outside capitalism—through means of reproduction outside the exchange of money and in the anachronism of enslaved peoples' historical advance beyond the European worker dispossessed of land. However, as Wedderburn knew quite well, what was lost in land by the English working poor became the recalcitrant habits that the Jacobin, industrialist, and philosophical materialist Joseph Priestley found so pernicious in the Romantic period. Of this dispossessed worker, Priestley writes that "whatever they do get by their labor more than is sufficient for their immediate needs, they too often waste in the most extravagant manner.... If the greater part of workmen can earn enough in three or four days to maintain themselves and their families for the week, they will never work anymore."[12] Even in Priestley's dismissal of what is spent extravagantly outside the time of labor, a surplus beyond what work provides and a sufficiency that does meet needs without any more work is still visible. It is such a manifold of excess, waste, and need all woven together that I mean by subsistence. Along with the upending of narratives of either industrial progress or historical decline that Wedderburn shows us, Priestley inadvertently loses his way in his condemnation of subsistence and wanders into a predicament of surplus. As even Priestley admits, workers' rejection of labor beyond what is necessary for subsistence is actually more than sufficient, enough to satisfy a week of reproduction *and* extravagance. Between Wedderburn and Priestley, we can begin to see that subsistence is never minimal in a measured way. Instead, subsistence is a continuation of existence (*subsistere*) from below (*sub-*). The conjuncture of dispossession I address here—as both a way of life and an originating discontinuity of capitalism—is a problem that will constantly be worked and reworked in Romanticism, and that continues its recursions in the present.

This language of simultaneity is in many ways familiar to us from rhetorical and deconstructive readings of Romanticism, particularly in the critical emphasis that has been put on apostrophe and lyric poetry. Significantly, however, such readings are framed as beyond the material and historical, in large part because they have remained locked in a narrow debate with New Historicism. While these approaches usefully remind us that the past is not a transparent body to be reanimated and that being is not a record of fullness and self-identity waiting to be revealed, they also treat New Historicism and its construction of ideology as false consciousness as the only framework for understanding the effects of capitalism upon Romantic sociality and life. In maintaining this delimited engagement with historical materialism, they reproduce a binary between rhetoric and history, because they remain focused on deconstructing a problem of abstraction and ideology of which Marx himself was quite critical.[13] These readings represent dispossession as a purely ontological refuge against the depredations of modern capitalism. Here the figural becomes the reserve of endless ontological difference, irrespective of the social and material differences that are cast as peculiarly fixed and determined. Somewhat ironically, such treatments of rhetoric are not far away from orthodox Marxist treatments of capitalism, as such readings tend to separate the difference, transience, and impropriety of poetic and rhetorical language from the presumed measure, fixity, and individuation of modernity.

To put this another way, strictly ontological approaches to dispossession forget that the cultivation and enforcement of individuated and self-possessed subjects is a historical, and thus a contingent and messy, process. Treatments of ontology as a reserve against modern subjectivity tend to buy into the Eurocentric discourse of the self-constituting or self-positing subject on its own terms, acting as if the discourse of such subjects banished all other ways of being to a lost past.[14] While de Man was himself obsessed with pushing such a discourse to its limit point of ironization, more recent deconstructive work has tended to enclose all possibilities of alterity within the ironic undoing of the subject. But this cedes too much to a liberal framework, requiring us to continue to invest in the subject and liberal institutions of representation as the only recourse to figural ways of being and living, in the form of projects that "give voice to the voiceless . . . and advocate simultaneously for cosmopolitan futures and local attachments."[15] Another way to say this is that a wholly ontological grounding of dispossession may be the epistemological effect of reading dispossession from entirely within the enclosures of (neo)liberal institutions such as the university. Through such enclosures, a primarily ontological and linguistic treatment of dispossession occludes the difficult but creative recognition that there is no alterity or identity in general; a concern with dispossession cannot prove useful if it does not get caught up in the impropriety of survival within capitalism that is not so clearly split between the premodern and the modern. What we need is an account of dispossession that is useful for struggles in the present, struggles that far exceed the confines of the subject and the aporia of liberal institutionality, and enable us to salvage those non- and anticapitalist ways of being so that they are not, in fact, left to a premodern past.

Such approaches get in their own way by idealizing the deviations of rhetorical language, making it impossible for us to follow noncapitalist ways of being that were and are at the crux of a dispossession in which no reserve, ontological or otherwise, is left pure and untouched. If rhetorical accounts of dispossession are to be useful for us in the present, it will not be because they continue to leave the subject or liberal institutions open to a project of further inclusion or expansion of difference but because they find ways to refuse the trap of idealizing rhetoric or homogenizing history. Rather than enclosing difference either in the past or in language, we might do better to approach subsistence as what Samuel Taylor Coleridge once described as a "something-nothing-everything."[16] Such a term is wildly appropriate to my survey of subsistence in this project, which ranges across scenes of leisure time and inactivity, domestic labor and provision grounds, theft and riot, species reproduction and idle wandering, dreams and gossip, sex work and stage performance, and witchcraft, superstition, and bodily capacities of susceptibility and impressionability. This is no straightforward definition of subsistence, which is why, as I argue, we need to approach subsistence as figural. As this "something-nothing-everything," subsistence is the coincidence of unmeasurable needs and the indirect and nonequivalent ways of their meeting, akin to what Fred Moten has called "the social economy of dispossession" of "the ones who [in] having nothing, have everything."[17] At once in excess and beyond what is necessary, more than what is needed and unmeasurable by necessity, needs and their meeting constitute the uncanny coincidence of lack and surplus that does not fit any economy but is, to borrow from Moten, "aneconomic."

One effect of the continued binarism of the rhetorical and the historical is that it has eclipsed the three interrelated senses of figure that appear consistently in Romantic writing: figures of speech as a feature of language in which opposites coincide rather than contradict in "the combination of uncombinables"; the late Enlightenment and early Romantic materialist sense of figure as the occurrence of being affected; and figure as the *use* of language. The first sense has long been central to deconstructive readings, while the second has recently gained some prominence as a way to critique deconstructive readings of figure by returning to a felt correspondence between the senses and language. But the third sense has largely gone unremarked and merits far greater attention. As I show throughout this book, we need a more sustained account of the ways figural language appears as a use value in Romanticism in order to historicize the dependency of capital accumulation upon subsistence ways of living. It is through this sense of figure as an association between rhetorical language, affectable bodies, and use that it is woven into the problem that Marx designated "so-called primitive accumulation" and the racialization and gendering of subsistence through that process.

Romanticism has often been the site of theorizing the possibility of coincident or simultaneous states of being and thus provides a unique vocabulary by which to reconsider these problems of the historical.[18] But the undoing, contradiction, and affordance of simultaneity that are most often associated with apostrophe is not restricted to lyric poetry. It coincides with recent work on a global commons that begins in the ambivalent figuration of Romanticism as a "red round globe hot burning [that] might refer *either* to what we would call the Anthropocene, with its planetary warming, *or* to the revolutionary struggles of the era and the fires on slave plantations," as well as Moten's discussion of Blackness as para-ontological dispossession of "difference in common" and "common differentiation."[19] Such work points us outside those sites of production that account for the extraction of surplus value and within the superfluous means through which needs are met in heterogeneous and unmeasured ways. Subsistence here is a deeply rhetorical form of life in which otherwise oppositional ways of living and ways of meaning coincide copiously in waste, redundancy, inactivity, reproduction, care-taking, child-making, reveries, chatter, and superstition. Such an account of dispossession requires the tools of rhetorical reading in order for us to understand the apostrophic, tautological, anachronistic, and simultaneous form that the history of capital accumulation takes. The possibilities enabled by such figures have everything to do with the dispossession of a history grounded in binaries of progress and destruction and a turn to the "messy, sensuous, gendered, raced, and unruly component(s)" of political economy in which "living human beings [are] capable of following orders as well as of flouting them."[20]

Figuring Subsistence, Historicizing Substitution

Following John Locke, we often consider figure as an ornamental excess to the conventional uses of language. A slightly different version of figure has it as an accepted deviation from convention. In both cases, rhetoric functions to allure, to persuade, and to fascinate listeners with sound rather than sense, with form rather than substance. But late Enlightenment and Romantic speculations on figure often associated it with subsistence. Indeed, associationist theories of mind and body, in which all human knowledge results from accumulated sensorial experience, often located the origins of language in the so-called primitive conditions of human existence. Especially in the Lockean, associationist tradition that was so influential even for early Coleridge, spoken and written language resulted from reactions to the pressure of external objects on the senses and the internal pressure of physiological needs. Language in this account was entirely material, even if histories of it were necessarily speculative. Setting us in the state of nature, Joseph Priestley, radical republican and aggressive proponent of industrialization, tells us that "it is natural to suppose that the first words which mankind, in the most early ages of the world would invent and apply, would be names for sensible objects, as of animals, vegetables, the parts of the human body . . . because these are the things that would first occur to their observation, and which their necessities would oblige them to have the most constant recourse to."[21] In contrast to a Rousseauian version, the origins of language here are tools of survival rather than social utterances. This early language is a response to things that "first occur" to our senses out of necessity. It emerges from the doubled nature of impression—that of outside objects and an internal dependency upon them. This sensational account of linguistic origins associates the subjection of European man to nature with the use value of language. This is not an initial figuration that establishes difference or sameness, as in the case of Rousseau's giant and man, but a figure in which sensible subjection carries the possibility of satisfaction.[22] However, this "primitive language, or that which was spoken by the first family of the human race, must have been very scanty and insufficient for the purposes of their descendants, in their growing acquaintance with the world."[23] In these speech acts, utterance associates need and speech, and so the utterance itself is "scanty" and "insufficient," barely meeting the threshold of the social relation of sense.[24] Priestley's conjectural history presents the origins of language not just in a state of nature but in a scene of subsistence.

That language is useful in its insufficient origins also means that language is originally figurative. After all, it is also "use and application" through which Priestley defines figurative language, which, in contrast to Rousseau, he understands as primarily bound up with sensible form. Indeed, while figure is understood to be a relation of substitution, for Priestley figure's originary substitution derives from the "correspondence" between the shape or *use* of two different things, and in particular the correspondence between the parts of bodies that enable sustenance. The mouth, first associated with the human, becomes a figure when attributed to animals, allowing for an association through function or application; it stops becoming a figure when the difference between these two things is forgotten. And in Priestley's edited and revised version of David Hartley's *Theory of the Human Mind*, figure and everyday subsistence are closely entwined: "It is evident, that if a language be narrow, and much confined to sensible things, it will have great occasion for figures: these will naturally occur in the common intercourses of life." In this origin scene, figurative language is rooted in "the uses and exigencies of human life."[25] Priestley extends this point in his own lectures, noting that in early, primitive languages, figures are useful because they can shelter more than one thing or idea. The mouth of a man can also be the mouth of a bird without implying the sameness or identity that will be assumed when figurative language is forgotten. Figure is useful because even in these scanty and insufficient conditions, there are too many things to say and not enough words for saying them.

Priestley continues to describe the development of language beyond this "scanty" form into "mere custom," as the complexity of an arbitrary system of signification comes to replace meager referentiality and sensorial touch. History is what is separate from such origins and is the artifice that makes language into a matter of understanding. Priestley's conjectural scene of language as it meets needs is prior to the emergence of a system of language as understanding, which is based in "arbitrary preference" and where "every thing is regulated by mere custom" rather than any "internal excellence."²⁶ Given this state of affairs, we can only consider language through "mere custom" and the "uses to which [it] is applied."²⁷ Figure occurs less as a metaphor that translates between binary oppositions of inside and outside and more as the coincidence of sensation and articulation, constellating impression, need, and sound. But this early language is also figural because, as Priestley notes, it is prior to convention, where signification is created. These figurative origins ground language outside the sense sanctioned by convention and developed over time. Figure is a priori in this sense but is not an a priori with sense. Such a ground is not the same as that of a system of differences that will emerge as the arbitrary grounds of language. Language in its use value, in its function of satisfying the necessity of need, is located in a place before signification, where articulation is a use value. Language here is not regulated by the (arbitrary) signification of the system of custom but inaugurated by the immediacy of need, which sits somewhere prior to the language of understanding. This "insufficient" language does not express but applies; it does not arbitrarily substitute but is used for meeting needs.

Setting figure in this scene of subsistence suggests another origin point for rhetoric, with a surplus that is distinctive from the excesses of ornament. Where ornament associates rhetoric with an excess that, as luxury, is superfluous, Priestley's scene articulates a coincidence of surplus and need that is foundational and insufficient, vital and scanty, necessary and "present in a greater quantity than is desired, permitted, or required," all at once.²⁸ In other words, this scene of subsistence is a deeply rhetorical one in which it is possible for a scarcity of substitution to disclose its own luxurious simultaneity. This kind of deviation is not a surplus in the sense of ornament but is rather a coincidence of opposites in which excess is both generated by need and is beyond what is needed. Such a coincidence of opposites has most often been associated with apostrophe and lyric poetry, but this holding together of oppositional conditions is precisely the state to which subsistence also refers us. As noted before, subsistence conjoins "senses relating to the basis or foundation of existence"; "Continued existence . . . the state of remaining in effect or force"; "senses relating to the maintenance and support of life"; and "often with reference to a bare or minimum level of existence."²⁹ Subsistence is a figure in which the very threshold of existence is coupled with a minimal form. It holds out the appositional possibility that minimality discloses a different form of surplus, the suspension of the necessary or requisite as defined only by what is said to develop after "a bare or minimum level of existence" has been satisfied. Figure and subsistence are rooted together in a coincidence in which our means of meeting needs are entirely illogical but without contradiction. This means that speech is, first and foremost, useful. In a way that will later irritate Kant, these associationist origins not just of language but of knowledge root human beings and their social relations in phenomenal pressures that are logically absurd.

Priestley's "use or application" of speech for the purposes of subsistence is already woven into rhetorical language, or a use of language in which "the combination of uncombinables" is possible.³⁰ In the rhetorical rather than logical origins of language, sense is made through a use of language that can maintain contradictions and oppositions not against the material world but by maintaining simultaneous senses of it. If language begins in figure, then there is no simple or bare form of language, only a sense of use that departs from mere functionality and remakes the empirical world into a dream in which chairs have feet and birds chatter. Such an association between use and these illogical absurdities—the sharing of a mouth by man and birds in these early days of language, for instance—suggests that we are not so much dealing with the essential meagerness of use as much as its essential vagrancy. It is in this origin scene of use, sense, and subsistence that we find imprecise affinities between the etymologies of the Latin *vagārī*, to wander, to *vagus*, wandering, inconstant, uncertain, and to the Old Saxon *weg* and the Old Swedish *vägher*. While no point of precise overlap is to be found, J. L. Austin carries us between these words when he suggests that "we are too prone to give ... explanations" of meaning that reduce it to "sense or reference." Instead, we must consider the "admittedly vague expression" of "what *way* we are using [language]."³¹ Many deconstructive and poststructuralist readings have emphasized the significance of force in Austin's theory of speech acts, but I want to draw our attention to the using of language as a "way" and this "way" as what has effects beyond the scope of "sense and meaning." In other words, there is no *use* of language that would not also be a *way*, no simple point of origin that was not also a style of doing woven into the uncertainty of its effects in a setting that is always more than the transparency of what the speaker intends. Meaning-as-use will always be bound to a manner of style or way, and in roots of meaning that are in their essence complex and transient rather than insufficient and scanty. This wayness of use takes us out of a bare circuit of communication in which expressions of need carry only reference to immediate satisfaction. The use of language to satisfy needs would always already be caught up in an inconstant passage between different ways of satisfaction that are figural. While Austin does not elaborate upon this vague expression, his use of it opens out to the uncertain motion of the history I follow throughout this book—that of the transformation of noncapitalist ways of living not as primitivized and prehistorical, which others have sufficiently shown, but as the criminalized, gendered, automated and animalistic, spatial and global, necessary and superfluous ways of living that constitute our capitalist present. Such a history requires that we seize the way of using language as a "manner or style" and as a "method of proceeding," or reading, that is vagrantly vague.[32] Such manners disclose an extravagance entangled with those indigent ways of living in an "extravagant manner" that Priestley described above, making good use of what is a waste to sense while also refusing to work properly.

While Priestley's distinctly non-Rousseauian origins of language might seem to be easily dismissed as non-Romantic, the most canonical of Romantic poets continue to remediate this scene of subsistence associated with the use of a language that is sensational and scarce of sense. Wordsworth is important here, as he remediates Priestley's conjecturally primitive scene of articulation into the present-day condition of the dispossessed and their sensationalist language, thus making a speculative past into the origins of a present, prepoetic feeling.[33] In contrast to a responsiveness subjugated to the immediacy of sensible things, poetry substitutes absence for presence and generates an elevated sense of feeling that is conjured by the poet "himself." Poetry elevates simple sensation into complex feeling, replacing the surround of stimuli with the effects of a recollection that are "far from the same." But Wordsworth's poetry is, of course, full of glimpses that mark this difference. Take, for instance, his prefatory note to "The Thorn." The narrator of that poem is a Captain, retired on an annuity in a place that is unfamiliar to him but that continues to operate on the social structure of the village. Wordsworth's depiction of our superstitious narrator and gossip-happy villagers is in many ways the effect of Romantic-era attempts to retroject superstition into a premodern past, a symptom of what Silvia Federici has argued was the entirely *modern* violence of the European witch hunts and their creation of gendered divisions of labor within capitalism. Our narrator is plagued by a tautological speech, the effects of a malleable mind, an affectable imagination, and the tendency to be stimulated immediately by, as Priestley wrote, "the things that would first occur to ... observation."[34] Remediated from the origin scene set by Priestley, the chatty, superstitious, and indolent narrator of Martha Ray's tragic story is overaffected by those sensible things to which he has most frequent recourse, to the gossip that circulates around him and by the landscape on which he discovers Martha Ray. Wordsworth's prefatory note to "The Thorn" is perhaps best known for its glossing of the difference between tautology and repetition, but the tenuousness of this distinction is crystallized in a figurative phrasing that recalls the coincidence of surplus and superfluity in subsistence. Wordsworth comments that our narrator is "sufficiently common," thus repeating that coincidence of excess and redundancy produced by Priestley, only now displaced onto the present-day primitivism of the village.[35] This phrase is a figure of excessive adequacy, of recursive commonness, and of sparse sufficiency. Speaking a language that is at once superfluous and in surplus, Wordsworth's narrator carries that rhetorical sense of subsistence beyond his own discourse of history, in which enclosure appears as people who are resolutely lost to the past.

It is probably Coleridge who is most concerned with the continuation of those doctrines in which an insufficient language originates in sensible things. For him, the difference between the imagination and fancy can be divided between "the mind ... affected by thoughts rather than by things" and language with "a ground, a firmament, a foundation" versus a language that was "mere ornamentation" and "paint."[36] Indeed, Coleridge's most famous distinction in *Biographia Literaria* between these capacities reiterates that origin scene of sensible subsistence. Fancy becomes a mode of conjectural history, a "memory emancipated from the order of time and space" that "must receive all its materials ready made from the law of association" in which all knowledge derives from the senses.[37] The *Biographia* also updates an earlier figuration of food rioters, engaged in noncapitalist ways of obtaining subsistence that Coleridge had used in 1795, whom he depicted as mechanistic and sensationally driven. Later, these rioters are substituted for critics, who instead of a "rebellion of the belly" suffer from "a debility and dimness of the imaginative power, and a consequent necessity of reliance on the immediate impressions of the senses."[38] Such a condition leads to "a deficient portion of internal and proper warmth" and a search "for a warmth in common, which they do not possess singly."[39] There could scarcely be a more apt figuration of that scene of subsistence set by Priestley, in which needs and their meeting appear scanty and insufficient while, at the same time, a sense of surplus remains. To satisfy this basic need through means that are not possessed by any body "singly," to exchange warmth externally through common and immediate senses, is to subsist figuratively. Ungrounded and without foundation, rhetoric and subsistence again find themselves rooted together.

Neither Wordsworth nor Coleridge locates such language in the past; rather, they find the response to "immediate external excitement" in everyday language used by dispossessed commoners and their kin—a retired sea captain, rioters, overstimulated factory workers, and, at least for Coleridge, literary critics. Impressed upon by need, the motley crew of the dispossessed must make use of language or use language in order to satisfy those needs. This need and its concomitant absence of foundation generate a language that is poor in feeling but surplus in its superfluity, producing "ideas and feelings [that] do not in that state succeed each other in accustomed order."[40] Across Priestley, Wordsworth, and Coleridge we can track a recursion to an origin scene that launches a narrative in which subsistence is both a form of life and a form of language. Such origins make subsistence into a way of using language different from but coinciding with the successive ordering of history as it is generated by regulated feeling. This scene grounds history in rhetoric, where the rhetorical is what enables the production of sense through the use of language that is not originally sensible as the development from simple to complex languages and forms of life.

The genealogy I have traced here is not meant to be a straightforward or even particularly continuous one. Rather, like the "circuitous paths" that Coleridge's *Biographia* is meant to warn youths against pursuing while itself performing endless ellipses, digressions, recursions, catachreses—in other words, rhetorical paths—it is meant to gather and hold together the constellation of sensation, figure, use, and need that echoes throughout a late Enlightenment associations tradition and a High Romantic one.[41] While separable in myriad ways, they both find that figure and subsistence share in more than historical origins and locate a rhetoric not of ornamentation but of an entwined superfluity that evades that historically developed system called sense.

This oscillation between a figural subsistence and a historical mode of subsistence is one that persists throughout the Romantic period and finds its way into Marx's historical account of the role of exchange in the development of capitalism. Marx joins this genealogy not only as the most important theorist of capital accumulation but also because it is with Marx that social relations in the form of substitution definitively surpass subsistence and use value as relevant to class struggle. One of the major revelations of *Capital* is that our means of meeting needs have been turned into a mode of production organized primarily around exchange, which makes possible the capture of labor power as surplus value through the measure of money. *Capital* explains how our meeting of needs outside relations of exchange has moved from being the driving force of production into a superfluous status. Social relations instead get subsumed by the abstraction of exchange as a socially necessary action of reproduction, while use is banished to the imagination. Marx does not deny the sensorial experience of use value. He affirms that the material form of commodities and the needs that they meet are incommensurate and nonequivalent. In fact, the problem he puts to us is how a world of difference became one in which everything is exchangeable for everything else. His analysis of the commodity form answers this problem by rendering those heterogeneous features of commodities negligible from the perspective of a historical development that has been driven forward by exchange. The distinguishing feature of the commodity form is its separation between the "motley natural forms of use value" and its capacity to be exchanged *despite* those material differences.[42] As Alfred Sohn-Rethel explains, "The banishment of use may be and can be kept in the private minds of exchanging agents (buyers and sellers of sodium chlorate might have gardening in mind or bomb making)."[43] It is the abstraction from material particularity that becomes determining for Marx, while "motley" use becomes superfluous to the commodity as well as its historical effects. This historical, material development reaches its apex with the money form, which is the form that surpasses the mere exchange of commodities to establish a "universal equivalent" in which a thing "appears to be immediately exchangeable with other things just as it exists for the senses."[44] Money, of course, does not develop out of thin air. It is the historical product of exchange and of the progressive separation between commodities as they are used and a single commodity—in this case, gold—that is separated from the motleyness of use and appears as a "pure form."

Labor too comes to be rendered in this value form of equivalence, through divisions of labor and the standardization of socially necessary labor time through mechanical production. But as Marx tells us, it is ultimately the fact that labor is abstract and general in its essence, and that this essence has been developed through the capitalist mode of production, that commodities are exchangeable in the first instance.[45] In other words, it is not the equivalence of money that determines the abstract sameness of all things but rather the fact that they are the products of human labor.

Thus it is not exchange as such that is of concern to Marx. It is the historical process that has led to the universal equivalent of the money form and a historical form of labor that can be represented by it. Labor is defined by the measure of what is socially necessary, and what is socially necessary is the historical product of a labor whose value is represented by money. The development of labor as a commodity determined by the form of equivalence is a violent historical process through which subsistence ways of living are destroyed in what Marx terms "so-called primitive accumulation" and in which the English enclosures play a central role. In order for populations to become dependent upon wages, and more important, money, for their survival, dependency upon communal production and heterogeneous ways of meeting needs had to be eliminated. In order for that to occur, workers had to be dispossessed of their means of subsistence and left only with their labor to sell, a process accomplished by the enclosures in England and "the extirpation, enslavement and entombment in the mines of the aboriginal population [in America] [and] the turning of Africa into a warren for the commercial hunting of black-skins."[46]

What Marx designates as the so-called primitive accumulation that forced labor power into the commodity form is no pure abstract analysis. It is a historical narrative bound to a logic of development—both the development of productive forces and of a capitalist system in which those forces produce exchange value. The development of labor power through the contradictory measures of exchange that can never fully compensate for its productivity renders the worker who has been entirely subsumed by this process the potential subject of historical transformation. One of the primary concerns of this book is how this narrative of capitalism's development makes the associations we developed above superfluous to our understandings of capital and history. The only needs that remain historically relevant for Marx are those held in the contradictions of exchange, because such needs are both produced by and met through generalized labor. All other forms of need, and in particular those identified with subsistence, as in the scene Priestley gives us, become insignificant in a world dominated by exchange and made in the image of money. As many others have noted, Marx's own Eurocentric model of history and his overdetermination of it by standardized, homogeneous labor led to the exclusion of other forms of labor—slave labor and reproductive labor in particular—as well as of the necessary heterogeneity that enables the superexploitation of workers through hierarchies of race and gender. Such a developmentalist logic excludes the unpaid labor of enslaved people, women, and nature as having any determining force in such transformation. My argument here is related but different. I am proposing that what Marx considers labor power has never broken free from its entanglements with necessarily figural ways of subsisting from one day to the next and that rhetorical relations other than equivalence and substitution are required for surviving the global process of capital accumulation. A more vagrant set of social relations remain historically significant and determining of the emergence and present-day occurrence of capitalist forms of labor. Use value has never been banished from the production of surplus value, because our ways of meeting needs within capitalism are still bound to the manifold thingliness of sensational bodies—human and nonhuman—and their effects upon a capital accumulation that is not "a teleology or an eschatology but a figure (an assemblage of points of entry)."[47] Thus, things like dreams and superstition, to which I turn in Chapters 2 and 3, are not peripheral to my analysis; they are the figural social relations through which both capital and labor are filtered.

As I argue in the concluding section of this chapter and in the rest of the book, use value and subsistence ways of living have not been banished to the past despite the tremendous violence wrought by dispossession. Both as a way of living and of language, subsistence and the rhetorical relations of simultaneity, anachronism, apostrophe, and tautology remain a part of our day-to-day lives under capitalism and our social reproduction within and against it. Exclusions of the persistent usefulness and necessity of incommensurate means of subsistence are the conditions that have kept Romanticism grounded primarily, if not entirely, in "the condition of England around 1800, specifically of its evolution into a culture governed by industrial time, machine-driven labor, and commodity form."[48] But use and its motley nature, its dispossession of the single, its essential wayness, persists elsewhere in Marx's account of capital—namely, in his account of dispossession in a more than historical mode and in a way that situates us back in Romanticism.

Dispossession and Rhetoric

Thus far we have followed Marx's narrative of the production of surplus value through the dialectics of labor and the money form, a narrative that is quite difficult to wrestle away from the historically determining power of capitalist forms of labor. Nonetheless, when Marx takes a moment to reflect on the relationship between language and money, he discloses something other than a historical separation of surplus and superfluity through equivalence.

> Language does not transform ideas, so that the peculiarity of ideas is dissolved and their social character runs alongside them as a separate entity, like prices alongside commodities. Ideas do not exist separately from language. Ideas which have first to be translated out of their mother tongue into a foreign language in order to circulate, in order to become exchangeable, offer a somewhat better analogy; *but the analogy then lies not in language, but in the foreignness of language.*[49]

Here we return to a scene of language, one quite different from Priestley's but no less bound up with figure. Marx is, after all, also interested here in the inseparability of language and knowledge (or ideas), and the relation to which he refers us for understanding the money form is analogy. One reading of this passage would be that language most resembles money in the translation of concrete ideas—the use value of language—into that other form of foreign language. Foreign language would be the money form, the form of equivalence that allows ideas to circulate beyond their immediate context. But this isn't quite right: if we follow this analogy, there is no universal equivalent to be found, only one language into which another is put in relation. Translation proposes an immediate problem here, because, as Marx knows quite well, ideas are not free-floating essences that are transparently represented by language. Ideas and meaning are bound to the materiality of language. Language, unlike money in its "pure form," is inseparable from the ideas it expresses, and ideas cannot be converted into a kind of homogeneous substance that language passively represents. Marx's distinction between language as it is used and money as it is exchanged reiterates, if only ever so slightly, that vague way of using language in which the rootedness of exchangeability in an abstract and homogeneous substance is put into question.

In this case the possibility of universal exchangeability would follow from a process more akin to the relationship between dialect and standardized language. Dialect, after all, does not derive from a standardized language. Rather, as Alice Becker-Ho has shown, standardization is the privileging of one dialect over others, a privileging that cannot cancel out the difference that constitutes it if it is to be used by the myriad living people using a standardized language. It remains composed of "all manner of mixed forms" so that it can circulate across national and imperial space, making it a hegemony through heterogeneity.⁵⁰ It is not standardization that makes an exchange of difference possible but rather the provisional accumulation of motley *ways* of use that make standardized language usable at all. Here Walter Benjamin's approach to translation proves indispensable. In "The Task of the Translator," Benjamin proposes that the totality of language—a "pure language" in which "one and the same thing is meant"—will only ever be realized by humans in the provisional form of proliferating ways of meaning that are "not interchangeable." This is because even a pure language is not "an identity of origin" in which language is grounded in an essential form for which words are transparent symbols. These ways of meaning are the "words, sentences, associations" and "syntax," and I would add figures, that make meaning possible through a historical materiality that is irreducible to meaning as essence or form. These aspects of language are archives of resilient *because* transient materiality and provide points of nonreferential relations between different languages based in this materiality of mutual exclusivity rather than sameness of meaning. That is, translation is made possible by the presence of foreign words, sentences, associations, and syntax in our own language that do not mean what we mean by them but supplement and transform a mother tongue over time. The totality of human language will only ever be composed of a paradoxical translatability that does not carry meaning as an essence or a form but carries *ways* of meaning as "fragments of a greater language" (261). Thus, translation can only ever work toward an expansive fragmentation, generating a totality out of the historically specific and "not interchangeable" ways of meaning that signal the existence of a greater language through the accumulation of what remains foreign in our own mother tongue. Here the *use* of language persists as a vital component of a nonuniversal translation, whereas equivalence produces poor translations that will not endure the test of time.⁵¹ Foreignness inheres in the translational relation between parts of language, establishing a totality in which even a universal equivalent would not be immune from the motley nature of a use value that is always a complex way rather than an immediate reference.

If, as Benjamin suggests, it is the nonequivalent and useful aspects of language that give us insight into the possibility of a historical and materialist account of translation, what does such an account offer to Marx's understanding of money through translation? What kind of history emerges from the sense of a constitutive foreignness at the heart of exchange and of nonequivalent uses that are not reducible to historical origins? As I want to suggest here, such foreignness requires a rethinking of use as a way rather than an object and of subsistence not through base needs but as the translation of noncapitalist ways of living to the present. When Marx gives us an account of the world of commodity exchange at the beginning of volume 1 of *Capital*, he privileges the development of money and of a socially necessary labor time dictated by the measure of equivalence as the meaning of capitalism. But if we take up the challenge of reading capital rhetorically, which I have suggested would also be to read it through translation, then we would have to begin at the end, or by starting backward, because it is there that Marx cues us to the differential and discontinuous preconditions of capitalism. It is this messier and more contingent, as well as more violent and constitutive, process of dispossession that Marx famously describes as "conquest, enslavement, robbery, murder, in short, force" that is the "actual history" of capital.[52] While the meeting of needs is subsumed by exchange in Marx's other historical account, this turn to foreignness as the illogical root of exchange likewise turns us to another one, where the *translation* of modes of subsistence becomes the possibility of the commodity form. Here ways of life and language are constantly interwoven through the undoing and remaking to which life and language are subjected by their transience, as well as through the forms of life instituted by capitalism.

Marx's analogy between money and language, when considered as something other than a narrative of transitions from subsistence ways of living to the dialectic of homogeneous labor and universal equivalence, potentially discloses a rhetoric of capital accumulation that draws our attention to scenes of dispossession rather than scenes of development. And indeed, Marx does turn to rhetorical language to deconstruct the mythic origins of primitive accumulation as propounded by political economists such as Adam Smith. Marx takes a famously ironic approach to that myth, in which it was the "riotous living" of the poor and the scrupulous saving of the bourgeois that enabled the latter's accumulation of wealth. Dubbing this so-called primitive accumulation, Marx upends this bourgeois narrative by demonstrating that "conquest, enslavement, robbery, murder, in short, force" is the "actual history" of the originary accumulation of capital by the bourgeoisie.[53] It is not only Marx who turns to figural language in order to understand this history. Rosa Luxemburg, perhaps the most significant theorist of dispossession and so-called primitive accumulation, gives us an acutely figural formation of dispossession in "The Struggle against the Peasant Economy," where she tells us that the interaction between capitalist and noncapitalist forms of life "cannot be expressed in the form of a precise schema," in contrast to the more abstracting modes under which capitalist production can be treated. Instead of the diagrams that can be used to calculate rates of profit as they fluctuate through the contradictions between wages, technology, and price, the necessity of "noncapitalist formations" to the formation of capitalism is a necessary deviation in design. In the emergence of a world organized toward the production of exchange values rather than use values to meet needs, capitalist designs cannot do without noncapitalist milieus, as "the movement of each intersects and is intertwined with each other at every turn."[54] It is this intertwining, according to Luxemburg, that creates new markets for commodities and relieves the impending crisis of overproduction.

But it is also the substance of everyday life from which capitalism emerges through dispossession, rooting it in an oscillation between an essential form and a deviating figure. Luxemburg's use of schema is already bound up in that oscillation, rooted as it is in the etymology of Latin *schema* and Greek σχῆμα, both form and figure, both the "recognized modes of deviating from . . . ordinary use" and "a plan of action devised in order to attain some end."[55] Dispossession is this material and otherwise historical intersection and entwinement, the coincidence of oppositions rather than simple contradiction. Luxemburg did not herself pursue the implications of this originary disruption at the center of capital accumulation to its full extent; she tended to focus instead on the potential effects of global dispossession upon the European proletariat.[56] Nonetheless, Marx and

Luxemburg's similar turn to the rhetorical suggests that we need figure in order to grapple with the necessity of so-called primitive accumulation to both the past and present conditions of capitalism. Indeed, the capacity of figure to maintain oppositions and combine uncombinables is a striking feature of work that takes up radical reconfigurations of capitalist and noncapitalist ways of living. For instance, Kalyan Sanyal addresses contexts of postcolonial capitalism in order to show that so-called primitive accumulation "leads to the destruction of the pre-capitalist sectors" and "simultaneously produces a space that necessitates the recreation of those sectors," such that "the complex of capital and non-capital [are] perpetually locked in a relation of contradiction and mutuality."[57] And writing in the context of Colombia and Bolivia in the 1970s, Michael Taussig returns us to the relationship between use value and way, describing dispossession as "a way of life losing its life."[58] Such a figural phrasing ought to indicate that dispossession is a figural operation that not only cannot be banished to the past but also demands attention to how noncapitalist ways of living are translated into and alongside capitalist forms of labor. Dispossession is not the historical rupture of enclosure or the mechanism that converts all historically significant labor into standardized form. It is, rather, the knottier entwinement of our motley and deviating means of subsistence with the process of capital accumulation, in a process that dispossesses history of any essential binaries or linear movements of past and present.

The work I take up in this book is chronologically prior to the processes of dispossession and so-called primitive accumulation discussed by Sanyal, who addresses the postcolonial nation, and Taussig, who addresses a twentieth-century South American context. The Romantic texts and contexts I focus on here instead appear in the period of what Marx called the "classic form" of expropriation, in which a mass of workers in England, dispossessed of noncapitalist means of subsistence, were made "free" to sell their labor on the market or be forced into the enclosures of the home and the workhouse, low-wage piecework, devalued reproductive labor, transportation and indentured servitude, or the carceral category of vagrancy. It might seem odd to return to this "classic form" for the purposes of dispossessing the history of capital accumulation of teleology or self-identity.

I do so in part to question how "classic" this form truly is and how well it holds up as the origin site of capital is on its way to becoming self-valorizing, or self-subsisting, with no outside dependencies. I also do so to return to the long-standing associations between needs, affectability, and historical origins that continue to persist in the most trenchant arguments for the ongoing nature of so-called primitive accumulation. Even analyses that are grounded in this historically disruptive process tend to reinforce the sense that need-based practices are reducible to immediate and meager consumption without any surplus and to the satisfaction of affectable bodies that are vaguely temporally prior to the development of capitalist modes of production. I am interested in undoing such presumptions by attending to the always complex and figural grounding of subsistence, in both Romanticism and the present. My use of subsistence throughout this book encompasses riots, dreams, unpaid and reproductive labor, vagrancy, Obeah practices, rural witchcraft, superstition, and finally, heterogeneous sensations and racialized need as necessary to the standardized time of capitalism. Such entanglements in the work of Romantic-era writers make it impossible to read subsistence as some simple or originary form of meeting needs. Figure, as we know, troubles any easy binaries between inside and outside, sameness and difference, through which modernity has often been cast by Marxist and deconstructive readers of Romanticism alike. Dispossession, recognized by many as a constitutive and ongoing process, needs to be read as more intimately caught up with those "not interchangeable" ways of living that do more than survive as remnants or remain in the present, and which also show up in ways of living that appear homogeneous to us unless read rhetorically. More than a separation of labor from soil, dispossession names the destruction of never simple, always complex ways of use, of which even the most standardized and abstract forms of labor are composed—which means that they are also inseparable from the global system of capital accumulation Marx set out to understand in *Capital*. I hope that in treating dispossession rhetorically we can come away with a constitutively wayward sense of that history in which every iteration, relaunching, and instance of reproduction is transposed onto the problem of how people maintain themselves from one day to the next in ways that are necessarily and ambivalently noncapitalist, and in which the use of force and the violence of social hierarchy are always required to eek out surplus value at a global scale.

Dispossessed of possession, subsistence as ways of living has its effects on capitalism too. As Taussig notes, one of these effects is "antagonis[m] to the process of commodity formation ... [and] the political action necessary to thwart or transcend it."[59] But another effect is the essential reorientation of how we understand capital to accumulate at all, through the dialectic of labor and exchange we saw above with a more imprecise schema. The rhetoric of Romanticism supplements our understanding of capital accumulation through the routine figuration of heterogeneous labors and ways of living as an articulation of past and present violences. The following chapters pursue the historical transformations of reproductive into unproductive labor, of subsistence as criminal activity, of the effects of the European witch hunts and English vagrancy laws as accumulated differences among dispossessed workers, of forms of resistance to slavery and enclosure as primitive and backward superstitions, and of racial and climatological variety into the colonized affectability of material bodies. At the same time, I follow rhetoric as it expresses the historical significance of subsistence beyond temporally successive accumulations. Each chapter of this book presents a specific constellation of subsistence in transformation, not strictly through its subsumption by substitution but rather as a disavowal of the reliance on needs in all their messy and heterogeneous excesses within what we call modernity. These chapters seek to hold open subsistence ways of meaning and ways of living in order to track a different understanding of the relationship between capital accumulation and the everyday from the narrative that industrial capitalism gives us. Instead, these texts provide a collection of transient ways of life and translational ways of meaning as the combined effect of enclosure and survival through it.

In both the first and last chapters of this book, I take up riots, turning to the 1795 riots in England not primarily as instances of disruption but as the spectacular expression of the intersection that Luxemburg describes. I read the 1795 riots not as the last gasp of what E. P. Thompson calls a moral economy of the past as it was making its way into the light of modern political consciousness but as a very contemporary expression of the articulation of surplus and superfluity bound up in subsistence ways of living. Certainly, as Edmund Burke's response made clear, the riots signaled the demand for a division between those labors that were productive of surplus and those that were "not capable of any equalization," specifically the labors of women and the aged.[60] Burke's proposal was part of early attempts to divide subsistence into categories of equivalence and nonequivalence, a division through which, it was claimed, wages could be used to meet certain needs while at the same time ensuring a natural equilibrium in the labor market through the exclusion of unmeasurable needs. As this chapter shows, what Burke and others designated as outside the market was the exogenous essence that was necessary in order for capital to accumulate—that is, rather than being a pure separation, the surplus of need was distributed as unpaid labor or criminalized ways of living. Following Marxist feminists, this chapter situates both Burke's and Coleridge's responses to the riots as indications of the extent to which labor performed by women was increasingly erased as labor while at the same time new punishments for obtaining subsistence outside exchange—for example, in cases of riot or theft—designated newly unproductive and criminal populations in the emergence of what Jackie Wang has dubbed carceral capitalism.

Such needs do appear, however fleeting, in Coleridge's "Letter to Famine" (1795). In the letter, appended to a series of lectures Coleridge gave during the height of the riots, he apostrophically appeals to Famine to end the crisis and, in a distinctly anti-Burkean turn, provide aid to the poor. In apostrophizing Famine, Coleridge holds an incomprehensible relation between surplus and superfluity in subsistence together, addressing scarcity as a source of satisfying needs. An allegory in which excess and lack coincide, this address to Famine provides a "way of meaning" other than syntax or sound, an inescapably rhetorical instance in which the maintenance of subsistence in modernity flashes. This bizarre address provides an occasion to reflect on subsistence as the radical and unmeasurable coincidence of oppositions instead of needs as a measurable scarcity. While the emergent free-market sensibility was reconfiguring the equilibrium of what Thompson has famously designated the "moral economy" of the food riot into the equilibrium of the free market, I argue that apostrophe gives us a better way to understand the historical force of need as necessarily beyond measure.[61] Coleridge's millenarian address to Famine helps us to recall an aspect of the riot that is not about the maintenance of an equilibrium but rather about what Luxemburg once called the "revolutionary romanticism" of the riot and its rejection of such an economy.[62] In the manner of millenarian radicalism, which was the language of the underground, this chapter treats the riots as a site of association between physiological sensation, a temporality of immediacy, and a messianic sensibility, making it impossible to recuperate equilibrium as the logic of the riot.[63] At the same time, however, apostrophe enables a more immanent reading of the transformation toward the wage form, one in which excess and unmeasurable needs remain crucial to the accumulation of capital as well as to the maintenance of noncapitalist modes of life.

Chapter 2 extends this focus on the unmeasurability of subsistence as it takes shape at the intersection of gendered labor and the criminalization of vagrancy, and as it gathers an impression of relations of solidarity rooted in Moten's "common differentiation" rather than universality. If Marx insists that capital accumulates through the standardization of labor, then this chapter follows the insights of the Romantic poet Mary Robinson and contemporary Marxist feminists and Black studies theorists to consider the significance of supposedly unproductive and unmeasured members of society that share in a history of differentiation. Mary Robinson's "The Maniac" (1793) holds together various noncapitalist modes of life as they are interwoven with the emergence of capitalism through the sensationalist memory of a dream. In this poem, different conditions of produced vulnerability are articulated together. The subjects of this poem include an abandoned mother; the spectacular life of a celebrity consort, actress, mother, and poet; and a vagrant driven mad by some unknown cause. While some have read sympathetic analogy as the meaning of this poem, I turn instead to anachronism as a "way of meaning" that both frames the poem and is the condition shared by its subjects. The dream frame of the poem sets us in what Romantic-era surgeon and body snatcher John Hunter once called the "ludicrous anachronisms" of the dream and asks us to read the relationship among its subjects in that light. I argue that this dream frame provides a memory of the nonlinear and contingent processes through which women's labor was degraded and became unpaid labor, leaving many women financially dependent upon marriage or superexploitative forms of labor. This degradation coincided at various points in time, both legally and culturally, with the criminalization of vagrancy as a means of subsistence outside the wage form.

I read these "ludicrous anachronisms" conjuncturally, following Angela Davis's argument that anachronism is the historical mode of capitalism. Stepping outside the supposed distinction between the temporality of "mature commodity capitalism" and the subsistence movements that have been made into a ghostly and lost presence, Robinson's poem insists on the contemporaneity of disrupted and disorderly temporalities. Within those other temporalities a present-day intersection and potential antagonism emerges between the gendered labor of reproduction and the status of the vagrant as unproductive in relation to commodity production. Robinson's poem is not a history, in any traditional sense, of those processes; rather, it constitutes a parallel and simultaneous space-time to that of commodity capitalism in which the anachronisms of unproductive labor and living take heterogeneous forms in the present. "The Maniac" demonstrates a form of enclosure in which differences are accumulated and organized rather than eliminated or subsumed. Robinson's poem is a poem of enclosure because of its indulgence in anachronism, an excess that allows us to see the contemporaneity of anachronism as well as the ways that so-called primitive accumulation renders gender and vagrancy as part of the displaced center of capital. Providing a version of what scholar Hilary Beckles describes as the "fertile soil of capital accumulation," Robinson's poem figures gender and vagrancy as transiently unproductive positions that define enclosure anew.[64] At the same time, this intersection retains the configuration of the only continuously discontinuous threat to capitalism, which is the failure of class to ever occur as a "singular social and historical entity."[65]

Chapter 3 begins with a reflection on Wordsworth's prefatory note to "The Thorn" (1800) and his attempt to distinguish tautology from repetition. Critical of its supposed redundancy, Wordsworth presents tautology as a form of unfeeling repetition. But etymologically, tautology provides the roots for much of Wordsworth's project, especially those poems with connections to witchcraft. Traceable as a repeated gathering or a collection of same-saying, this trope holds together a variety of words, bodies, and things in Wordsworth's poems, as well as in "The Three Graves," a poem begun by Wordsworth and completed by Coleridge. The Romantic poetic concern with same-saying as it coincides with the practice of witchcraft also crosses the ocean to Jamaica, appearing in Benjamin Moseley's part medical treatise, part history of sugar, and part defense of slavery, "Treatise on Sugar" (1799). All three of these texts share a concern with the supernatural and the scientific together with the extent to which hearsay makes history impossible to track. What is associated in hearsay is, I argue, a "sufficiently common" way of living that for Moseley appears as manna falling from the sky and the hospitality of slaves to mysterious practitioners of Obeah, and shows up in Wordsworth and Coleridge as the superstitious effects of repeated and unmeaning sayings. The syncretic nature of Obeah practices in Jamaica further helps us to read the persistent images of witchcraft in Wordsworth and Coleridge not as residual practices but as yet another expression of the contemporary necessity of the superfluity of needs to a colonially capitalist present. Crossing and weaving together medical practices, religious belief, underground communiqués of slave rebellions, and nonlinear images of history, Obeah and witchcraft draw our attention away from historical narratives of colonial capitalism, in which commodity production is at the center, and toward the accumulated manner in which material bodies continue to subsist in noncapitalist ways.

Running through each of these texts is an interest in the tautological thingliness of material bodies in their simultaneously dispersed and affectable existence. For Moseley, this takes the form of Obi[66] objects as well as slave's bodies, which are overly susceptible to the kinds of superstition that also take hold in "The Thorn" and "The Three Graves." For Wordsworth and Coleridge, such affectability is a condition of rural inhabitants of England as well, marking that kind of primitivized but not yet settled sense of otherness that Saree Makdisi has located in the process of "making England Western." This global commonality also holds out potential solidarities still embedded in an affectability that is associated with ways of living and speaking that are "sufficiently common," that are paradoxically both just enough and excessively enough.[67]

Throughout Chapter 3, I treat the commons as a tenuous indistinction that was constructed between the transience and redundancy, the surplus and superfluity, of subsistence as thingly bodies, and the ways in which representations and criminalizations of witchcraft in England, Jamaica, and Africa function as crucial sites of dispossession. Reading the transformations of the commons as a tautological repetition allows us to see how the gathering of affectable bodies, gendered and raced knowledge, and the nonsense of speech are all part of the dispossessed history of a contemporary commons.

In Chapter 4, I return to riots as they leap across centuries and find Romanticism embedded in the present. Here the Black Audio Film Collective's 1985 film *Handsworth Songs* provides a way to read the disruptions of linear, chronological history of the kind often imputed to the emergence of capitalism during the Romantic period. They do not present such disruptions as utopian but rather as immanent to capital's colonial and racial formations. *Songs* is a film in which apostrophic (in)direction is the only way to tell the history of the riot. Arguing that its experimental style, which plays with collage and montage, is not avant-garde but rather a "straightforward"[68] way of telling history, the BAFC provide images of a capitalism that cannot be understood outside so-called primitive accumulation. Such a history is not a product of the imposition of progress but a matter of discontinuous accumulations that are the "straightforward" history of capital.

Handsworth Songs sets the frame for my reading of work by Joseph Priestley and Erasmus Darwin, two members of the Lunar Society, a prominent group of Romantic-era scientists, philosopher-poets, and industrialists who were all deeply committed to liberal and capitalist development. More recently, rereadings of both have located them in a different materialist tradition, one concerned with horizontal ontologies.[69] In contrast, I focus on their penchant for presenting history as a flash, much in the manner of the BAFC's own presentation of Priestley in *Songs*: he appears for a flash on-screen, in an initial montage that associates him with scenes of deindustrialization and diaspora. This momentary location of him in this "straightforward" montage prompts my reading of Priestley's "New Chart of History" (1769) against most assessments of it as a sign of the impending subsumption of modern history by standardization and homogeneity.

Against such readings of the chart, I show how figure functions in the chart, allowing as it does a simultaneous coexistence of different spaces and a rapidity of impression. Following from the work on affectability in Chapter 3, I show that the modernity of Priestley's history depends not only on the linear time it constructs according to a geographically balanced scale but also on the translation of race as coexisting and differentiated space in the chart. This figural coincidence maintains spaces and times that are alternative to an industrialized logic as significant to the present, thus opening a dialogue between Romantic history and racial capitalism. The figural opens out to a way of reading these coinciding spaces and temporalities through Denise Ferreira da Silva's notion of historical and scientific modes of racism, in which the former operates through temporal plotting, while the latter creates a discourse about empirical bodies.[70] The coincidence of these opposing temporalities and different spaces provides the coordinates by which to read the status of subsistence in relation to more recognizable features of industrial capitalism. The enclosure of subsistence ways of life across the globe becomes contemporaneous, primitive, and racialized through such simultaneity. Race here is not the product of essentializing sciences but rather of the distribution of noncapitalist modes of life as coincident with but mythically other to the present.

It is because those forms of life labeled as subsistence are the target of so-called primitive accumulation that it must be presented in such figural terms—not because the violence of primitive accumulation destroys an ideal form of life that existed before but because capital becomes tangled up with the roots of subsistence as it works to enclose them. As we have seen in Priestley, Wordsworth, Coleridge, and Marx above, such a use, rooted in subsistence—in the way of life of subsistence—remains in a tenuous relation to the historical record of development. A "way of life losing its life" brings these roots and relations into the present but also enforces the continual articulation of rhetoric and subsistence together in a way that should change the way in which we, as literary critics, read if we are concerned with how language does anything. It is this coincidence between the use of language, ways of meaning, and ways of living that constitutes the dispossessions that are worked and unworked in this book. Through my reading of Romanticism, I hope that Romanticism will be seen as a way of reading history as a combination of uncombinables and as a desire to live in that history rather than to write it as otherwise and elsewhere.

Throughout these chapters, I make a case for subsistence that is not primarily grounded in social histories or in anthropological terms. Subsistence here undoes straightforward accounts of history, creating genealogies of ways of living that "weave roots endlessly, bending them to send down roots among the roots, to pass through the same points again, to redouble old adherences, to circulate among their differences, to coil around themselves or to be enveloped in the other."[71] In treating subsistence rhetorically, I hope to show that while concrete forms of life were and are continuing to be destroyed by the accumulation of capital, we must also work to locate, as Benjamin suggests, the foreign in our own ways of use and the ways those can be seized upon for the purposes of anticapitalist, antiracist labors of social reproduction, mutual aid, and ludicrous dreams in the present. This proposal is by no means meant to reduce or obscure the extreme violence of dispossession as a colonizing, racializing, and destructive process. Rather, it is meant to locate a more primary or originary dispossession at the root of subsistence, where the ways in which we meet needs have the capacity to reorder history because needs and their meeting hold together extravagance and insufficiency. These are roots of subsistence in which the destruction of the commons and riotous ways of everyday reproduction "mix with each other in tempestuous measure," to borrow Percy Shelley's language of materiality, preventing any pure recuperation of ontological privation or enclosure of the commons by the past.[72]

CHAPTER 1

Apostrophe and Riot

Apostrophic Subsistence

Since the seventeenth century the conception of the human body as a machine has been central to our understanding of the development of capitalism. As Silvia Federici puts it, "The human body and not the steam engine, and not the clock, was the first machine developed by capitalism."[1] Some of the most significant work on the relevance of the Romantic period to capitalism has made this same case, demonstrating the various ways in which bodies came to be newly disciplined and their labors increasingly standardized. It is, after all, for this reason that William Blake stands as such a formidable and formative poet of the period, for his recognition of the social devastations wrought by the making of the human into a uniform and clock-managed machine. I do not mean to dismiss this claim, but I am interested in what our account of capitalism would look like if that machine, and its outputs and inputs, became a bit stranger. As Wordsworth's depiction of the unnamed Vagrant who "Stoops her head and shuts her weary eyes; / Or on her fingers counts the distant clock, / Or, to the drowsy crow of midnight cock," suggests, the counting of the clock could still be construed as distant, and other ways of measuring the passing from one day to the next were still possible, in the Romantic period.[2] In this chapter, I pursue a reading of the coincidence of such ways in riots, unmeasured labor, and the criminalization and gendering of means of subsistence that were outside the wage form. Turning to the surprisingly apostrophic ways in which the human machine was understood to meet its needs in sites as distinctive as the nursery and the riot, apostrophe will be shown to be a constitutive trope both of riotous subsistence and a capitalist system that cannot do without it. In contrast to the sometimes binarizing opposition between the mechanical and the unmeasured body, or the disciplined and the wandering body, that derives from an identification of capitalism with industrialization, here a consideration of apostrophe allows us to see the ways in which surplus populations, carceral infrastructures, and the necessary excessiveness of subsistence ways of living coincided in the Romantic period and continue to do so today.

Apostrophe has, to my knowledge, never been associated with the mechanistic tradition, and certainly not with that tradition as a precondition of industrial capitalism. Instead, apostrophe has tended to be read as central to a Romantic discourse of life and subjectivity that carries over into the present, pervading constructions of legal personhood, human rights, and lyric poetry. But apostrophe as presented in a rhetorical tradition offers the terms through which to read the relation between subsistence and capitalism outside phases of development. Barbara Johnson tells us that apostrophe is a "deviation from convention" in which speech is "both direct and indirect, based etymologically on the notion of turning aside, of digressing from straight speech, it manipulates the I/Thou structure of address." Or, as Sara Guyer puts it more succinctly, in apostrophe "direct and indirect are not merely opposites: they coincide with, rather than exclude, one another." Jonathan Culler has famously described apostrophe as a trope of the "circuit or situation of communication itself," in which the drama of subjects of address and their overhearers is staged. Even in this scene, oppositions coincide. The "O" that marks apostrophe is also an embarrassment that "will provoke titters," an unmeaning letter and mark of extreme emotion, and the simultaneous launching of and resistance to narrative. As minimalist as a lone letter, apostrophe is also an embarrassing surplus of emotion and an outburst of the "gross body of life." This "O" always seems to signal too much and too little at the same time. In contrast to the equilibrium and homeostasis through which life is often characterized in critiques of Romantic organicism, the life of lyric entities capable of addressing one another and being addressed as subjects is always produced through a coincidence of otherwise oppositions.[3]

But setting the coincidences of apostrophe strictly within a discourse of subjects and persons forecloses the possibility that it made its way in from elsewhere, smuggled in from a history in which there were no subjects to be found. Turning elsewhere, we might find that the configurations of excess and minimality, of surplus and superfluity, through which life has been thought to be discursively sustained in lyric terms were already woven into the means of subsistence of the working and wandering poor of the Romantic period. If we attend to the figural ways in which certain forms of subsistence were addressed in the Romantic period, we will also find that the figural is historically produced through the satisfying of needs and not through the formation of subjects. Historically speaking, subsistence ways of living were already indexed by the Romantic period as if they were prior to the inauguration of history and its civilized subjects. But day-to-day life in England, both city and country, would have proved otherwise, as riots, theft and pilfering, and the criminalization of such means of subsistence produced other, ongoing experiences of subsistence that coincide both directly and indirectly with capitalism. And it is from these means that a rhetorically informed historical materialism can be gathered, along with a rhetoric that is inseparable from ways of living. If, as Marx instructs us, the minimal condition of history is subsistence, then history as we approach it here is inextricable from the figural relations that afford subsistence, the indirections and coincidences that afford reproduction in a quotidian key. Such renderings of the historical leave us with conditions of subsistence that, as I argue here, accumulate as an excess of the indirection and directness of needs, of regulated habits and deviations from convention, and of measured and unmeasurable labors that keep material bodies in motion. These deviations allow us to read beyond the often presupposed transition from mechanism to organicism, and from subsistence ways of living to industrialized labor, in order to track a persistent reconfiguration of subsistence and our riotous ways of meeting needs in Romanticisms both past and present.

Such ways of meeting needs flourished in 1795, as "the efflorescence of a regional consciousness ... as vivid as that from a hundred years before" responded to massive price inflations for provisions and "crop failures, unseasonable cold, diminished imports, and dwindling supplies." As E. P. Thompson writes, "Roads were blockaded to prevent export from the parish. Wagons were intercepted and unloaded in the towns through which they passed.... Threats were made to destroy the canals. Ships were stormed at the ports."[4] Coleridge's 1795 lectures, titled *Conciones ad Populum, or Addresses to the People*, were given amidst such upheaval. But Coleridge's addresses are not only a straightforward appeal to enlightened subjects given in the context of the riots. These texts are a rhetorical experiment in the different modes of subsistence that show up in the intersecting discourses of political economy, science, and associationists' hopes for a better future. The lectures try out different combinations of that characteristic trait of apostrophic "deviation from convention" and capacity for coincidence, locating the features of apostrophic address as being immanent to rather than a stylization of competing means of subsistence in the early Romantic period. In the version of the lecture given to a public audience in Bristol, Coleridge associates rhetoric and subsistence through the need for indirect speech to be used with those most affected by food shortages. But in the published version of the lectures, he includes an apostrophe to Famine, almost directly contravening the injunction against direct speech to famine-inflamed rioters he presents in the body of the lectures. In its published form, then, *Conciones* as a whole articulates material conditions through different configurations of apostrophic relations, holding out a riotous means of meeting needs outside relations of exchange while also articulating them with the dispossessions of unpaid labor and the carceral conditions that Peter Linebaugh has called a Romantic thanatocracy.[5]

Throughout the "Introductory Address," which was delivered as part of a set of public lectures, Coleridge says that without the minimally assured barrier of secure reproduction, the poor will fall away from social equilibrium and succumb to the impulse of pilfering. A direct response to physiological stimulation, the riots indicate the extent to which "Want" makes machines out of men and bars them from the softening conventions instilled by domestic association and education. In the "Introductory Address," Coleridge makes an appeal for strategic indirection to those without adequate means of reproduction, because those who "live *from Hand to Mouth*, will most frequently become improvident." "Possessing no stock of happiness," he writes, "[the poor] *eagerly seize* the gratifications of the moment, and *snatch* the froth from the wave as it passes by them. Nor is the desolate state of their families a restraining motive, unsoftened as they are by education, and benumbed into selfishness by the *torpedo touch* of extreme Want."[6] Troped as riotous machines, the oppressed grasp at superfluous things in instances that indicate their own status as appendages to an otherwise softened and sensible social body. In response to such hyperstimulation, Coleridge suggests that "we ... should plead *for* the Oppressed, not *to* them."[7] The mechanical movements of the poor turn them into objects of rhetorical indirection. In contrast to "men" who have "encouraged the sympathetic passions till they have become irresistible habits," "the Oppressed," "whom Plenty has not softened," do not have "minds susceptible of reason" and thus cannot sustain the excitation of a rhetoric that is not mediated by sympathetic habit.[8] Coleridge's address here participates in what Ian Balfour has described in Coleridge's better-known *Statesman's Manual* as "enforc[ing] a regime of hierarchy and exclusion" by virtue of a politics constructed "as a matter of truth (rather than power or justice)."[9] Turning the oppressed into indirect objects of address—spoken *of* rather than spoken directly *to*—these mechanistic entities become as superfluous to this scene as the froth they seize for satisfaction. "The Oppressed" cannot be addressed directly because direct address would have the same effects as the stimulation of Famine, enticing them to snatch only more insubstantial satisfactions. But in this case, bodies are not simply troped as machines; rather, figures of speech are also mechanized, becoming subject to the same economy of lack as material bodies and acting as a stimulating force akin to hunger. Direct speech is yet another species of that stimulation that the famed Enlightenment mechanist Julien Offray de La Mettrie worried would turn mechanically regulated men into devouring machines. In this distribution of rhetorical relations, "the Oppressed" are positioned as superfluous entities of address because they are most immediately stimulated by it. Thus, this troping is no mere mystification; it attests to language as a material force subject to the fluctuations of subsistence. Like a human body, figures of address can also be reduced to the stimulations of subsistence.[10] What E. P. Thompson famously once satirized as "rebellions of the belly" can just as easily be sparked by mouths, in "O"s that are uttered by the force of the oppressed.

Rhetoric and material bodies get stuck in the space of apostrophe, living—subsisting—in the immediacy of surplus and superfluity. Coleridge's admonition of those who would speak directly to the poor, rather than for them, thus directly links the rhetorical with economies of subsistence, warehousing speech in times of scarcity. If in these times "men" become machines, "living *Hand to Mouth*," then so too do figures of speech become entangled with the force of need, withheld from speech to prevent rampant pilfering. Laying the groundwork for a later social-historical consensus, the very same at which Thompson took aim in the "The Moral Economy of the English Crowd in the Eighteenth Century," Coleridge finds the cause of riots to be the immediate and unthinking reactions that link figures of speech and subsistence. Such subjugations of bodies and language to a vulgar economism of stimulation and reaction turn both into a precarious coincidence of lack and surplus. The surplus force of direct speech only amplifies the needs of the poor, already stimulated by want; and inflamed by oppressive want, the poor react excessively, seizing whatever pleasures are passing them by. Coleridge's "Address" here seizes on the etymological roots of riot, as referring both to luxurious enjoyment and to dissipation, to extravagant revelry and to wasting away, but it can only see in such figural holding together a matter of scarcity.

The rhetorical indirections meant to keep the oppressed from further stimulation were no tropological flourishes atop an economic base, however. The developmental effects of indirection were drawn from David Hartley, along with the aims of habituation and utopian associations it was meant to produce. In Hartley's theory of association, direct seizures and superfluous wants provide the originating impetus for a materialist economy of reciprocal relations. This theory presented the immediacy of needs as a stimulus response that, over time, became superfluous to actions regulated by social and environmental interactions. When Coleridge addresses "the Oppressed" and the immediacy of their needs indirectly, he does so with the sensibility that such needs are originary but superfluous and that they occur as deviations of, as indirections from, the development of harmonious social interactions. He draws this sensibility from Hartley's *Observations on Man* (1749), in which Hartley depicts the movement from a purely mechanistic to a socially habituated subject through the allegory of a child learning to express his desires, much in the manner of the poor's frothing seizures. Hartley writes that, in the first instance, "the fingers of a young child bend upon almost every impression which is made upon the palm of the hand, thus performing the action of grasping, *in the original automatic manner*. After a sufficient repetition of the motions which concur in this action, their ideas are associated strongly with other ideas, the most common of which, I suppose, are those excited by a favorite play-thing which the child uses to grasp, and hold in his hand."[11]

Here Hartley presents us with an initial form of automated seizure in an infantile state of nature. Far from a harmoniously self-regulating operation, the bending of a child's hand is a mechanistic response to external stimuli. But the relation between mechanism and motion mutates over time and in response to "a sufficient repetition of the motions" in which an object impresses the hand. The response reaction begins to change, as the child accumulates a variety of sensations that occur at the same time—sound, sight, memory—and over time. Through repetition that cause is replaced by an economy of associations, turning the effect of reaction into the cause of will. The direct sensation of impression is replaced by the association of conditions in which it first occurred:

> By pursuing the same method of reasoning, we may see how, after a sufficient repetition of the proper associations, the sound of the words *grasp, take, hold*, &c. the sight of the nurse's hand in a state of contraction, the idea of the hand, and particularly of the child's own hand, in that state, and innumerable other associated motions, i.e. sensations, ideas, and motions,

will put the child upon grasping, till, at last, that idea, or state of mind which we may call the will to grasp, is generated.[12]

This association inverts stimulation from an external to an internal force; it replaces an object with its absence, touch with sight, the child's hand with a memory of a multitude of hands. The grasp of direct need is replaced by the indirection of will and the complex associations that generate it. It is here that superfluous want develops into regulated need, not by virtue of the object of desire but by virtue of the way it is obtained. But the instance of will passes away, too, as a different mode of repetition emerges. This is the formation of what Coleridge calls habit, and which Hartley describes in the following way: "[The child] comes, at last, to obtain a sufficient connexion with so many diminutive sensations, ideas, and motions, *as to follow them in the same manner as originally automatic actions . . . and consequently to be automatic secondarily.*"[13] What was mechanistic becomes economically equilibrating, as secondary automation transforms sensational causality from an immediate grasp into a harmonious system of associations. It transforms mechanical repetition into economic associations and immediate reaction into a series of reciprocal interactions, of "worlds harmoniously moving to minds, and minds to worlds."[14]

Key to this chiasmic transformation is the separation—through temporal sequencing—of direct need and the indirection of habituated stimulation. In Hartley's schema, desires that are met in this secondary, diminutive fashion take leave from their originary form. This transformation carries over to Coleridge's address as well, where he figures direct satisfaction as a deviation from habit to which the best response is indirect speech to a secondarily automated audience. Coupled with Coleridge's understanding of rioters as grasping at froth, Hartley's allegory of associationism provides the backdrop against which the riots could be situated as a deviation in the indirections of social harmony. Such figural arrangements were the empirical foundation for socially regulated subsistence. The material association that bodies developed over time had everything to do with the rhetorical configuration of deviation and the forms, dispositions, and postures that bodies took in relation to others involved in the second form of meeting needs. Here bodies became subjects through a certain passage from direct need to indirect habits, in a passage from the immediate grasps of want to the equilibrium created by interactions of the kind that Coleridge refers to as the softening effects of education and domestic association. Figures of address were woven into the fabric of material relations and into the economy of how such relations were reproduced over time. Thus, our social means of subsistence are not economic in a purely reductive sense. Rather, subsistence is a figural operation even in this account of automation, a passage from direct sensation to indirect motions. Needs are met through a social semiotics in which indirections—diminished sensations, memories, frequent repetition, the sounds of words—substitute for and defer immediate grasps of desire. Their rhetorical positioning is not limited to Coleridge's immediate address but are inseparable from the arrangement of material conditions and the articulation of needs as they are met through progressive indirection. Subjects here emerge from the noncoincidence of direct and indirect, through a series of successful substitutions that ensure the chiasmic relation of minds moving with the harmonious world and vice versa.

Coleridge's appeal for indirection to those riotous children "liv[ing] Hand to Mouth" in the case of the riots is no simple analogy. It is grounded in the rhetorical relations of material bodies, the figural arrangement of needs and their fulfillment understood as the progressive movement from riotous stimulation to secondary automation. Coleridge's rhetorical indirection is embedded in the material relations of sensation, time, repetition, habit, and relational equilibrium, and derives from a materialist account of the directness of needs and the indirections through which they are met. Unlike the secondarily automated hand of the child, the grasp of the poor remains stuck in, seized by, the static condition of mechanical reaction, ungratified by repetitive satisfaction that leads to habit. Such seizure is an imbalance in an economic subsistence, caught in that messier coincidence of direct needs and deviations from convention or habit. Immediate needs, as Coleridge has it, are outside an ideal equilibrium of secondary automation, and those possessed by them cannot help but react arbitrarily, grasping for gratification, moments, froth, or playthings.[15] Figured in this mechanistic manner, direct material needs become a deviation from within the movement toward an economic indirection of habit.

The associationist development posited by Hartley and put into play by Coleridge puts Romantic materialism into dialogue with Malthusian castings of the poor, as well as with Marx's later critique of it. For Malthus, the poor were always surplus in a superfluous sense, exemplary of the ways in which populations could be necessarily and unnecessarily excessive at the same time.[16] Famously, Marx intervenes into Malthus's construction of surplus populations in order to show that they are not the necessary effect of a natural cycle of abundant labor and agricultural scarcity but rather the "lever" of capital accumulation.[17] In contrast to the Malthusian line in which surplus populations are an expression of natural scarcity, Marx shows that the populations that fall in and out of or that never enter into the paid workforce are actually the historically produced condition of possibility for capitalist profits. To be sure, the accumulation of wealth in a capitalist mode could not have functioned without the coincidence of the surplus and superfluous population that Marx figures as the "lever" that ensures that a mass of potential workers are always on hand during technological "leaps." And while Marx tends to figure the effects of capital accumulation in chiasmic polarities, with "an accumulation of misery . . . corresponding to the accumulation of wealth," I want to suggest that it is also the apostrophic coincidence of subsistence as it is met simultaneously through the indirection of the wage and in ways that remain outside its measured means that makes accumulation possible.[18] The coincidence, and not the opposition, of these different means gives new meaning to Marx's sense that within capitalism the worker becomes "an appendage of a machine."[19] More akin to Hartley's conception of the mechanical expression of need, workers in their surplus form are both foundational and superfluous, balancing both sides of a noneconomic relationship. At the level of the social, the "lever" of surplus population is a direct indirection, in which the mediation of waged reproduction and needs met otherwise have to be in play at the same time.[20]

Coleridge's indirect speech—which automates the bodies of the poor while simultaneously turning figuration into a subsistence-style stimulation—thus accurately, if ironically, figures the actual unfolding of subsistence within the machinations of capital accumulation in the Romantic period. Not a matter of mechanization in a reductive, or even literal, sense, this figuration works like a "lever," as the coincidence of being on both sides at once, simultaneously existing as lack and surplus for capital. Drawing heavily from Hartley's mechanistic materialism, these appeals do not straightforwardly attest to the mechanization of the human body for the purposes of labor. They introduce the necessity of the direct indirections of apostrophe to the mechanisms of capital accumulation. The superfluity of needs is at the center and to the side, both cause and (mechanistic) effect, of the conditions for such accumulation.[21] The maintenance of subjects developed through proper indirection is inseparable from the continuation of subsistence in a direct mode for surplus populations, which continued to play a central role in the conditions of the accumulation of capital.

Like Coleridge, Edmund Burke argued during the riots that "the cry of the people . . . ought, in *fact*, to be the *least* attended to upon this subject; for citizens are in a state of utter ignorance of the means by which they are to be fed."[22] Deeply wedded to Smithian and Malthusian economics, Burke argues for a separation between those needs that can be met through exchange and equivalents and the exclusion from the market of those that cannot, but in so doing he cannot help but hint at a fact that even Adam Smith and David Ricardo understood: that needs are not measurable and that meeting them entails deviations from the convention of the wage. It is the unavoidable acknowledgment of this coincidence of what cannot be measured with what bears equivalence that opens us up to struggles over subsistence that are not reducible to economically distributed forms.

Indirect Reproduction in Burke and Coleridge

Without conflating Coleridge and Burke's attitudes toward the 1795 riots, what is significant here is the way in which their understanding of the riots as a direct expression of need is met with a sense that needs should be met through a self-regulating equilibrium; otherwise, satisfactions turn into dangerous grasps on the margins of economic relations.[23] Both Coleridge and Burke address the immediate seizures of "Want" through rhetorical indirection. When not delivered by the self-regulating price of labor, according to Burke, or directed through sympathetically habituated subjects, according to Coleridge, the subsistence of the working poor turns into spontaneous direct action. These depictions, while distinct in their principles, both render subsistence obtained outside the equivalence of price or the equilibrium of the social as superfluous—in excess and necessarily unnecessary. The direct needs of the working class are, in this sense, met through a circuitous deviation from the automatic operations that otherwise supply demand. Exited from the process in which survival is sustained by reasoned exchange, nonequilibrating forms of subsistence become mechanistic parts and superfluous extremities on the periphery of animating circulation.

As Joshua Clover has recently reminded us, riots are a struggle over the direct means of reproduction. In contrast to the strike, which Clover understands as a struggle over the indirect means of subsistence that are wages, riots are a struggle over commodities. If for Thompson the eighteenth-century food riot was a way of "setting the price" of commodities in an inherently anticapitalist manner, then for Clover the riot is, more generally, a struggle over reproduction outside what waged labor could ever provide in a system so dependent on that "lever" of the surplus population. It is a circumvention of the indirection of the wage and a contestation over the status of those positioned as economically superfluous by their lack of access to it. From this perspective, the riot is a direct action that seizes the items most necessary to subsistence and enacted by those who are presumed to be the most supplemental to the capitalist labor market. The riot suspends the measure of needs by the supposed equivalence of the wage and instead opens subsistence up to the coincidence of necessity and superfluity, of what is enough and what is beyond measure. In this sense, we can see that the riot is not a response to overstimulation or the meager directness of need. It is an expression of the constitutively direct indirection of needs and of the ways in which they are necessarily met through deviation. In the riot, necessities are met by "not taking the straight or nearest course in view; not going straight to the point," and on a way, path, or course," that is "crooked, devious."[24] The riot is an alternative construction of the direct indirection of the meeting of needs, one that contests any proper separation between direct needs and their satisfaction through the indirection of the wage.[25]

These scenes of struggle over subsistence cross back over into the rhetorical scene set by Coleridge, expressing the material relations of social reproduction as they are organized—spatially and temporally—in the terms of direct and indirect relations. That is, the riot highlights the ways in which needs can be met directly through deviations from the convention of the market rather than as affirmations of it. Rendered as rhetorically indirect because it is a direct seizure, the disorderly and disorganizing grasp of the riot is situated as a deviation from the means by which subsistence might otherwise be ensured economically. For this reason I want to stay with Coleridge's figuration of the oppressed as deviating from the conventional means of subsistence in their frenzied froth-grabbing. Much in the manner that apostrophe creates an indistinction between subjects and objects, Coleridge's looking away from the oppressed leaves them at the periphery of his vocal field, like a phenomenophiliac specter of satiety.[26] Rather than reading such deviations as mystifications of previously established convention, I am interested in Coleridge's association of a certain mode of subsistence—namely the riot—with an extreme instance of direct indirection.

When published, *Conciones* was accompanied by an address to that stimulus of seizure, famine, titled "A Letter from Liberty to Her Dear Friend Famine," which prefaced the "Introductory Address."[27] In publishing the "Letter to Famine" prior to the "Introductory Address," Coleridge introduced a meditation on secondary automation in the context of scarcity with an apostrophic association between indirection and immediate need. In a distinctly anti-Burkean mode, Coleridge's Liberty appeals to that overstimulating source of deviation, Famine, asking her to bring about her own demise by ending the grain crisis. After repeated appeals by Religion, Prudence, and Conscience addressed to the "Majesty," Liberty realizes that each is a "perfect ventriloquist who could throw her voice into any place she liked." Liberty next turns away from those masters of indirection and instead apostrophizes Famine. The letter ends with a closing apostrophe: "O Famine, most eloquent Goddess! Plead my cause. I meantime will pray fervently that Heaven may unseal the ears of its viceregents, so that they may listen to your first pleadings, while yet your voice is faint and distant, and your counsels peaceable."[28]

The letter shifts the figural arrangement of subsistence that later arrives in the "Introductory Address." Restyling "the Oppressed" as the allegorical "Famine," Coleridge pleads to Famine to intervene directly—to speak directly to—the state. Here he rhetorically indulges the coincidence of direct and indirect in the form of needs and of speech, establishing an economy in which needs are not a matter of direct satisfaction but are caught in an economy of unmeasured indirection, in which the surplus and superfluity of needs coincide. The "torpedo touch of Want" is met in this instance not by the equilibrium of habit that renders such need as superfluous but through an apostrophic deviation from convention in which surplus and lack coincide. In contrast to the distribution of direct and indirect that we saw above, the apostrophic arrangement of Coleridge's letter embraces the indivisibility of the surplus and the superfluous, of satisfaction and froth. This apostrophe directly contravenes Burke's Malthusian convention, appealing to an allegorized version of that overstimulating source of "rebellions of the belly."[29] If apostrophe creates direct relations through deviation, through a split between the "by" and the "to," then Coleridge's address to the riot(er)s makes it impossible to sever the connection between excessive need and its deviating satisfaction. The separation between the direct and indirect collapses here, with an articulation of subsistence as their inseparability. Such subsistence is not measured by a progressive equilibrium but by a radical coincidence between surplus and lack figured here as Famine.

Elsewhere this coincidence can also be found in the London underground, in the debate clubs hosted by Robert Wedderburn that become a refuge for so many, including his predecessor Thomas Spence, who made his way circulating trade coins (without the value imputed to universal equivalence), homemade liquor, and incendiary declarations to dispossess the wealthy; in the washerwomen who would take time to write defenses of their free time, their labor, and their poetry; in the middle-class runaways making not much of a living writing letters and the sex workers and working poor who would become sources of their imaginative surplus; and in the "rushing multitudes" who would pour flour gleaned from riots into waterways, burn Newgate, and fill the pages of Dickens with fascinated abjection in his depictions of Romantic riots in *Barnaby Rudge*.

Strangely enough, in its own way, Burke also attests to the coexistence of equalized and nonequalized labors of meeting needs in his "Thoughts and Details on Scarcity." Such labors are, in his own telling, the labors of a different kind of repetition from the ones Hartley describes, although they also occur alongside that development of self-regulating habit. In his memoranda Burke distinguishes between the labors of those "who are able to perform the full work of a man" and the labors of those "who are able to work, but not the complete task of a day-laborer." The second group includes men after the age of fifty, who are "every year more sensible to the period of debility and decrepitude," and "*women*, whose employment on husbandry is but occasional, and who differ more in effective labor one from another than men do, on account of gestation, nursing, and domestic management."[30] The distinction Burke makes here is between those whose labor is regulated by equivalence (wages) and those whose labor is too "occasional" and chaotic to fit within the measures of supply and demand:

> This inferior classification is introduced to shew, that laws . . . never can provide the just proportions between earning and salary on the one hand, and nutriment on the other: whereas interest, habit and the tacit convention, that arise from a thousand nameless circumstances, produce a tact that regulates without difficulty, what laws and magistrates cannot regulate at all. The first class of labour wants nothing to equalize it; it equalizes itself. The second [is] not capable of any equalization.[31]

For Burke, this second class of laborers, "not capable of any equalization," exists as a deviation from the convention of equivalence, while remaining, separately, as labor. Such labor is partial, unmeasurable, and occasional, and outside the motions of disciplined habit. Its classification is based on an equivalence in relation to which all kinds of things—gestation, nursing, social reproduction—fall outside. But as Coleridge's apostrophe helps us to understand, such labors do not so much fall outside what can be measured as they coincide with it. They occur alongside yet at the same time without being reducible to the convention of equivalence.[32] They are the lack and surplus, the superfluous and the excess that coincide with a commodified labor that for Burke can only be regulated by the invisible hand of habit and convention. In this sense, such kinds of labor are constituted in a separation through equivalence and through an association that, again, figures them as unmeasurable, in contrast to indirectly measured waged labor. Subsistence always involves an unmeasurable set of relations through which needs are met, beyond the reductive classification of what Burke terms "nutriment," in excess of equalization. It is disorderly in regard to the time of the working day and the habit and convention of market-based price setting.

The embarrassment of Coleridge's apostrophic gestures is not containable by the continually blinded insights generated by economies of equivalence; these gestures indicate a different kind of economic embarrassment. Embarrassing in the sense of "an (overwhelming or encumbering) excess or abundance of riches [and] resources," apostrophe rewrites the Malthusian sense of subsistence not as "a bare or minimum level of existence" but as the excessive and nonequivalent direct indirections of survival. When Coleridge addresses Famine, these relations are reorganized not through the progressive divisions made by Burke and Hartley but through the inseparability that characterizes apostrophe. The indirection of this moment is not a mark of superfluity in separation but of a deviation in which superfluity and surplus, of unmeasurable labors and daily subsistence, can coincide without the separation of equivalence. Coleridge's apostrophe here presupposes a different economy of subsistence, in which conventions are set by constant deviations from measure and the meeting of wants and needs requires labors without measure and relations of nonequivalence. Apostrophe makes it possible to center direct indirection as its own mode of reproduction rather than understanding it as superfluous to subsistence and direct demands for survival.

Such obstructions are historically accurate: after all, subsistence as measured by exchange was hard to establish, since, contrary to classical political economics, subsistence-style production was actually good at meeting needs. Indeed, "dependence was often forced not because production of subsistence goods in household agriculture was inadequate, but precisely because it was adequate. If households were independent of the labour market, the laboring population—once it produced what it needed for consumption for exchange in order to pay rent—would choose leisure instead of more production."[33] Subsistence, understood as that mode of life which provides enough to repeat it again the next day, is an economy that constricts the measure of exchange in favor of unmeasured time. But it is precisely for this reason that it takes an apostrophic form in relation to an exchange economy, operating simultaneously as a source of maintenance outside measure and being treated as a cost or lack within the sphere of productive labor that always demands measured surplus.

Instead of a seizure of goods for that most quotidian need—reproduction for the day—this figuration of the riots gives way to a transient economy over which it is the arrangement of an always indirect nature of subsistence that is contested. Apostrophe thus marks a distinction from Burke's and even Thompson's understandings of the riots, which, while opposed on all other terms, refer us to convention as a matter of measure, either of the feudal past or the free market economy. From Thompson's perspective, food riots were a return to, not a deviation from, a conventional sensibility that was noncapitalist and antiprofiteering, and supported by the memory of common law.[34] But the 1795 riots as I have read them show an apostrophic arrangement of subsistence, in which superfluity and surplus coincide. Here, the inseparability of what is in excess and what is necessary is what is contested in the riot. To this extent, struggles over that reproduction from one day to the next cannot be about the direct "stuff" of mere subsistence. Rather, they are contestations over the figural arrangement of subsistence, the minimal and the maximal conditions of passing from one day to the next. Apostrophe fuses, or renders coincident, the measured proportion of the working day with what Kristin Ross has called the communal luxury of address as it declares "an understanding of the present, in its unfolding, as historical, as changing."[35] Eighteenth-century and Romantic-period poetry is full of such figural subsistence, and the practices of subsistence alive in them are full of poetry: the "chattering" of women between breaks in labor against which Stephen Duck railed, the songs and dances that erupted around the

Albion Mills as it burned in 1791, the unaccounted counter–clock time of Wordsworth's Vagrant and the "recessive action" of his poetry more generally, and the inexplicable coincidence of the "maddest people" of the Gordon Riots with a knowledgeable crowd that "broke open the doors" of Newgate Prison "as if they had all their lives been acquainted with the intricacies of the place to let the confined escape" before burning "the strongest and most durable prison in England . . . in the space of a few hours. The list could go on, immeasurably. The figures that we often consider constitutive of Romantic rhetoric are themselves images of the economic arrangements of subsistence, in which the meeting of needs operates through deviation and indirection, what Saidiya Hartman has recently called the "social poiesis" and "art of survival" of that "activity required to reproduce and sustain life," rather than any measured or direct manner.[36]

This figural nature of the subsistence that we find in the riot presents a different historical understanding of the rhetorical than Amanda Jo Goldstein has recently described as a "materiality . . . marked [sic] by the tendency to trope." While materiality is marked by the tendency to trope, the form of that trope is conditioned by the historicity of subsistence. The relations of giving and taking form, of reciprocity and interdependence, that ontological readings impute to figure need to be supplemented with figure's inseparability from the conditions of reproduction, which are, in Marx's figural language, "concrete because of the concentration of many determinations" in a particular conjuncture.[37] While materialist conceptions of irreducibly relational reproduction are inextricable from the rhetorical, the rhetorical is also deeply enmeshed in the material conditions of subsistence. As shown above, such rhetorical materiality shares its conditions of existence with historical modes of reproduction. But these historical modes are not direct, nor are they reducible to the economic directly, or at least not in the traditional Marxist sense of historical modes of production. The ontology of "worlds moving to minds, and minds to worlds" that we saw in Hartley was formed in the conditions of contestation over the figural nature of subsistence and the organization of its vital indirections. Never purely a logic of the commodity, such struggles had to do with the distribution of the indirections of unmeasured labor, free time, nonequivalent objects, and "social poiesis," as superfluous, together with the figural sensibility around such excess.

Erasmus Darwin's Articulation of Reproduction

Thus far we have been following a more well-known affiliation between mechanistic associationism, which Coleridge would later vehemently reject, and the physiological, psychological, and social developmentalism it assisted in cultivating. But as our inquiry into Coleridge and Hartley also suggests, such a mechanism was never so straightforward. Rather, it involved a negotiation with a rhetoric of indirection, bringing it closer to an apostrophic economy where clear divisions between what is necessary and what is excessive, what is harmonious and what is superfluous, break down. With this apostrophic "aneconomy" in mind, we turn to another site where its coincidences become further involved with the material conditions of the production of Romantic science and articulated with what critical race scholar Jackie Wang has recently dubbed "carceral capitalism."[38] Here the stakes of considering the riot as a way of subsistence and as the coincidence of a necessary superfluity in the meeting of needs, come into view more fully as the immanent domain of capital accumulation outside the confines of sites of labor.

With this sense of subsistence, let us turn away from Coleridge's address in the Bristol Corn Market and to an anatomy theater in Lichfield. More than thirty years before the 1795 food riots and four years before an earlier wave broke out in 1766, the following announcement was published in the *Aris Gazette*:

> October 23rd 1762—The body of the Malefactor, who is ordered to be executed at Lichfield on Monday the 25th instant, will be afterwards conveyed to the house of Dr. Darwin, who will begin a Course of Anatomical lectures, at Four o'clock on Tuesday evening, and continue them every Day as long as the Body can be preserved, and shall be glad to be favoured with the Company of any who profess Medicine or Surgery, or whom the Love of Science may induce.[39]

This immediate conveyance of "the body of the Malefactor" from the gallows to the home, coupled with the movement from an execution by the law to an address to lovers of science, provokes an unsettling material site of extraction for Erasmus Darwin's otherwise fluidly figural theories of living bodies. Far afield from recent readings of his *Love of Plants*, this announcement to lovers of science entangles such theories with the well-documented savagery of capital punishment in the eighteenth century.[40] As Peter Linebaugh and Jordy Rosenberg have shown, dissections of the kind that pushed anatomical and physiological knowledge "forward" in the eighteenth century were made possible by the long-term fallout from enclosure and the legal structures that were put in place to protect property from those who could not turn even their labor into a commodity.[41] Without the ability to do this, the dispossessed turned to theft, vagrancy, and other crimes that often led them to the gallows. It was in their deaths that such dispossessed bodies became productive. As Rosenberg documents, Bernard Mandeville argued in favor of harvesting anatomical knowledge from these otherwise unproductive bodies.[42] "The body of the Malefactor" that arrived at Darwin's home on October 23 was an example of the prison-to-physician pipeline that subsequently developed. Already separated out from the sphere of equivalence in which labor counted as a commodity, this "Malefector" came to "count" as a source of epistemological value by virtue of dispossessions of subsistence.

Physicians' access to cadavers for dissection was limited, but it was more heavily supplied in the late eighteenth century owing to what Linebaugh argues was the conversion in the late eighteenth century of waste products into property. He accounts for the excessive use of capital punishment in London, at least in part, as a result of the recategorization of waste into commodities, a transformation that made a means of subsistence outside equivalence into a capital crime. What had previously been considered a customary right to the excess materials of production, free to take home, became criminalized as theft. Such "perquisites," the nonagricultural version of gleaning, reduced the reliance on the commodified form of wages, thus freeing up time and enabling limited autonomy from labor.[43] Such practices, much like Thompson's conception of the riot as a setting of the price of commodities, worked to preserve some plasticity and dynamism within the overall economy of subsistence, allowing an outlet from its subsumption by exchange value. But decades of the Bloody Laws, which between 1660 and 1815 made threats to or expropriations of private property such as theft punishable by death, and shifts in the vagrancy laws made such practices, along with access to free time away from labor, punishable by death or transportation.[44] This was, effectively, a transfer of superfluous excess into a lack in terms of workers' access to a noncommodified means of reproduction. What had been considered waste became a means of increasing the surplus labor of workers in yet another instance of the reorganization of noncapitalist means of subsistence as superfluous to the market. In another reweaving of the relations of direct and indirect in the economy of subsistence, the criminalization of such "theft" meant that another direct way of meeting needs outside an exchange economy, through waste products, was shifted into a form of deviance.

This history of deathly hierarchy and exclusions in which bodies were separated on the basis of their subsistence within or outside relations of equivalence filters ambivalently into the radically non-Cartesian and materialist theory of life for which Darwin is well known. In his most famous scientific treatise, *Zoonomia*, Darwin theorized an interdependent ontology of animated beings, leading him to declare that "the whole of nature" was a sensorium patterned like congeries, "a collection of things merely massed or heaped together," in which relations between the vegetable and animal worlds were formed like "the branches of coralline."[45] Darwin argued that "the whole of nature may be supposed to consist of two essences of substances . . . motion, considered as a cause, immediately precedes every effect; and, considered as an effect, it immediately succeeds every cause."[46] Along with other members of the Lunar Society, in particular Joseph Priestley (the subject of Chapter 4), Darwin was part of a significant shift in British empiricism through which such essential substances became contingent and open to change. Such empiricism, predicated on the fundamental inability to directly access the structures underlying phenomena, went so far as to upend hierarchical distinctions between essential structures and phenomena. Darwin's extension of Hartley's materialism is a forerunner to the kinds of Simmelian science that suspended binaries between nature and culture, rendering them instead into an interactively determining relationship between the social and the natural in which, over time, they came to stand in the place of cause and effect at different points.[47] Such reinterpretations of Hartley function to de-center agency within any pregiven agent (the human or the social) and displace it onto forms of relation. Nature, in Darwin's conceptualization, was articulated, jointed together through relations that are not ordered hierarchically but could be differentiated from one another.

What made such interconnected order possible was the *je ne sais quoi* that characterized animated matter in much the same manner as we saw in Hartley. But whereas for Hartley such interconnection was primarily social and psychological, for Darwin it extended into an ecology of species. Darwin and others in his Lunar Society were interested in the capacity for systems to self-organize and for living bodies to be immanently generated by material interdependency, although subject to deviation at times. Like Hartley's allegory of the transformation from instantaneous reaction to the choreography of second nature, Darwin's account of such bodies, what Maureen McNeil calls a "biological learning process realized through habits," is narrated as the development from a localized mechanism of physiological reaction to an interconnected, dynamic environmental and social equilibrium.[48] Through a combination of fluidity and repetition, animated bodies constructed convention through a dynamic give-and-take fixed only by the ability to maintain, at various scales of bodies, a balance of excitation.

Between Darwin's basement in Lichfield and his writing in *Zoonomia*, we have two seemingly opposed processes at work. One is the effect of the violent divisions of living bodies between those who live and those who die, another an account of all bodies as the effect of interconnected motions. The materialist ontology theorized by Darwin emerges through and alongside a hierarchy of bodies divided by the conjuncture of dispossession and eighteenth-century carceral capitalism. These interconnected but differentiated routes turn Darwin's figure of coralline connection away from the purely scientific and toward a more historically material coincidence with those contested economies of subsistence we saw in the riot.

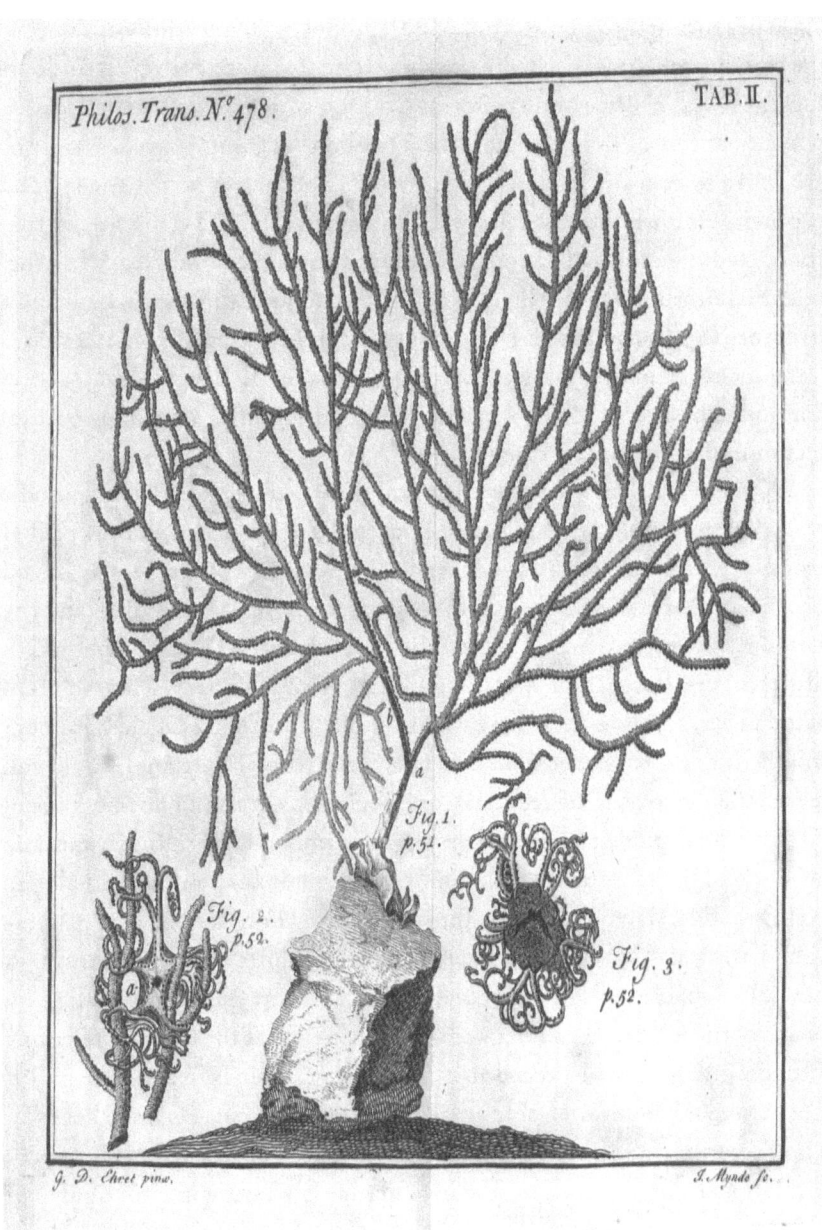

Hans Sloane, *A Description of a Curious Sea Plant. Philosophical Transactions of the Royal Society* 44 (1746). Reprinted with permission from the Royal Society.

Darwin's own figure of interconnection proposes an uncannily apt one for the structures through which superfluous bodies were conveyed to doors such as his. Like the coralline forms through which he articulated the interconnections of living bodies, the relations between dispossession, the law, and a science of sensibility came together at certain points and split off at others. Neither entirely designed nor formed arbitrarily, the sinews that connected the criminalization of nonwaged subsistence and Darwin's theories of living bodies were branching and congeried. And they articulated a structure that encompasses Darwin's treatment of a radically shared sensorium, inclusive of dreaming plants, together with the history of dissection that made bodies available for knowledge through the circuitous path of accumulation-by-dispossession.

In this sense, Darwin's deeply figural theory of nature gives us a model of capital accumulation while also highlighting the *material* form of that process, dependent as it is upon the coralline structure of nature. Organized like the jointed dispersions of coralline, this model captures more about the material conditions of reproduction than he meant it to. Developing through "different practices [that] operate as a series of interconnected but differentiated processes," the coralline structure that links the Lichfield basement and the theories of *Zoonomia* turns us toward what Stuart Hall would call the articulated nature of economic and social, cultural, and juridical structures within capitalist economies. Sharing etymological origins that mimic those of coral, the term "articulation" comes out of anatomy and botany, as well as rhetoric, later developing the mechanical connotations Hall primarily had in mind.[49] In each use the term implies a connection of parts through joints that enable motion and movement. Darwin's figuration of nature by means of the jointed skeleton of coralline also figures the indirect relations through which, in Hall's account, exchange value comes to organize multiple vectors of life as "a variable amalgam," and in Brenna Bhandar's words, is both "noninevitable yet nonarbitrary" precisely because it must be reproduced materially.[50] Coralline and articulation are both material figures of a natural history in which there is "no historical category without natural substance, no natural substance without its historical filter."[51]

A product of the articulation of "interconnected but differentiated" processes of reproduction—of labor, of physiological motion, of historical modes of subsistence—Darwin's extension of a Hartleyan materialism provides a way to understand the emergent entwinement of capital accumulation with the reproduction of living bodies, in a dialectic between nature and history. That is, the indirect but interconnected mode of nature posited by Darwin is not ontologically opposed to the structures of capital, as has often been suggested.[52] Such a figure provides a model for the ways in which means of subsistence are both rendered as deviations—mechanized indirections—visible in riots and theft alike, and come to be articulated as the branch that turned bodies into sites of knowledge about nature while simultaneously suturing them to an economy ordered by exchange value. Darwin's notion of a coralline ontology of nature and Hall's notion of an articulated structure for the social locate the historical relations of capital in coincident figures.

This articulation also makes it possible to read the otherwise binarized assessments of Darwin's work and its relationship to industrial capitalism differently. Presented as a direct relation between the mechanization of industrial capitalism and the quantification of material motions by McNeil, and between commodification and imperial science by Alan Bewell, Darwin's contributions to capitalism seem relatively straightforward. As McNeil writes, Darwin's understanding of the body as a machine led him "to a quantitative medicine in which political economy and the organic economy were fused."[53] From this perspective, attempts to measure the "excitability" of living bodies made by Darwin, and others similarly working in the materialist tradition popularized by Scottish physician John Brown, are immediately legible within an increasingly commodified, as well as classified, form of life and mechanized mode of production.

But as others have argued, Darwin's scientific work made major contributions to a science of life that challenged binaristic formations and dehierarchized fixed classifications. In Kevis Goodman's words, Darwin was part of a rearticulation of Newtonian mechanics through a "detailed, material imagination" that "offered him and others a way of fending off the specter of man as machine [and] a physiology of relative freedom from outer forces."[54] While these more rhetorically and figurally attentive readings of

Table of Excitement and Excitability, illustration by Samuel Lynch. *The Elements of Medicine, to John Brown, M.D. Translated from the Latin, with Comments and Illustrations, by the Author* (London: J. Johnson, 1795). Reprinted with permission from the American Antiquarian Society.

Darwin might seem to be at odds with those that situate Darwin directly in the context of industrialism, this is not necessarily the case; rather, they highlight the articulated, that is, coralline, nature of capital accumulation that is missed in an emphasis on capital's mechanically commodifying drive. While Darwin was certainly an enthusiast of industrialism, most significant about his work for understanding the emergence of industrial capital might be the ways in which seemingly oppositional tendencies and organizations of life coincide throughout his corpus. Such an apostrophic configuration reinforces Darwin's own figural onto-epistemology of nature not in opposition to capital accumulation but, in Hall's words, as "a series of interconnected but differentiated processes."

The opposing tendencies of Darwin's work provide a dialectical image of the coincidence of the relative freedom and quantified motions of bodies, the sensorium of nature and the hierarchy of unfree humans through which capital accumulated beyond the frame of straightforward binaries. Rather than being an imposition from the outside, in which the transcendental and idealized relations of supply-and-demand economics come to dominate the transient and messy material means of subsistence, the heterogeneous conditions of the emergence of capitalism can "in retrospect seem almost entirely fortuitous," as Cedric Robinson has extensively historicized it. Not a pure drive for commodification, the collision between Darwin's science and the state's response to expropriation demonstrate how means of subsistence came to be differentiated from one another, separated through the measurability of their economies. It also articulates the relations between nature and the social through those apostrophic terms of direct and indirect relations. The arrival of an anonymous "Malefactor" on Darwin's doorstep coincides with the mechanistic movements of rioters through the figural status of their means of subsistence. Such histories are connected by the conversion of relations of nonequivalence into scarcity and of unmeasured time into either bare life or criminal status. The conditions that led to the outbreak of riots in the late eighteenth century were also the conditions through which this body-without-equivalence came to Lichfield, through "a series of interconnected but differentiated processes" that can be found in nature, like the structure of coralline.[55] The minimal relation of equivalence as it separates certain means of subsistence from others marks the boundary between rioters, criminals, cadavers, and otherwise interconnected species.

Coleridge and Darwin's Convention of Deviations

In his *Phytologia; or, The philosophy of Agriculture and Gardening*, Darwin describes the difference between the development of trees and that of coralline-like insects as the difference between exogenous growth and eternal decay, writing that "the caudexes of buds, which compose the barks and afterwards the timber of trees, differ from the nests or cells of the coralline insects, which compose their calcerous [sic] insects, like the shells of other sea-animals, become harder by time" and eventually are "converted into limestone and flint, and remain eternal monuments of departed animal life."[56] Here depicting the growth of coralline through layers of calcareous decay, Darwin distinguishes trees from such growth-by-death through their annual expansion as exogenous, or "grow[ing] from the outside." A figure of indirect reproduction, of generation from the outside in, this organic exogeneity occurs circuitously.

Thus, through another figural form of growth isolated in nature, Darwin points us to the indirect relations through which reproduction occurs. Not an organic growth from within, the annual growth of trees occurs multidirectionally, both "from" and "by" relations that develop from the outside in. With this figure Darwin crystallizes another way of thinking the relation between nature and history. In directing us to the historical nature of growth that operates exogenously rather than through decay, Darwin offers another instance of the figural as it is bound up with the historical conditions of subsistence, of day-to-day reproduction. But as we have seen in the discussion of forms of subsistence as demonstrated in the riots and the transport of bodies to Darwin's door, such figures were at the center of reproduction as it was articulated through exchange value. Both Coleridge's address to rioters and Darwin's address to the lovers of science are instances of such historically configured and contested figuration. They provide dialectical images of subsistence and deviation, of the ways in which the deviations immanent to subsistence were externalized as aberrations in convention.

The examples gathered in this chapter attest to an accumulation that operates in this more figural mode, through a history of interventions into the apostrophic arrangement—the unmeasurable labors and indirect relations—of subsistence. Coleridge's tropings of subsistence, Burke's division of unmeasured labor, and Darwin's claim over the "body of the Malefactor" provide occasions for reading the ways in which such accumulation occurred through interventions into the apostrophic affordances of everyday reproduction and the indirect mediations of capital punishment. Riotous struggles over the cost of reproduction, nonequivalent labors that do not fit the measure of the wage form, and laws that separated the equivalent from the nonequivalent modes of subsistence all attest to the negotiation with the directly indirect nature of subsistence. Collected together, they constellate the array of ways in which subsistence is an apostrophic relation and the ways in which the historical production of certain forms of subsistence provided the materials for a sphere of knowledge production about the articulated interconnectedness of life.

In other words, subsistence is an economy of deviations. Coleridge's riotous face-off between apostrophic indirection and arbitrary directness aptly captures the differences of indirection as it is structured between two different economies. Struggles over subsistence in the Romantic period highlight a sustenance that occurs through repeated deviations from convention rather than adherence to it. Figured in Coleridge's declaration to Famine is the history of direct indirections that constitute subsistence—those defenses of leisure time, of the affordances of perquisites or waste, and of the transient economy of needs and desires that are recorded in the historical record as riots, theft, executions, and labor disciplining. Translated into a subsistence reduced to necessity and the maintenance of bare life in the "Introductory Lecture," the apostrophic letter indicates a more radical mediation between direct needs and the indirections through which they are met and in which the means of maintaining life are essentially indirect rather than mechanistically direct seizures. Subsistence of this kind is more aligned with that "flagrantly disorganized and disorganizing effect" of material life, hinged on "an obsolescent and transitive expression between bodies that multiplies their relations and exacerbates their contingency."[57]

But this figural account of subsistence also suggests that such life is not entirely "outside" more measured and equalizing forms of reproduction. According to feminist and colonialist accounts of capital accumulation, capital expands in a more rhetorically material fashion than our more familiar accounts of industrialization and commodity production suggest. Capital "grow[s] on the outside" of modes of reproduction and forms of subsistence that are nonidentical to its own logic. Understood from this perspective and woven through the figural nature Darwin offers us, the accumulation of capital can be seen as inseparable from the figural, inasmuch as the figural is material. While we tend to separate figuration from the process of accumulation, presenting it as disordering to capital's drive for homogeneity, it is the figural—that is, the apostrophic—nature of subsistence that affords capital accumulation its necessarily exogenous mode of expansion. In other words, capital accumulation occurs more figurally than we have often portrayed it, which means, vice versa, that the rhetorical is more historical than we have often portrayed it as well.

It was this deviating nature of historical subsistence that Adam Smith and David Ricardo understood to be the primary point of antagonism, as well as loss of profit, for capitalists. As Antonella Picchio writes, they understood that "the material standards of living expressed in the natural price of labour . . . are determined by the consolidated habits and tastes of the laboring population."[58] Habits, contrary to Burke's account, were always deviating from the calculations of a supply-and-demand market. In other words, the means of subsistence for the working class was understood to be deeply historical, subject to the contingencies and fluctuations of a material system. The economy of subsistence was a deeply figural one, understood to be both outside and inside commodity production in its capitalist mode and irreducible to the measure of equivalence.[59]

Even this classical assessment of the relation between capitalist production and social reproduction was openly configured along apostrophic lines, of an integrally indirect and contingent relation over which struggle would always ensue in the drawing of lines between the necessary and the superfluous. Only later was reproduction "transformed into the idea of a supply-and-demand equilibrium (in the limited sense of work done in the workplace)."⁶⁰ Toward the mid-nineteenth century, more Malthusian-inspired political economists established a mechanistic supply-and-demand calculation that dislocated the contingent and historic nature of the material needs of a laboring population outside the costs that capital would bear. Everything that could not be reduced to the wage form was pushed into the domain of the social and transferred as a cost onto an array of social and ecological relations. Such calculations located reproduction outside the labor market, but as others cited throughout this chapter have shown, made reproductive labor all the more invisibly central to the possibilities of capital accumulation. After all, as more Malthusian and mechanistic formulas of supply-and-demand economics were put forward, the reproduction of labor power became excessively cheap, enabling greater profits to accrue. In this mode, the further social reproduction is divided from the cost calculations of capital, the more integrated it becomes with it.

Capital accumulation thus occurs from the outside in, articulating spheres of equivalence and excess through indirect relations that are necessary for the "direct" object of commodification. Accumulation occurs, in other words, in a figural manner in which the "thing" of capital—exchange value—can only derive from what grows outside, proliferates beyond, and exceeds it. The historically contingent means of subsistence are necessary for the production and accumulation of capital, but they are also necessarily indirect with respect to capital. The trick of the organization of labor under capital, however, is its translation of such excess into a cost that capital refuses to bear. As is visible in the rhetoric of riots and the articulation between science and the state, the innately transient and contingent nature of subsistence became a primary lever for a capital accumulation that increasingly relied on the externalization of reproduction to its own processes. Figural disorder and indirection are not outside such accumulation, then, but are instead the outside through which accumulation grows exogenously.⁶¹ In this division, the excessively deviating nature of subsistence was externalized from the market, transforming it into a superfluous matter unrelated to the profits and costs of capital. In other words, the transience of habit and the unmeasured reciprocity of subsistence became an appendage, an arbitrary feature of the necessary cycles of supply and demand. To borrow

Hartman's phrasing, the art and poiesis of survival is turned from a surplus into a scarcity economy, and the excessively tropological nature of subsistence is turned into a supplemental activity. But it is the essentially figural nature of subsistence that makes its projection as supplemental possible.

Coleridge's response to the 1795 riots crystallizes the competing organizations of indirection emerging in the shift detailed by Picchio. On the one hand, it figures struggles over subsistence outside the harmony of habit. On the other hand, in apostrophizing Famine, Coleridge puts the extremity of material need as simultaneously a source of surplus. Figured through apostrophe, surplus furthermore becomes a condition not of equilibrium but of a direct indirection, of deviations from the kinds of market-regulated habits described by Burke. But such a figural construction of reproduction is not outside the processes of capital accumulation. They are exogenous, meaning that capital accumulation remains dependent on the apostrophic, which is to say, figural, arrangement of subsistence. Capital can only accumulate through a surplus value that is derived from the indirect nature of the production of those things we need most directly to survive. Not simply the excess of labor time that is stolen from the wage worker, value is produced through the unmeasured labors that accumulate outside wage labor and the coralline carceral structures put in place to ensure their superfluity. Developing through the "web of life," capital accumulation staves off crisis by the deferral of commodification through unpaid labor and forms of subsistence that space out the time of an inevitable decline in profits.[62] The means of reproducing labor power, otherwise a cost that capital has to bear, have been divided from what measures of equivalence will provide. This means that a proliferation of labors, temporalities, and ways of meeting needs that do not fit within the container of equivalence exist as both an unmeasurable surplus of and an excessive cost for the social.

The innovation of Malthusian-inspired political economy was not a simple, straightforward division between a figural form of life and a mechanical and quantifiable one. It was a *negation* within the figural nature of subsistence, a rearrangement of its indirections and outsides through the logic of supply and demand. What had been a transient and unpredictable cost set by the historically variable habits of the working class was reorganized as indirectly related to the means of subsistence guaranteed by exchange. But this did not do away with the relationship between capital accumulation and the messily unmeasurable ways in which labor power was reproduced apostrophically. Indeed, as histories of carceral capitalism and a long history of feminist scholarship has shown, it intensified capital's reliance on the surplus of indirection through which material life is maintained while making such subsistence appear as incidental to its own growth. Those means of reproduction outside the exchange form became the "hiddener abode" of capital, the site of labor more invisible than any factory floor.[63] The necessarily indirect nature of subsistence, already "exogenous" to exchange value, became superfluous and contingent to the machinations of the market. Along with this shift, as we have seen, direct needs that lie outside the sphere of exchange come to appear as spontaneous and mechanical, allocated to a position outside a calculating market that only designates exchange as the proper means of subsistence. But the rhetorical arrangement of such relations helps to show the ways in which the constitutive transformation documented by Picchio was not a break with the figural nature of reproduction but rather a reorganization of it, a rearrangement from the inside out.

Such an account of capital accumulation provides a rhetorically nonbinaristic history of it in which figure's relationality becomes historically complicated. Those relations that do not fit into the logic of exchange and equivalence as articulated by Burke are not outside or other to that logic in some kind of ontological way. Rather, as Picchio makes clear, they are divided at the level of organization, rendering such relationality into an exogenous form. In such a reorganization, the totality of subsistence becomes a site of scarcity, turned into an economy that is either too much (as a surplus population) or too little (as poverty). In this sense, such relations remain coincident with rather than opposite to those more recognizable relations of capital accumulation. This is a history that holds together and divides through a "separation-with-equivalence."[64] Apostrophe, together with its economy of indirections, is not a simple analogy or an allegory for the struggle over subsistence in the Romantic period; it is part of the historically produced repertoire of indirections requisite for the maintenance of life, as well as reproduction's vulnerabilities to separation and classification historically produced by a system of subsistence organized toward exchange value.

As presented here, Romantic rhetoric and Romanticism more generally are inextricable from these historical oscillations in subsistence, as well as the inseparability of the direct and the indirect, the surplus and the superfluous, that ensures it. In this sense, the histories of struggles over subsistence and the forms they take are already a part of our critical sensibilities. Coleridge's "Letter to Famine" demonstrates how central these struggles were, not just to the historical period of Romanticism but also to our pre-existing understanding of Romantic rhetoric. After all, as Ian Balfour has said, the fundamental conundrum of such rhetoric is that it intermingles "conscious action and volition" and forces "beyond... control and comprehension."[65] Balfour's description is an apt one for the history Thompson was trying to provide for the food riots. And, like Thompson, we often strive to write Romanticism away from the "compulsive, rather than self-conscious or self-activating" aspects of the figural, that more mechanistic power of language that de Man once described as "a random event whose power, like the power of death, is due to the randomness of its occurrence."[66] Balfour is not describing the rhetoric of Romantic riots here, however; he is dealing with the problem of the prophetic nature of such rhetoric. But, by way of concluding, it is worth noting that Coleridge's apostrophe to Famine shares a prophetic genre of indirection with a genealogy of politics that does not, as Thompson and Coleridge did, force a division between the compulsive and the free.

Coleridge's letter joins another way of historicizing subsistence, not through an increasingly self-activating political tradition but one in which the minimality of reproduction was also immediately aligned with the prophetic and messianic. In this tradition, the quotidian is inseparable from direct action, forms of mutual aid, a millennialist spirit, and guerilla sensibilities that defined a Romanticism that never fit well into a more progressive convention.[67] This was the time of Robert Wedderburn's *The Axe Laid to the Root*, in which he issued eschatological appeals to the English poor through an indirect address to Jamaican slaves. It was the time of anonymous letters that infused demands for material needs with a radical religiosity. Always anonymous, these letters were apostrophic in all but the "O": "Downe with Your Luxzuaras Government both spiritual & temperal Or you starve with Hunger Downe with your Constitution Arect a republic Or you and your offsprings are to starve the Remainder of our Days dear Brothers will you lay down and die under Man eaters and Lave your offspring under that Burden that Blackguard Government which is now eatain you up."[68] Coleridge was, in 1795, disposed toward such a rhetoric, as he was, in John Thelwall's words, a "young man of brilliant understanding . . . desperate fortune, democratick principles, and entirely led away by the feelings of the moment."[69] Subject to sympathy with riotous dispositions, Coleridge also points us to the importance of a language beyond control and comprehension not just in the riot but in the apostrophic nature of need and the means by which we meet it.

This more riotous rhetoric of subsistence prefigures the crucial paradox of collective life today, in its fusion of everyday needs with apocalyptic contingency. In this moment it seems we cannot but think this paradox in its inverted form, as we are surrounded by figures of life living through extreme precarity. Living constantly at the end of things—namely, of economic upheaval and climatic crisis—we must find ways to invert the relation between contingency and death that de Man proposed. My turn to figures of subsistence and its histories of indirection in this chapter is meant to rethink that relation in the light of today, to see in 1795 an address to the present.

CHAPTER 2

Anachronism, Dreams, and Enclosure

Enclosure Poetics

Mary Robinson's poetry tends not to be read in the context of enclosure. Neither a working-class poet nor a poet with any attachment to the commons, Robinson is perhaps best known for her skillful translation of the public scandal of her relationship to the Prince of Wales into a celebrity asset. Far from the historical space of enclosure, Robinson is most legible in relation to it as a successful participant in the new economy of commodified reproduction that was, in large part, the long-term effect of expropriation. Here I shall not read Robinson in the context of but as a theorist of enclosure, which, in its sense as the originary violence of capital accumulation that disorders the progressive narrative of capitalist production from within its own processes, her poem "The Maniac" (1791) works out in its twenty stanzas. In so doing, it shows us the relevance of anachronism for understanding connections between scientific epistemologies, vagrancy laws, and gendered divisions of labor in a Romanticism that continues into the present. Set in a dream, the framing of "The Maniac" draws from the radical relationality of emergent scientific epistemologies while simultaneously maintaining attention to the differential effects of dispossession. This framing helps us to think through the ambivalence of terms such as "relationality" and "contingency" in the context of accumulation by dispossession. While the poem uses the trope of analogy, which has returned as the signal trope of nonhierarchical relationality in recent scholarship on Romantic science, it is also structured through the "ludicrous anachronis[m]" of a dream.[1] And it is through anachronism that the poem associates a poet, a wandering "maniac," a sorceress, and a series of anonymous and abandoned women, in an accumulation of figures that is particularly significant to capital accumulation if we understand it not through the lens of industrial production but through what I referred to in the previous chapter as the articulation of different social, economic, and political spheres.[2]

According to Mary Robinson's *Memoirs*, the poem was written upon her return from a convalescent treatment for a mysterious partial paralysis that had recently afflicted her.[3] On the way home she witnessed "an elderly man, hurried along by a crowd of people, by whom he was pelted with mud and stones." As the *Memoirs* imply, this man, "mad Jemmy," was "an unfortunate maniac" with whose "miserable being" and "emaciated countenance" Robinson had reason to empathize. The poem offers "an example of the facility and rapidity with which she composed," as her daughter described it, under the influence not just of empathy but "near eighty drops of laudanum" prescribed by her doctor on an evening in which she suffered more than usual.[4]

Suspended from the regulating forces of memory, external sensation, and habit that otherwise organize the experience of waking life, Robinson spontaneously dictated the poem in full, recalling none of the process when she awoke the next morning. Framed as an involuntary and unconsciously composed work, the poem is written as if it was a product of an invisible hand in the sense that Sheehan and Warhman have recently used. For them, the eighteenth-century trope of the "invisible hand" does not refer solely to the Smithian doctrine of the free market but to a more general epistemology defined by "causal links that were discontinuous and nonlinear; appreciation for the constructive possibilities of chance and randomness; understandings of providence with latitude for indeterminate events; unintended consequences of actions cumulatively leading to beneficial outcomes; and the mysterious emergence of order out of the chaos of discrete particulars."[5] The trope of analogy enabled this new epistemology because it establishes "loose, nonhierarchical connections" and "assume[s] a principle of nonidentity between things" as the basis for open-ended social relations and nonteleological scientific methods.[6] Analogy was not a homogenizing or transcendentally ordering logic, then, but a way of knowing that "brazenly assumes what it needs to prove, relying on endlessly circular accounts of order" and indulges transitional forms and a lack of coherence in systems.[7] More generally, analogy has returned within and beyond Romantic-era scholarship as a way to cast differential relations as something other than hierarchical or binarizing. Part of the postcritical turn, analogy has resurfaced as a method for injecting contingency and instability within disciplinary thinking in a way that for many critics mirrors the discursive porosity of Romantic-era science. Late eighteenth-century science and literature come to be part of what Devin Griffiths has recently designated the age of analogy, implicitly displacing the tropes of metaphor or apostrophe that have tended to guide the critical reading of Romantic-era poetics and the science of life.[8]

More than just an expression of empathy, the analogy developed between poet and subject in Robinson's flawlessly unconscious composition points to a more fundamental effect of the unplanned events that yielded surprisingly harmonious outcomes or unintended consequences that had the appearance of design—of that other "invisible hand." And yet, as Romantic-era surgeons and physiologists, as well as their predecessors, made clear, dreams of the kind in which Robinson dictated "The Maniac" pushed analogy to its limits. Exploited in dreams, the conditions presumed to establish order out of chaos—namely, assumptions about time as successive and space as divisible—were given a riotous reign without the force of self-organization.[9] Rather than replicating the spatial and temporal conditions of succession that typify empiricism, dreams result from a simultaneity of impressions held together at the same time. According to David Hartley, in dreams "[associations] rise up quickly and vividly one after another, as subjects, predicates, and other associates" are "affirmed of each other and appear to hang together." Instead of unfolding cumulatively, the space-time of dreams renders sequence absurd: "Thus the same person appears in two places at the same time; two persons appearing successively in the same place coalesce into one; a brute is supposed to speak[;] ... any idea, qualification, office, &c. coinciding in the instant of time with the idea of one's self, or of another person, adheres immediately, &c. &c." Dreams are a series of discrete images disconnected from the causal or explanatory logic of sequence, as "the recurrence of ideas, especially visible and audible ones, in a vivid manner, but without any regard to the order of past facts."[10]

John Hunter would later emphasize this same temporal discontinuity of dreams, as a disregard not only of past facts but of the larger metaphysical and historical framework that succession provides: "One of the most remarkable properties of dreams, is that we have no idea of time or place, or sometimes of our personal identity; in consequence of which we commit the most ludicrous anachronisms, imagine ourselves dead and alive, or in two places, at the same time, or else that our spirits have transmuted into some other bodies."[11] In Hunter's account, anachronism reigns supreme, turning space and time into "an error in computing time, or fixing dates; the erroneous reference of an event, circumstance, or custom to a wrong date"; "of a date which is too early, but also used of too late a date"; "anything done or existing out of date; *hence*, anything which was proper to a former age, but is, or, if it existed, would be, out of harmony with the present."[12] Ordered by the simultaneity of different, even opposing conditions rather than the succession of a continuous one, identity and the space-time that affords it is undone. In dreams, two or more bodies may inhabit the same frame of time "at the same time," inhabiting space simultaneously. Or one person may be rendered as composite, the result of random ideas forged in an instant. Instead of a continuous organization of impressions and memories, personhood becomes instantaneous and discontinuous: "any idea, qualification, office, &c. coinciding in the instant of time with the idea of one's self, or of another person, adheres immediately." And perhaps most surprising, the organizing principle of second nature, language, may be rendered as anachronistic too, when "a brute is supposed to speak."[13] Animals, generally understood to be capable only of sounds and not of language, no longer mark the originary difference of second nature between human and nonhuman.

David Hartley's full assessment of the disordering effect of dreams on the normative conditions of space, time, and cognition also includes them in the field of orderly outcomes, however. As he makes clear, the differential, anachronistic motions of dreams perform an important labor in maintaining and reproducing the nonanachronistic and measured motions of waking life: "The wildness of our dreams seems to be of singular use to us, by interrupting and breaking the course of our associations. For, if we were always awake, some accidental associations would be so much cemented by continuance, as that nothing could afterwards disjoin them; which would be madness."[14] Here, what we otherwise might be tempted to read as the threatening or disruptive potential of dreams becomes productive, dividing "accidental associations" from regulated associations, splitting them quite literally into different times of the day and building in a break from the successive "course of associations." For Hartley, regulated motions can only be maintained through the continual repetition of other kinds that disregard the order of the past. Accidental associations are not repressed here but divided into different spheres of labor through the difference in hours of the day; but in this division different economies of time uncannily inhabit the same body. Indeed, in the case of daydreams they may even function simultaneously, as dreams invade our waking hours.

But Robinson's poem is not only framed through the dream; it exploits the spatial and temporal anachronisms described by Hartley and Hunter as the condition of possibility for analogies to be drawn between its different poetic subjects. And these subjects hold among them a distributed and collective history of enclosure; the possibility for their poetic analogy is given by virtue of their sharing the anachronisms particular to the enclosures of vagrancy and gender. Walter Benjamin has argued for dreams as a site in which we can gain access to a forgotten collective history. For him, dreams are the physio-psychological analogy to the Parisian arcades, an infrastructure of history located in the body rather than the ever-changing, ever-static capitalist world. While for Benjamin dreams are an index of the effects of commodified experience, dreams also provide a framework and form for understanding enclosure as more than a historically or geographically specific event of landed dispossession. They do so by pushing analogy to its limits, where we can see a history of capital accumulation that is ordered by simultaneity and anachronism rather than succession and by the preservation of nonidentical and nonhierarchical relations.[15] Recent readers of analogy such as Sheehan, Wahrman, and Griffiths have tended to focus on its emancipatory effect in the realm of science, where an absence of intentional design is read against the grain of the ostensibly rationalizing projects of industrialization and colonialism. But the history of enclosure, a history that takes the form of a dream more than a design or than reason, uncannily follows the same contingent and immanent relations readers have recently found in analogy. Enclosure, in other words, is the dream of industrial capital, one that, as Hartley might tell us, it cannot do without.

Consider, for instance, that the money form can also be understood to work as an analogy. For Celeste Langan, analogy is the figure that allows money to move in Romantic-era poetics. Analogy enables a nonlinear and recursive movement that is without origin or termination: "the logic of analogy . . . is neither progressive nor retrospective, but rather *the logic of infinite circulation*," and it is this kind of movement that money makes.[16] The money form and its infinite circulation appear as a form of undirected and indeterminate freedom, the absence of fixed order for which analogy has recently been so celebrated. The conjuncture of freedom and money that Langan locates in Romantic poetry forces a more Nietzschean sense of analogy, in which nonequivalent things are forced into relations of equivalence. But this violent mode of analogy should not be confused with the full enforcement of identity between two things. Langan makes clear that, instead of a relation of identity, through money different things "are placed in an absolute relation, which is why, finally, *the logic of their equivalence cannot be fully determined*."[17] Gavin Walker has described the effects of enclosure in a similar way. Rather than the production of identity, enclosure has the effect of making commensurate: "Commensurability, that is, the possibility of an articulation between two things based on a shared or common measure, *does not mean equivalence*. It means two things are 'enclosed' in the same way, that through the emergence of 'enclosure' two things appear where there used to be simply contiguous planar space."[18] Enclosure actually produces what Langan describes as "contiguity into sequence" or renders what had been "touching," "in contact," or "neighbouring, situated in close proximity; dwelling near" as a particular order.[19] In contrast to the enforcement of equivalence, where different things become identical for the purposes of exchange, commensurability preserves the difference of entities so long as they share a "common measure." Sharing in a relation but not forced into the same identity, commensurability carves out a sphere of analogy that operates alongside the sphere of the money form and its "infinite circulation." Enclosure is both the production and accumulation of differences where they did not exist before, a process that Silvia Federici has most famously described as the racializing and gendering origins of capital accumulation.[20] In other words, capital accumulation and its "infinite circulation" can occur only because of the nonidentical process of accumulated differences of race, gender, and ethnicity, which emerge through contingent historical processes that inform the development of capitalist production and exchange.[21] Rather than a fixed and determinate process, such theories of enclosure point to shifting and contingent designations of difference that emerge in tandem with but are not only caused by spheres of equivalence and exchange.[22] In this sense, analogy is even more the proper figure of enclosure, given that, as Taylor Schey writes, it "enables a logic of relationality that might be valued precisely because of its failure to establish clear-cut identities and differences."[23]

Let us return to Mary Robinson and her dream. If analogy has recently been read as a way to set epistemology and history free from the mechanisms of design and determination, then the dream frame that Robinson gives her poem suggests a deep ambivalence about such freedom. "The Maniac" is not only set in the frame of a dream; it also exploits the capacities of the dream to collapse identities, reorder space and time, and allow one person to be in two places at the same time. Enclosed in a dream, the figures in Robinson's poem are not exemplars of the beneficial outcomes of contingency but of the consequences of enclosure and its logic of analogy, a logic that is inseparable from the patterns and harmonies through which it has recently been recuperated. If this is the case, then a deeply ambiguous setting for the epistemological shift toward those contingent and transient models of life and history in the late eighteenth century and the Romantic period appears, one that is not as straightforwardly nonhierarchical or open-ended as we might like it to be. Uncannily, the definition of analogy as "brazenly assum[ing] what it needs to prove, relying on endlessly circular accounts of order," actually repeats Marx's critique of so-called primitive accumulation, of which enclosure was a part.[24] Primitive accumulation was "so-called" for Marx because the classical economic narrative that attempted to account for the initial accumulation of capital through thrift rather than through violent dispossession was itself a "brazen assumption" and an endlessly circular account that assumed what it needed to prove—namely, how the capital required for industrialized production came to be accumulated. In contrast to those assessments of the "invisible hand" of capital as entirely predetermined or mechanical, from which Sheehan and Wahrman are attempting to decouple it, the process of so-called primitive accumulation and enclosure operates much more like the "loose and nonhierarchical," "bottom up," and "reciprocal" relations of analogy to which recent scholars have drawn our attention.

Contrary to most critical depictions of capital accumulation in the Romantic era, as the imposition of standardization, equivalence, homogeneity, and so on, we might do better to think it through the "messy, sensuous, gendered, raced, and unruly component(s)" of political economy that operate through contingency and a certain kind of heterogeneity.[25] Critically accumulated notions about capital accumulation in the Romantic period have forced us to choose between an affirmation of messy, sensuous relations and a critique of abstraction and homogeneity. In the reading of Robinson's "The Maniac" below, enclosure and its histories of accumulation-by-dispossession are read as indeterminate and relational, thus forestalling such sedimented binaries.[26] The poem presents such a messy and unruly history by establishing relations of analogy through the anachronistic effects of enclosure. Cultivating the same terms by which analogy has recently been shored up as an ethical and political good, Robinson's poem demonstrates that at the limits of analogy and its "loose and nonhierarchical connections" we can find an often unattended-to history of dispossession, along with its accompanying history of subsistence.

Dream Economies

Locating the poet in the limit conditions of the dream state, Robinson makes use of the possibility in which "the same person appears in two places at the same time; two persons appearing successively in the same place coalesce into one":

> One night after bathing, having suffered from her disorder more than usual pain, she swallowed, by order of her physician, near eighty drops of laudanum. Having slept for some hours, she awoke, and calling her daughter, desired to take a pen and write what she would dictate. . . . [Robinson] lay, while dictating, with her eyes closed, apparently in the stupor which opium frequently produces, repeating like a person talking in her sleep. . . . On the ensuing morning Mrs. Robinson had only a confused idea of what had passed, nor could be convinced of the fact till the manuscript was produced. She declared that she had been dreaming of mad Jemmy throughout the night, but was perfectly unconscious of having been awake while she composed the poem, or of the circumstances narrated by her daughter.[27]

This dream state creates an analogical possibility between the poet and Jemmy through a physiological correspondence, establishing a commensurability between opiatic reverie and madness through a "loose and nonhierarchical connection." As the poem tells us, mad Jemmy evinces "sense, unchain'd by DESTINY" and "hot brain consum'd," leading him to "Now laugh and sing, then weep and rave," while Robinson, for her part, has no recollection of "what had passed" during the night of her spontaneous and rapid dictation.[28] While Robinson dictates at rapid-fire speed with "eyes closed," Jemmy's "eye-balls roll / Like *Heralds* of the wandr'ing soul" and he utters an "agonizing shriek" as "the mind's unpitied anguish speak."[29] Dreams and madness may manifest differently but are rooted in the same cause—namely, an imbalance in stimulation that leads to an inability to sustain memory and its successive order.

These conditions are not identical, but they do establish an analogical relation. The subjects of the poem—Robinson as speaker and Jemmy as addressee—are disassociated from each other and the typical conditions of sympathy. But the formal constraint of the poem proposes a mediating medium, providing a frame that can accommodate and even regularize their different states of insensibility. Written in a meter that has been described as "regular irregularity," Robinson's Horatian ode uses a regular tetrameter that is modified by the pentameter of its third line and the hexameter in the final line of each stanza. The form and sound of the poem presents a regulating infrastructure for the sensational irregularity and excess of its subjects, creating a mediation that prefigures Wordsworthian sobriety.[30] It establishes coherence between otherwise disordered content and arranges the absence of memory and lack of successive trains of thought.[31] In this sense, it is the form that enables analogy, bringing dissimilarity into a relation of formal continuity.

The initial stanzas of the poem also work to establish the possibility of sympathy in the absence of its typical, physiological requirements. That is, the first six stanzas of the poem rely almost entirely on a direct mode of address that reinforces Robinson's refusal to turn away from the subject of her poem.[32] The first line of the poem is an apostrophic address, "AH! WHAT ART THOU, whose eye-balls roll / Like Heralds of the wandr'ring soul."[33] The next six stanzas also directly address "mad Jemmy" with questions of causation: "Why dost thou rend thy matted hair"; "Why dost thou from thy scanty bed"; Why dost thou climb yon craggy steep"; "Why does thou strip the fairest bow'rs"; "Why dost thou drink the midnight dew."[34] These first six stanzas of the poem open with lines that directly address Jemmy, most of which appeal to him to disclose the source of his suffering. But the poem also ends with the same gesture of sympathetic identification, as the poet appeals, "Oh! let me all thy sorrows know; / With THINE my mingling tear shall flow, / And I will share thy pangs, and make thy griefs my own."[35] Such mediating gestures, both formal and figurative, establish the kind of analogy that Devin Griffiths has argued "reworks diverse aspects of the intelligible world into a more coherent whole."[36]

But as we saw in Hunter and Hartley, dreams suspend the presupposed psychophysiological conditions of coherence. Coherence and sympathy are effects of empirical conditions that do not hold in the absence of external stimulation and the regulating effects of continuous memory. Instead, in dreams, identities are split, bodies collapse into the same space, and otherwise impossible states of being ("a brute speaks") become simultaneous with one another. Dreams push that particular feature of analogy that Schey describes as an epistemic and rhetorical "failure to establish clear-cut identities and differences" to its limit.[37] Dreams install this "failure" in the operations of body and mind. And dreams fail in a very particular way in Robinson's poem, emphasizing that certain material conditions, and bodies and minds, are put into relation or made analogous through what Barbara Johnson has suggested is the violence inherent to figurative language. In dreams, the violence attendant to analogy is disclosed through what was described in Chapter 1 as that coincidence, rather than opposition, of direct and indirect address, which is the mode of address that turns the poem in a different direction at its halfway point.

In stanza 6, Robinson turns away from a direct address to Jemmy and instead addresses a self-figuration of the poetess "in her solitary tow'r / The *Minstrel of the witching hour*" as she "Sits half congeal'd with fear, to hear thy dismal moan."[38] Abandoning "the real language of men," Robinson pivots to the kind of personification that Wordsworth would later eschew.[39] Robinson's turn to the figure of the "Minstrel of the witching hour" holds together, or associates, a difference between the poet and Jemmy, brought together indirectly. This turn of indirection, which does not so much address the Minstrel as bring her into a "half congeal'd" relation with both the poet and Jemmy, creates a constellation of figures in that simultaneous and coalescing language of dreams (where "a brute is supposed to speak"). Figuring herself in the poem not as speaker but, like Jemmy, as a silent subject of address, Robinson half-congeals herself in a dream, or as two figures at once. She is both sympathetic speaker and supernatural fixture, a figure at once bewitching and paralyzed. What had appeared as the possibility of a direct, sympathetic exchange of sensationalized bodies is immediately threaded through a turn elsewhere, in which the poet and Jemmy are articulated through oscillating positions. In such "half congeal'd" states, they are dispossessed of any direct identification, and their potential association is made only indirectly. Enabling a more vagrant mode of association than waking associations can afford, this turn sets aside the demands of recognition and instead indulges a coincidence constructed indirectly.

Such figuration highlights the indirect nature of address and enables the coincidence of, rather than straightforward analogy between, different entities. This threading of indirection within direction allows otherwise oppositional states of being to persist at the same time, establishing a relation more akin to enclosure, in which two nonidentical entities are enclosed "in the same way." But then again, so does the dream, which serves as a shared frame in which the infrastructure of identity is suspended. Robinson's indirection does at the level of figure what the dream does at the level of form: it creates a dispossession in which relations are only "half-congeal'd." This kind of dispossession is not fully captured by the terms of labor through which Langan describes it, in which the feudal laborer's stable self-representation is alienated by the daily sale of his newly "free" labor. If according to Langan material dispossession is replaced by the "possession" of labor power, then the figures in Robinson's poem cannot lay claim to such possession—or such productivity, for that matter.[40] Instead, their enclosure within the same regular irregular form, as well as their always partial and indirect relations, evokes a dispossession that, to borrow from Marx's ironic twist, frees them from the strictures of self-possession and for an oscillating array of positions in the poem.

At the halfway point of the poem, when Robinson momentarily turns away from Jemmy to indirectly figure herself as the Minstrel, Jemmy seems to be subject to the bewitching powers of Robinson's meter, much in the manner Coleridge once suggested any reader would be.[41] But toward the end of the poem, Robinson displaces the figure of the Minstrel through another indirect reference to the poet. The hint of horror within an otherwise capable figuration (she "Sits half congeal'd with fear") returns, figured as the potential violence enacted by "the Maniac" on a gendered personification of ORPHAN and WIDOW. This time, the position initially held by the poet-as-Minstrel shifts as Robinson imparts the delusive powers of the witching hour to the subject of the poem in its penultimate stanzas:

Or hast thou stung with poignant smart,
The ORPHAN's and the WIDOW's heart,
And plung'd them in cold POVERTY's abyss;
While CONSCIENCE, like a VULTURE stole,
To feed upon thy tortur'd soul,
And tear each BARB'ROUS SENSE from TRANSITORY BLISS?

Or hast thou seen some gentle MAID,
By thy deluding voice betray'd,
Fade like a flow'r, slow with'ring with remorse?
And didst though THEN refuse to save
Thy victim from an early grave,
Till at thy feet she lay, a pale and ghastly CORSE?[42]

The first mention of that "Minstrel of the witching hour" marked the shift from direct sympathy to indirect relation. This second one introduces the end of the poem as well as an agentic inversion. In the first, although "half congeal'd with fear," Robinson figures herself as the "Minstrel" of an incantatory and supernatural power. In the second, she asks if Jemmy's madness has been caused instead by the deluding power of his own voice and his abandonment of ORPHAN, WIDOW, and MAID. What had been figured as a potential power of the poet shifts into the vulnerability of woman and child, and what had been supernaturally agentic becomes a subjection to violence.[43] Robinson's auto/biography, remarkable for the fact that she publicly pursued a court case over her financial abandonment by the Prince of Wales, along with her support of her children when her husband squandered their money, is here loosely linked in another way to the "half-congeal'd" figurations in the poem. But more than any autobiographical reference, it is more the coincidence of nonidentical figures through different forms of precarity and their different exposures to violence that indirectly bind them to one other.

Such indirection is crucial to the historical dimensions of Robinson's rhetoric, however. That is, Robinson does not directly locate herself as the subject of abandonment by Jemmy. Nor does she directly locate herself as the bewitching and deluding force that acts upon him. Instead, she turns to allegory to draw uneven connections between forms of violence that put them into relation while maintaining a difference between them. Robinson's use of allegory to associate and divide her own conditions from that of a CORSE, the Minstrel and the Maniac, the Maniac and the Maid, and so forth, does not strictly figure their adjacency as assembled bodies or the nonidentity that keeps open the possibility of their inclusion in a community. Instead, Robinson's poem teases out a series of inversions in which the poet and Jemmy inhabit analogous positions while rendering those positions of reciprocity or open-endedness as conditions of differentiated vulnerability. Analogy works here, as Schey has described it, to "suggest a relation of both identity and alterity without establishing either."[44] This leaves the poet and Jemmy, the Widow and Maid and poet, the Minstrel and Maniac, as coinciding and adjacent figures. The poem's translation of disordered and materially differentiated content into an economy of sympathy, regularity, and "a more coherent whole" depends on figures that are nonidentical to it and sit both inside and outside it—that are, to refer us back to the Introduction, never entirely a matter of equivalence. As the poem continues, the figural "freedom" that enables the poet, the Minstrel, and Jemmy's coincidence with one another also becomes the condition in which they are indirectly entwined through their exposure to different kinds of social violence. Bringing them together is a series of turns of doublespeak and an indirect association of an uncertain exposure to harm.

Amanda Jo Goldstein offers an account of allegory in Shelley's *The Mask of Anarchy* that is quite useful here. In contrast to readings of allegory as a mask of ideology, she argues that allegory is a literalization of otherwise abstract forces. As such, it provides a way to read bodies as assembled through material conditions of shared vulnerability, through "a relation of metonymic contiguity, of physical and causal contact and context." Expressing what she calls a poetic materialism, allegory of this kind helps to render stories that are "pulled apart at the seams by composite back-stories that require a kind of double-speak, an allegory, to be told at once," thus enabling democratic assemblies of bodies that are "similar in their dissimilarity."[45] Allegory works similarly in "The Maniac," but here it indexes a different kind of simultaneous composition. Its "divergent back-stories" are assembled not as the possibility of democratic space-holding but as an accumulation of differences figured by the doubling of relation and division, of shared conditions and differential violences. Robinson's use of allegory does something slightly different with the figuration of "distinct and adjacent bodies" assembled in the dream space, which similarly enables the simultaneity or at-onceness of different "back-stories." It does so by showing those backstories to be made adjacent through a discontinuous continuity and the accumulated and intermingled violences of enclosure.

In other words, Robinson's poem differentiates commonality in a more ambivalent mode, demonstrating the ways in which conditions of survival and solidarity can also be inverted as sites of structural violence. These inversions point to what Barbara Johnson once queried as "the politics of violence already encoded in rhetorical figures as such."[46] If analogy enables a poetic address, or figuration, of subjects rather than objects of reflection, then Robinson's poem troubles any easy treatment of such sympathetic relations by suggesting that a shared condition can also be inverted as a hierarchical relation. In the context of a dream, a common condition can be inverted into differently distributed vulnerabilities, thus tilting rhetoric from a poetics of assembly to a poetics of expropriation. It is through the frame of a dream that the shared history of expropriation can perhaps be best understood.

Sensation Histories and Witching Hours

David Hartley, whose account of dreams has been discussed above, understood ideas to originate in memory. According to Hartley, the remains of certain physiological sensations, what he called vibrations, would contingently leave an "effect, trace, or vestige" of a "single sensation."[47] With enough repetition and with a proper balance between sensation and the nervous system, ideas would be generated over time. Hartley's principle of vibration, and his theory of cognition, relied upon what Sheehan and Wahrman call "sensation histories," which provided a necessarily nonmechanistic way to understand the dual preservation and combination necessary for the formation of complex ideas.[48] For Hartley, such sensation histories were secured, despite their contingent happening, by virtue of a correspondence between the matter of the body and events in the world, a "mutual indefinite Implication" between human vibrations and the impulses of nature.

Coleridge had a term for such sensations when displaced into the realm of aesthetics. In his famous distinction between Imagination and Fancy, Coleridge renders the latter as essentially Hartleyan vibrations, only in this case freed from the "mutual indefinite Implication" of space and time. In contrast to ideas based on materialist Memory, Fancy was a "mode of Memory emancipated from the order of time and space."[49] It was based on this distinction that W. K. Wimsatt Jr. and M. C. Beardsley formulated their influential account of poetic interpretation against a Hartleyan materialism, one that had to dispel the "gross body of life, of sensory and mental experience" that would always be delimited by the privations of history.[50] In a curious reading of Coleridge's dictate, Wimsatt and Beardsley endorse an aesthetics of imagination in the hopes that it could transcend the "the order of time and space" set by historical and psychological specificity, creating a poetics that would become "public" through its emancipation from the fixity of the past. If for Hartley it is the materiality of time and space that enables a transient endurance through "sensation histories," then for Wimsatt and Beardsley it is the constraints of material sensation and history from which poetry must be emancipated for the survival of poetry in a public mode.

This puts Robinson's poem in an interesting position between Hartley's account of memory on the one hand and Coleridge's and Wimsatt and Beardsley's account of imagination on the other. For the latter, the only way to make poetry collective was to emancipate it from what they saw as the privation of history and sensation. For Hartley, the preservation of ideas was only possible through a "Memory" delimited by time and space, which provided the basis for Coleridge's notion of degraded Fancy as that "mode of Memory emancipated from the order of time and space."[51] Robinson's poem creates a third option, which is a collective sensation history or memory that is, contra Hartley, emancipated from the order of space and time. Such a history would be most closely indexed to what Coleridge dismissed as Fancy. For Coleridge, and later Wimsatt and Beardsley, Fancy was impoverished in its poetic power, whereas Robinson's emancipation of sensation and memory from the order of space and time indicates a collective, if forgotten, history embedded in dreams. "The Maniac" weaves together a novel sensation history, suggesting a double bind of freedom akin to the one Marx invokes to figure dispossession and the freeing of labor. "Emancipated" from the space and time in which subjects were mutually imbricated with a waking world of harmoniously sympathizing vibrations, the dream state conjured in Robinson's poem presents us with certain vestiges of dispossession that are held in anachronism.

It is precisely through this figure that Angela Davis encourages us to understand the relationship between gender, enclosure, and capital accumulation.[52] The history of capital accumulation is an anachronistic one for Davis because it requires the dialectical preservation and re-creation of certain features of a precapitalist society. Most important to Davis's "Fancy"-ful history of capital accumulation is the reconstitution of reproductive labor as gendered and nonproductive, a transformation that left women both central to and outside the historical narrative of progress under a capitalist mode of production, by virtue of their absorption of the immense costs of reproducing a labor force.[53] This counterintuitive possibility of capital accumulation highlights the necessary preservation and combination of "forms of exploitation or cultural practices which appear to be residual, pre-capitalistic, anachronistic elements of the social formation [that] are in fact absolutely contemporary, but they are also deeply ambiguous."[54] Rather than a smooth train of successive events, this history of capital accumulation takes the form of a dream, in which people can be split into two (temporalities) and residual forms and practices are entirely contemporary, or to use the language of dreams, appear "at the same time."

It is also such anachronistic temporalities that yielded commensurabilities between the different figures that populate Robinson's poem. The laws that defined and criminalized vagrancy from the twelfth to the nineteenth century offer one such anachronistic history. As William Chambliss writes, "for a substantial period [in the fourteenth century] the vagrancy statutes were dormant," but "when social conditions create a perceived need for legal changes . . . these alterations [were] effected through the revision and refocusing of existing statutes."[55] Vagrancy laws fell dormant for decades and were reconstituted to address entirely new historical conditions, reusing the language of and laws against vagrancy to create a new meaning. This reconstitution of older vagrancy laws to suit the present was marked by the shift "from an earlier concern with laborers to a concern with *criminal* activities."[56] The practices condemned anew by the same vagrancy laws were entirely contemporary, the product of a long arc of enclosure, but by virtue of the fact that they were practices of subsistence outside commodified ones, they appeared as a threat to a society now organized around property and possession.

This translation of the vagrancy laws demonstrates a peculiar form of anachronism. What Chambliss's work suggests is that the remaking of contemporary means of subsistence and habits of life was punished through the anachronistic logic of the law but also produced populations just as anachronistic through their enclosure by the law. What appear as residual forms from the past function in an entirely modern fashion, and the mode of transition from the past to the present is one of "violen[t] disarticulat[ion]."[57] In other words, what appears as archaic from the vantage point of developmental or progressive narrative is, in fact, entirely contemporary, leading to the combined and uneven histories of the assemblage of bodies swept up by those histories. These anachronistic histories are the conditions in which those analogizing, or commensurating, processes described above must be situated. The vagrancy laws organized a motley assembly of bodies in which gendered divisions of labor were instituted at the same time as the criminalization of mobility. For instance, the 1503 vagrancy laws included under the heading of criminal vagrancy those "lurking in any house, or loitering or idle wandering by the highway side" and those "using subtil, crafty and unlawful games or plays; and some of them feigning themselves to have knowledge of... absurd sciences."[58] Moreover, as C. S. L. Davies writes, the 1530 vagrancy laws provided that "only university scholars begging without permission, counterfeit shipwrecked seamen, fortune-tellers and quacks were subject to the more extreme measures of mutilation" than generally idle vagrants.[59] According to Chambliss, "with minor variations... the statutes remain essentially of this nature until 1743," when they were expanded to include, among others, "all persons who run away and leave their wives or children." Even in 1824 the vagrancy laws stated that "every person pretending or professing to tell fortunes, or using any subtle craft, means, or device, by palmistry or otherwise, to deceive and impose on any of his Majesty's subjects . . . every person wandering abroad and lodging in any barn or outhouse or in any deserted or unoccupied building, or in the open air, or under a tent, or in any cart or wagon, not having any visible means of subsistence and not giving a good account of himself or herself" could be committed to a correctional house.[60]

This dual enclosure of witches and wanderers testifies to the accumulation of differences that Federici defines as the key feature of so-called primitive accumulation, only one aspect of which was the enclosure of common lands. She writes, "Just as the Enclosures expropriated the peasantry from the communal land, so the witch-hunt expropriated women from their bodies, which were thus 'liberated' from any impediment preventing them to function as machines for the production of labor."[61] So-called primitive accumulation was first and foremost the accumulation of the differences of race and gender within the dispossessed working class in Europe. Rather than a criminalization of socially rejected practices, Federici argues that early modern witch hunts created high crimes out of previously accepted social practices of reproductive and medical labor. Such transitions inverted women's former position of social power to one of vulnerability, which was a necessary precondition for modern capitalist divisions of labor of concern to Davis. In other words, what had been socially privileged positions of caregiving were converted into supernatural forces enacted, quite literally, in that time of the "witching hour" shared by both the Minstrel and "the Maniac." Crucial to the criminalization of witchcraft for Federici is the creation of the new, gendered distributions of paid and unpaid labor to which Davis also refers, themselves predicated on the anachronistic "preservation" of reproductive labor as unproductive. From this perspective, it is not coincidental that Marx figured the heterogeneous processes attendant upon primitive accumulation as the "midwife" of history.[62]

Saidiya Hartman ushers this anachronism into the establishment of "the plantation, the ghetto, and the prison" in the United States. Drawing a line of discontinuity between English jurist William Blackstone's 1765 definition of "vagrants as those who 'wake on the night and sleep in the day ... and no man knows from where they came or whither they go'" and a range of resistances to labor in the present, Hartman shows that, far from being a historically specific event, enclosure is a form of accumulation emancipated from the order of space and time.[63] For her, the criminalization of unwaged means of subsistence and social life that began with the Bloody Laws in fourteenth-century England are preserved and re-created as "coeval" forms of criminalization that punished "the right *not* to work."[64]

> While the legal transformation from slavery to freedom is most often narrated as the shift from status to contract, from property to subject, from slave to Negro, vagrancy statutes make apparent the continuities and entanglements between a diverse range of unfree states—from slave to servant, from servant to vagrant, from domestic to prisoner, from idler to convict and felon. Involuntary servitude wasn't one condition—chattel slavery—nor was it fixed in time and place; rather, it was an ever-changing mode of exploitation, domination, accumulation ... and confinement.[65]

Hartman here makes clear not only the continuous discontinuity of the long arc of enclosure but also the double bind of subsistence and exclusion we took note of in Chapter 1. Across Federici, Davis, and Hartman, we can see the anachronistic conditions in which reproductive labor becomes unpaid labor. Composed through anachronism, that "ever-changing mode of exploitation, domination, accumulation ... and confinement," these writers collectively show that it was, in fact, possible for one body to collapse into another and for one person to inhabit two places at once.[66] Fixed in neither time nor place, the continuous discontinuity of enclosure shows how a nonwaged worker can become a criminal, how a body can be split between a productive and an unproductive subject, and how the enslaved human can tell the anachronistic history of capitalism.

In contrast to a critical tendency to understand "excessive or wayward conditions—madness, hysteria, melancholy, addiction" as "threat[s] [to] the ability of society to function efficiently, productively, and, in the increasing dominant model of political economy in the late eighteenth century, profitably," Federici's, Davis's, and Hartman's analyses of enclosure and criminalization suggest that it is, in fact, the designation of such conditions that make profit possible.[67] What is more, their work allows us to read the wayward arc of expropriation not as past but rather as that peculiarly productive anachronism through which forms of life outside the seemingly rigid and fixed hierarchy of exploitation remain utterly contemporary through their continual reclassification as residual or disorderly and thus subject to being enclosed "in the same way" without becoming identical.[68] By designating certain forms of labor as unproductive by virtue of their reproductive nature and by punishing potentially productive bodies through incarceration, different forms of enclosure from the fifteenth to the nineteenth century came to ensure that subsistence outside the capitalist mode of production was deeply entwined with it. Enclosure, we might say, is ambiguously coupled with subsistence in such a way that myriad forms of reproduction that have been pushed outside the costs of what capital pays are also, as Picchio argues, a crucial cost-saving technique of capital accumulation. Such enclosures also produce analogies, as we have seen above, including the "loose, nonhierarchical" assembly of fortune tellers, university scholars, shipwrecked sailors, and barn sleepers, all punished with the same gruesome equality. Organized spatially, either in the home, the bedroom, or the workhouse, and temporally, as the residue of a previous era, the supposed nonwork of reproduction and vagrancy constitute the dream that, to paraphrase David Hartley, the waking workings of industrial, commodified capital cannot do without. The habits of subsistence outside capitalist labor have to be maintained in a form "emancipated from the order of time and space" and in an enclosure of their nonidentity in the same way.

These subjects are at once of the past and of the present, but so are the laws and legal terms that accumulate, that pile up and are translated to suit the demands of different historical moments. Such laws have created an entangled and open-ended assembly of bodies that are "similar in their dissimilarity" by virtue of being equally subject to gruesome physical punishment.[69] In the transformation from the power of the witching hour to the violence of vulnerability shown in the stanzas above, an impression of gendered divisions of labor and uneven histories of incarceration endures. It is this kind of sensation history—one that is collective and (dis)continuous—of enclosure that Robinson's "ludicrous anachronisms" helps us to think.[70]

In the transition from feudal to capitalist labor, wandering bodies were inseparable from the precarities of reproduction, both linked by the increasingly difficult conditions for subjects left in an indirect relation to waged means of subsistence. Activities and statuses that range from resistance to labor stretched across centuries and continents to the catch-all of reproductive labor divided from the equivalences and exchange of paid labor became "two things enclosed in the same way."[71] In these cross-sectioned inversions, the contemporaneity of wandering madmen and precaritized reproduction intersect, indirectly and unevenly. Inhabiting the space of dreams and the time of anachronism, ambivalent figurations that link speaker and subject(s) indirectly point us to the ways in which the "loose, nonhierarchical connections" of analogy that Sheehan and Wahrman describe emerge alongside combined and uneven sensation histories. Such uneven entanglements are highlighted by the impasse between different assessments of analogy as a relation of equivalence and more recent turns to the capacity of analogy to hold together differences. In the logic of enclosures I have offered above, it is altogether crucial that analogy does not operate as a relation of equivalence, as Langan suggests, but rather as a relation that preserves difference and nonequivalence through simultaneity and anachronism.

The paradoxical coincidence of analogy in enclosure and scientific epistemologies here suggests a more wayward approach to the harmonic, creative, and democratic aspects of analogy recently celebrated by critics. Literary critics tend to approach the history of capital accumulation through the language of sameness rather than difference and of progress rather than contingency. It is for these reasons, in part, that the turn to analogy and toward its affordances of relationality and nonidentity are often made to appear as if they were outside the processes through which resources are extracted and commodities are produced. Recent readings of analogy as composite and nonidentical means of assembly and relation are crucial to understanding the resources Romantic poetry gives us for historicizing life, social reproduction, and law. But they are most useful when read more immanently, as a way of constellating the ways in which such poetic renderings of life capture an ongoing struggle over the relation between subsistence—or modes of life outside relations of equivalence—and its configuration as an anachronism necessary for the emergence of a social world driven by relations of equivalence.

Enclosure is, then, always the holding together of two different processes, one of equivalence, one of commensurability, or as I have argued here, analogy. Its time is the time of simultaneity rather than succession, of anachronism rather than progress. Primitive accumulation, as Jackie Wang has recently described it, rather than being the interplay between standardization and equivalence (socially necessary labor time and exchange value), is the simultaneous operation of two different axes, one of exploitation (equivalence) and one of expropriation (difference).[72] These two axes appear as a division of spaces and the bodies that inhabit them, often loosely configured, and the infrastructures that develop over time to sediment and naturalize such enclosures. Not a history of equivalence, quantification, and circulation, then, the origins of capital accumulation in enclosure—what Marx referred to more generally as primitive accumulation—must be understood in a deeply Nietzschean sense, as a matter of force and violence perpetrated upon origination itself. In this sense, enclosure is a process of continuous reopening, of the reconstitution of differences, and the (re)ordering of past and present—never fully closed, never fully open.

The recent turn to analogy can, perhaps unexpectedly, help us to create new concepts and languages for the history of capital accumulation as it operates in a more poetic and affective fashion. The process of enclosure being tracked here suggests as much, pointing to the centrality of "half-congeal'd" labors, both potential labor and gendered labor, to produce and reproduce the possibility of commodified equivalence and commodity exchange. From this perspective, our understanding of enclosures and of capital, more specifically primitive accumulation, is perhaps most historical when it approximates a dream—as that process in which two different bodies inhabit the same space, in which two bodies become one, in which brutes are made to speak. Read through the lens of the anachronisms of enclosure,

Robinson's poem and the "regular irregularity" of its form may be counted as one vestige of the doubled conditions of such histories, one that marks a site of mutuality and vulnerability simultaneously but differentially.[73]

The "half-congeal'd" figures of capital's anachronisms oscillating between fixity and movement refer us to a primary dispossession of ownership, sovereignty, and proprietorship as such. For Fred Moten, such dispossession is found "in the figure of the slave, [where] capitalism depends on the eclipse, or liquefication, of proprietorship even as it demands the reemergence or, better yet, the transfer of the very forms proprietorship takes."[74] Rewriting the history of capital through the violence of origination in slavery, Moten points out that this origin makes a fundamental dispossession the very possibility of capital's possessed products. Significantly, in Moten's view, the slave demonstrates not just the history of dispossession that lies behind the production and sale of commodities but also the rich and subterranean world of the noncitizen, the nonworker, the nonsubject, to which expropriation is always secondary. The "half-congeal'd" nature of the surplus of such figures exposes the fragile economy in which those separated out as signs of a cost that capital will not bear also constitute the countergenealogy of the only means of subsistence we really have. The "half-congeal'd" figures I have read above point us to a related countergenealogy of reproduction that lies behind Marx's hidden abode of production and the production of "coagulated, congealed, objectified, inanimate" commodities. The radical dispossession of the slave—as noncitizen and nonworker—is also a record of "certain submarine, subcutaneous areas of unfamiliar resemblance" that are necessarily differentiated, such that we must not "los[e] sight of the best place to look for them" and "where they can change."[75] This grounding of such dispossession in the slave as the "best place" to look for unfamiliar resemblances takes us back to the potential uses and abuses of analogy, together with the problems attendant upon a too easy embrace of it as a way out of the violence of origins. I turn to Moten not to make an analogy between a Romantic poet, a wandering vagrant, and the slave body but to locate analogy squarely within the problematic of enclosure sketched above, through the vestiges of differential dispossessions as they point to different processes that operate at the same time, becoming the conditions for hierarchies where they had not existed in the same way before. The history of the witch hunts, of the brief reestablishment of slavery in England in the fifteenth century for anyone found to be without employment, and the various laws instituted in the United States to divide indentured servants from slaves all retain vestiges of de Man's "palimpsest of dreams, some of them individual, some shared with others, all grafted upon each other."[76]

What might be emphasized through a more ambivalent reading of what Sara Guyer has titled the "biopoetics" of the Romantic period is the "inherently [sic] affirmative process" of reproduction and Moten's sense of dispossession. While, on the one hand, the nonequivalent and incommensurate labor of reproduction is the reproduction "of the subject to be exploited or cast off by capital, the reproduction of gender," on the other hand, it is "also a reminder of its potentiality as a site of resistance [that] 'restores to the economic process its messy, sensuous, gendered, raced, and unruly component: living human beings capable of following orders as well as flouting them.'"[77] Robinson's poem thus establishes analogies not only between poet and subject but between dreams and enclosure, between nonhierarchical association and commensurable dislocations. Robinson offers us messier and more contingent analogies than we are used to, showing us the capacity of what appear to be loose or nonhierarchical relations to be frontier zones of so-called primitive accumulation in which new kinds of hierarchies are forged. Analogy provides a rhetorical index of the "pollution of nonwork," both unpaid and criminalized alike, that functions simultaneously as the condition of possibility for and site of struggle within (ongoing) primitive accumulation. It is this kind of accumulation that George Caffentzis has described as "washing, fucking, cooling tempers, picking up the trash, lipstick, thermostat, giving birth, kids, teaching them not to shit in the hall, curing the common cold, watching the cancer grow, even lyric poems for your schizophrenia," and last of all, "sleep and dreams."[78] The point here is not about some always already capitalist relation embedded in the social, nor is it about the subsumption of everything under capital, if by that we mean a mode of production and circulation organized strictly through homogeneity and equivalence. The point, rather, is to deal with the ways in which relational resources of material bodies—their transience, contingency, capacities, and vulnerabilities—function simultaneously as reserves for collective survival and distributed violence.[79] It is this politically charged analysis of analogy's anachronisms as it brings together the messy and sensuous with the gendered, raced, and unruly that may help us to best work through the possibilities and limits of changing conceptualizations of bodies and history, both in that transitional period from the late eighteenth century to the Romantic era as well as in our own return to it in literary criticism today.

CHAPTER 3

Tautology, Witchcraft, and a Thingly Commons

> This heap of earth o'ergrown with moss,
> Which close beside the thorn you see,
> So fresh in all its beauteous dyes,
> Is like an infant's grave in size
> *As like as like can be*:
>
> "The Thorn," William Wordsworth

> To market she on market-days,
> To church on Sundays came;
> *All seem'd the same: all seem'd so, Sir!*
> But all was not the same!
>
> "The Three Graves," Samuel Taylor Coleridge

Tautological Gatherings

In 1797, shortly before the publication of *Lyrical Ballads*, a group of fortune-tellers were arrested in the Norwood forest. They were not charged with the practice of witchcraft, however. Laws against palmistry and divination had been struck in 1736, when it immediately became illegal instead to make accusations of witchcraft, thus effectively inverting the crime of witchcraft from one of serious practice to the threat of superstition. Instead, the

Norwood group, primarily women and children, were charged with a section of the 1597 Vagabond Act under which certain practices formerly criminalized as witchcraft could still be punished, not out of fear of the efficacy of the supernatural but as an explicit condemnation of undisciplined ways of living associated with the "backwardness" of superstition.[1] The power and threat of witchcraft having been disavowed, a much older form of criminalization was resurrected to deal with the presence of the unmarried and the unemployed. In 1760, only fourteen years after the passage of the Witchcraft Act in England, Obeah, a practice that was often labeled as witchcraft by Europeans, was criminalized in Jamaica.[2] After Tacky's Rebellion, considered the most threatening attempt to overthrow the plantocracy in Jamaica, "An Act to Remedy the Evils arising from Irregular Assemblies of Slaves" included a "clause designed to 'prevent the practice of Obeah.'"[3] According to Diana Paton, this act was significant in two ways: first, it both reasserted and "creolized" the power of the supernatural that had been explicitly rejected by the Enlightenment mindset of the Witchcraft Act; second, it used an African-derived term, Obeah, in the naming and consolidation of a range of practices that, as Srinivas Aravamudan describes it, include "medicine, symptom, fetish, or trope," as well as "a full-blown information system that named pharmacological knowledge, political conspiracy, religious practice, or literary construction."[4]

This shifting and paradoxical legal and cultural terrain involves continuous reinventions of the supernatural within the history of capital accumulation. Of particular interest is what the reanimation of the vagrancy laws in England and the European claims that African practices had been reanimated in Obeah have to tell us about the global destruction and remaking of subsistence ways of living that are the concerns of this book. These overlapping reanimations fold together a more figurative process in which superstition was simultaneously targeted for destruction, remained necessary to the production of capitalism in its present-day form, and provided a resource of noncapitalist ways of living that were immensely recombinatory. Romantic literary critics often understand the transformation of responses to the supernatural in an English context as part of the transition from sovereign to disciplinary power through the emergence of medical and patriarchal expertise. They tend to suggest that such relationships were nothing more than remnants of a past that is no longer relevant to modernity. But such accounts do not help us understand the less straightforward entwinement of the supernatural with subsistence ways of living that persists in canonical writers such as Wordsworth and Coleridge, as well as defenders of slavery such as Benjamin Moseley.[5] Silvia Federici's account of the European witch hunts in Chapter 2 provides a counterreading. Central to and determining of modern capitalist divisions of labor and interclass hierarchies of gender, the European witch hunts and their aftermath are an example of what she has described as "a classic instance of how, in the history of capitalism, 'going back' was a means of stepping forward" and the production of modernity through the affirmation of the power of the supernatural.[6]

Helpful as Federici's dialectical reading of capitalism's "going back" and "stepping forward" is, it still clings to a primarily temporalized account of capitalist modernity in which later claims to enlightened science and social order would remain indebted to an indulgence in the backward rather than the reconstituted, or to borrow Paton's term, the "creolized." This chapter takes up contemporaneous representations of what English writers understood to be beliefs in the supernatural in England and Jamaica in order to show that such beliefs continued to be far more defining of capitalist modernity than previously thought. Further, such beliefs are not reducible to the realm of the spiritual or even what M. H. Abrams famously termed natural supernaturalism—they are, instead, entangled with the material relations of subsistence and its remaking by the violent processes of capital accumulation.[7] Here we shall stay within these knots of superstition, not simply to identify the ways in which superstition was historicized to banish people and practices to a mythic past but also to ascertain all of the ways in which it carries an archive of subsistence that does not fit into narratives of past and present, loss and progress.

We might take a different cue from Federici here, drawing not from the binarizing timeline of backward and forward but from her claim that capitalism develops by taking the "bricolage" of available discourses, beliefs, and practices and turning them into hierarchical social relations. Bricolage already suggests a different arrangement of things through which to understand the historical process of capital accumulation. Made famous by Claude Lévi-Strauss, bricolage remains a useful term by which to approach so-called primitive accumulation because it describes "the continual reconstruction from the same materials" in which "earlier ends... are called upon to play the part of means."[8] What had been a conclusion, perhaps even a telos, becomes repurposed as a way elsewhere and of doing otherwise. While this formulation of bricolage has a distinctly Hegelian bent to it, it also enables a more contingent arrangement in the English sense of bricolage as "odds and ends" rather than "remains and debris."[9] It is this former arrangement that best suits descriptions of objects used by Obi men and women to work their science, at least as we see in versions passed down to us from British travel narratives and parliamentary reports.[10] In Benjamin Moseley's description, likely lifted from Bryan Edwards's then already well-known *History, Civil and Commercial, of the British Colonies in the West Indies*, these objects are

> made of grave dirt, hair, teeth of sharks, and other animals, blood, feathers, egg-shells, images in wax, the hearts of birds, liver of mice, and some potent roots, weeds, and bushes of which Europeans are at this time ignorant, but which were known, for the same purposes, to the ancients. Certain mixtures of these ingredients are burnt; or buried very deep in the ground; or hung up a chimney; or on the side of an house; or in a garden; or laid under the threshold of the door of the party, to suffer; with incantation songs, or curses, or ceremonies necromantically performed in planetary hours, or at midnight, regarding the aspects of the moon. (*Treatise on Sugar*, 191–192)[11]

This description of Obeah objects bears a remarkable resemblance to the abject arrangement of body parts and fragments of organic matter seen in *Macbeth* and earlier representations of female witches' talismans in early modern European treatises. Certainly, such abjectifying observations of Obi objects were important parts of the hierarchical classification of Obeah as a practice of sorcery rather than a science in the manner that Federici suggests; these necro-epistemological arrangements find an uncanny resonance with Enlightenment and post-Enlightenment hierarchies of empirical sense experience.

Indeed, Erasmus Darwin's materialist scientific treatise *Zoonomia* presents a similar composite configuration to evoke the bricolage of superstition. A materialist and empirical approach to symptoms and diseases was the best tool in the fight against "fictions of fancy, of witchcraft, hobgoblins, apparitions, vampires, fairies; of the influence of stars on human actions, miracles wrought by the bones of saints, the flights of ominous birds, the predictions from the bowels of dying animals, expounders of dreams, fortune-tellers, conjurers, modern prophets, necromancy, animal magnetism, with endless variety of folly."[12] His empirically driven model of medicine offered a way to treat bodies that were overly prone to influence from external bodies, which for him meant being able to distinguish between superstitions and a science of influence. As we see here, Darwin expresses a deep, almost excessive concern over "the influence" that certain objects and things (bones, birds, bowels) have upon the fancy, that faculty of association that organizes and orders sense experience. Such things can create false perceptions of the natural world (of hobgoblins and vampires and fairies, oh my!) as well as of false causal agents (fortune-tellers, conjurers, modern prophets, etc.). As Darwin clarifies in *Zoonomia*, pathological associations result from the imputation of external sensation to what is actually caused by an internal problem with the imagination.[13] But we also get the sense from the passage above that, as with Moseley's depiction of Obeah, there is something lurking in the mere arrangement of these things: there are disturbing relations of likeness and sympathy between stars and human life; of metonymy between necrotic parts and living processes; and of chaotic contiguity in Darwin's own manner of constructing these associations, where stars sit beside bones and dying animals alongside animal magnetism. This passage does more than describe—it performs relations of magic in which "like produces like; contact results in contagion; the image produces the object itself; a part is seen to be the same as the whole."[14] This transatlantic concern with heterogeneous forms holds together shared concerns over the order of things and the influence things can have upon susceptible bodies, whether those be of slaves or the rural villagers we turn to below.

The associations through which we receive knowledge are crucial here, because it was often the moment of sensation that seemed to lead superstitious folks astray. This instance was a deeply precarious one, since according to Darwin it is the influence of external things upon the senses that constitutes the building blocks of all knowledge of the world and of healthy bodies. As he describes it, empirical sensations arrive initially through some degree of contiguity, contact, or likeness: "As the constituent elements of the material world are only perceptible to our organs of sense in a state of combination; it follows, that the ideas or sensual motions excited by them, are never received singly, but ever with a greater or less degree of combination."[15] Human perception of "the material world" is confined to an experience of the "constituent" as manifold. The ground of sense experience is an originary gathering from which temporal order is constructed over time into successive causality and habituated sensibilities, epistemological progress and physiological equilibrium. Darwin uses sugar, a thing that likely came to him from Moseley's plantocratic Jamaica, to exemplify this process in which "sweetness, and whiteness, and solidity are received at the same time from a lump of sugar." "I cannot," he writes, "recollect any of these qualities without thinking of the others, that were excited along with them."[16] Primary sensations—while more boring than superstitious perceptions—are nonetheless instances of influence from the outside and associated in a combination of simultaneous difference, contagious contact, and metonymic materiality. Never received singly, these empirical instances are composed instead through what David Lloyd has described as a "peculiarly exterior internal constitution" of the thing, in contrast to the object or subject.[17] Lloyd is not commenting on Darwin's sugar here but Hegel's salt. In his *Phenomenology of the Spirit*, Hegel wrote of salt in this tauto-thing-ical fashion: "The salt is a simple Here, and at the same time manifold." For Hegel, such a "Thing" "is white and *also* cubical, *also* tart, and so on. . . . The Thing is the *Also*, or the *universal medium* in which the many properties subsist apart from one another, without touching or cancelling one another."[18] As for Darwin, here Hegel shows us properties and the sensations they provoke as never single but always in a combinative state that is experienced in a simultaneity that is impossible to capture in language. The thing here is defined by its also-ness, its auto-repetition of a variety of phenomenal features that are not gathered into an identity. Prior to the realization of self, sense perception yields this crystallized likeness of relations in which entities subsist without the imposition of identity. Held together simultaneously, they are also spaced out, defined by a coexistence that is simultaneous but separable, that constitutes neither identity nor habit but combination.[19] Salt, like Darwin's sugar, is in an externally associated state of combination, as well as being an adverbial essence—"the thing is the also," a structure of becoming that is additive, supplemental, and potentially redundant. Our experience of things is initially gathered from the multiple qualities and generated impressions of sensational encounters that uncannily reproduce, in a subdued manner, the depictions of supernatural things such as bones, birds, feathers, and teeth we saw above.[20]

But Hegel adds to this associationist structure a reference to subsistence. Not quite substance, Hegel invokes subsistence as existence in a less substantial way, as a continuation in a base, nondialectical mode. And it is with this composite thing that subsists in its "peculiarly exterior internal" manner that we also hear a likeness with Moseley's abject depiction of Obeah, which reflects these subsistence relations and the superstitious forms of knowledge that can always emerge erroneously from those forms. In contrast to the regulated bodies that were Darwin's medical aim and the self-consciousness that would come to find sense experience ultimately alienating for Hegel's Subject, these originating scenes of influence contaminate the material basis of knowledge through the external, metonymic, contiguous, and simultaneous relations of magic. Smuggled into the foundations of a modern subject with connections to and effects on the material world are the motions of a magical view of a potentially "anarchic, molecular conception" of the world.[21] While these features of sense experience would be neutralized hierarchies of experience in their texts, the constellated and crystallized figuration through which things subsist in Darwin's and Hegel's accounts gives us an association by which to read the persistence of superstition within the empirical process of becoming subject.[22]

While Darwin and Hegel leave out the slave mode of production through which sugar and salt arrived upon their empirical and phenomenological taste buds, Moseley's engagement with superstition in his *Treatise on Sugar* is meant entirely as a defense of slavery. In returning to Moseley, I want to constellate the associations between sense experience and external influence, superstition and things, and subsistence both as a way of life and a form of knowledge within the global process of capital accumulation. It is not only in the thing of Obeah that Moseley sees a problem of loose gathering, of things that neither touch nor cancel each other out, remaining an unordered mass. It is also in the history of sugar that Moseley tells us he confronts an overly superstitious arrangement of knowledge. For Moseley, the production of modernity hinges on the association between superstition and subsistence, or the superstition that sugar is available outside the form in which it is exchanged for money in Europe.[23]

Moseley finds himself caught up in the messy and meaningless hearsay of what has, up to this point, been accepted as the historical taxonomy of sugar. The bulk of Moseley's treatise, 173 pages in all, is an attempt to sort through the heap of words that have been used to signify that empirical thing, sugar. Struggling against an adhesive mass, Moseley declares that he will create a hierarchy out of what we've called bricolage, beginning with "the surface of the mass": in order to "discove[r] a foundation, on which order and arrangement may rise, I must toil through trackless regions of obscurity," to arrive at "the more certain and determinate history of the sugar cane."[24] The problem Moseley immediately confronts is an unmapped landscape in which no history of sugar can be found. On the one hand, "the incorrect account of the first West Indian discoveries" make it "impossible to ascertain in which of the islands the cane was found, and which it was not."[25] On the other hand, "every thing [Arabs] have said pertaining to the subject" is unreliable, because "there is such a want of discrimination among the Arabian writers, which their editors, translators, and commentators, have further perplexed with various texts, interpretations, and conjectures, that is it impossible to know exactly the precise distinctions, intended by the original authors, in their different appellations of *honey, manna,* and *sugar.*"[26] The problem, as Moseley puts it, is a manifold of words used to signify more than one sweetener. No pure line can be extracted from the origins of sugarcane and its production by slaves in Jamaica. Moseley lays most of the blame here on Arabic writers, who, in the process of writing down the location, function, and features of various sweeteners, have indulged in "interpretation and conjecture," mystifying the true source of sugar in sugarcane. This is at least in part due to what Moseley offers as the fact that "the Arabian medical writers were chiefly compilers and copiers from the Greeks; and seem to have known but little, even of their own country. Their account of *manna* is as fabulous as that of their *tabaxir*, and has given rise to as many speculations. They supposed it was a dew, attracted by certain trees, plants, and stones, and there concreted."[27] The history of sugar provided by Arabic writers may as well be a magical gathering of elements. It is the result of external influence that has confused things by suggesting that sugar might be gotten for free—dropped from the sky like manna and attained without labor, as if stars have sweet influence upon human action. Repetition gathers heterogeneous things, as the "*sacar-mambu* of the Indians" and the "*tabaxir* of the Arabians" are equated with sugar, and as signifiers float freely away from the proper and nonexistent history of sugar production.[28] These signifiers produce an adhesive mass that binds time in a nonsuccessive pattern, making it impossible to find in sugar a signification of history. Instead of history, prior writing about sugar yields only accounts of magical substances falling from the sky.

The form of speech through which we derive such superstitious relations between things is at the center of Wordsworth's "The Thorn," which is famously narrated by a superstitious sailor with an "adhesive" mind. While this may seem a rapid leap from Moseley's *Treatise on Sugar*, to say nothing of Darwin and Hegel, I hope to show that a more than transatlantic context is needed for grappling with the history of superstition. What Moseley calls the "interpretation and conjecture" of Arabic writers shows up in the "The Thorn" as the hearsay and gossip of rural villagers. Circulated through versions of superstitious chatter, the poem tells of an abandoned woman and the mysterious death (or murder?) of her newborn child, passing along a history in which eighteenth-century misogyny derives from rural ignorance.[29] Most of what we learn about Martha Ray is given through a version of hearsay, through a series of stanzas held together by "they say" and "'Tis said" and "I heard" and "some say," by "I've heard" and "some had sworn." It is through such sensational chatter that Martha has been tried by a village politics and nearly put to death: "And some had sworn an oath that she / Should be to public justice brought; / And for the little infant's

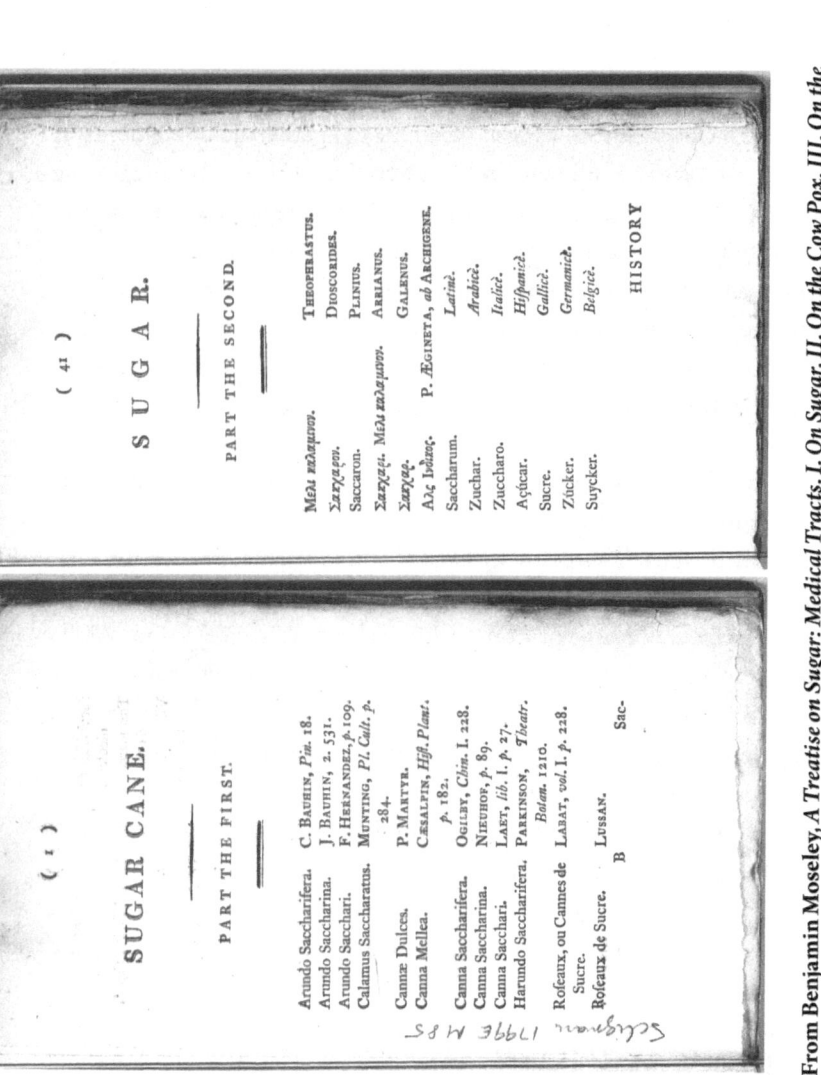

From Benjamin Moseley, *A Treatise on Sugar: Medical Tracts. I. On Sugar. II. On the Yaws. IV. On Obi, or African Witchcraft. V. On the Plague; and Yellow Fever of America VI. On Hospitals. VII. On Bronchocele. VIII. On Prisons*, 2nd ed. (London: Printed by J. Nichols, 1800), 3, 4. Reprinted with permission from the Columbia University Rare Book and Manuscript Library.

bones / With spades they would have sought."[30] It is this near-sovereign decision that retroactively confirms that we are not just dealing with loose lips but with a superstition that situates us in the narrative created by the 1736 Witchcraft Act. Like an echo chamber, these unverified reports are how we learn of the location of the thorn and mysterious heap (like a grave), of the timing of Martha Ray's movements, and ultimately, after many digressions, a combination of the motions—"never received singly" as Darwin said of sugary perception—of "some say." This repetition passes from neighbor to neighbor, from narrator to us. Chatter here is the figurative matter of things, in which we can hear Hegel's "also, also, also" strung together against the woman who sometimes appears as a thing in the poem: "And, as I am a man, / Instead of jutting crag I found / A woman seated on the ground."[31] These tautological sayings uproot Martha Ray, banishing her to crags and hills, where she seems to become a thing herself.

Repeated as the hearsay of "some say" throughout the poem, superstitions sparked by sensational experience are socialized as "information received by word of mouth, usually with the implication that it is not trustworthy; oral tidings; report, tradition, rumour, common talk, gossip."[32] Tradition and rumor, report and gossip, hearsay is discredited upon arrival but binds the social at the same time. As a form of language, it expresses the deeply noneconomic and superfluous subsistence that maintains community life through the routine spread of an expression that immediately undermines its own veracity. It is perhaps because it derives solely from what one has heard from others that it circulates so easily, making no claim to knowledge that would require the checking of facts. It is precisely in this more than double bind of surplus circulation and the baselessness of what is said that Wordsworth's "The Thorn" indulges, working as it does to remediate superstition into sympathetic feeling. The sufferings of Martha come to us and, Wordsworth suggests, are also caused by a kind of common talk that spreads like a contagion. Shifting the etymological possibility of samesaying, "The Thorn" positions offside speakers in the poem as same-sayers, repeating words that create a supernatural aura.

Such hearsay and chatter are historically relevant to Wordsworth's poem and its skirting of the supernatural. Hearsay was central to the operations

Henry Ninham, *The Hethel Thorn*. From *The Eastern Arboretum* (London: Longman, Brown, Green, and Longmans, 1841), 282. A depiction of what has long been considered one of the oldest thorn trees in England. Reprinted with permission from The British Museum.

of the European witch hunts, through which village gossip, a distinctly feminine form of sociality attached to the commons, was transformed into a tool of class warfare.[33] It took a sustained campaign to transform the social life of chatter into the divisive acts of accusation. This campaign can be seen in the source text for *Macbeth*'s weird sisters, James I's "Newes from Scotland." There we read of Gilles Duncan, who "took in hand to helpe all such as were troubled or grieved with anie kind of sickness of infirmitie." Suspected of witchcraft because of such care, she was "committed to prison, where she continued for a season, where immediately she accused these persons following to be notorious witches."[34] As Federici's landmark, and controversial, book *Caliban and the Witch* argues, the witch hunts often designated caregivers as threats to communities that were "already disintegrating under the combined impact of land privatization, increased taxation, and the extension of state control over every aspect of life." But it was "only as the persecution progressed, and the fear of witches (as well as the fear of being accused of witchcraft or 'subversive association') was sowed among the population, did accusations come from neighbors."[35] In addition to the slow violence of this cultivated ideological campaign, a sustained effect of the witch hunt was also the erasure of communicative spaces and social bonds between women, as the absence of common lands took away a crucial site of feminine congregation. The construction of the kind of mob politics that threatens Martha Ray in "The Thorn" was the product of time and concerted efforts by the European ruling class, who were desperate to establish social discipline in the wake of the widespread peasant uprisings of the sixteenth century. The gossip of neighbor against neighbor and the prepsychiatric demand to confess were crafted through a sustained legal and propagandistic campaign, which could only become effective in the aftermath of the enclosures, the ensuing wild spikes in prices caused by inflation, and the crushing of the peasant rebellions. The witch hunts took a gathering of differences and organized them into hierarchies, transforming the medical, care, and reproductive work done by women into a mark of gendered inferiority and consolidating gender differences that preexisted the rise of capitalism as essentializing features upon which inviolable divisions of labor could be grounded.

For Wordsworth, however, it is not just hearsay that carries the influence of superstition. Rather, it seems to be a kind of pathological repetition of the kind we saw above, a repetition that is no less concerned with thingly bodies and their sensations. In his prefatory note to "The Thorn," Wordsworth engages the repetition of words in poetry, distinguishing between a repetition that communicates feeling and a repetition of the same meaning, even in the use of different words: "There is a numerous class of readers who imagine that the same words cannot be repeated without tautology: this is a great error: virtual tautology is much oftener produced by using words when the meaning is exactly the same. Words, a Poet's words more particularly, ought to be weighed in the balance of feeling and not measured by the space they occupy upon paper."[36] Here Wordsworth seems to suggest that most readers conflate repeated meaning with repeated words, and his aim in "The Thorn" is to show that the repetition of words, paced out in certain meters, may come closer to remedying the deficiency of language in communicating feelings than any other kind of language. Whereas virtual tautology hews to an identity of meaning, repetition of the kind Wordsworth produces in "The Thorn" is calculated to generate sympathy, more specifically a likeness between sound and feeling. The repetition of words can establish a "balance of feeling" through their thingliness—through the psychophysiological effects upon readers of "words . . . as *things*."[37] Such things have the capacity to affect readers through sense experience rather than stimulating in them a temporal redundancy.

Martha Ray's repeated "Oh misery! oh misery! / Oh woe is me! oh misery!" is the best-known example of such tautology. But it is in the loose resemblance between the narrator and the villagers through a shared susceptibility to a less regulated thingliness of language that the most significant form of tautology appears in the poem. As Julie Camarda has argued, Wordsworth's "Note to the Thorn" potentially sets a trap for critics by caricaturing their "hostility and limitations" toward a speaker with "a mind that is . . . not loose but adhesive" and by doing so associates our loquacious narrator with the repetitive Martha in order to establish a "mutuality and sympathy" that is not based on an absence of narrative knowledge. But we cannot avoid the fact that Wordsworth similarly aligns the narrator with the villagers through a shared credulity and talkativeness derived from indolence and an overstimulated imagination that "produces *impressive* effects out of simple elements."[38] Like others, our narrator amplifies the power of external things and recounts events through relations of loose likeness. Impressed by the thingliness of words as "simple elements" upon "adhesive" minds, the narrator carries out the task of passing along village gossip. Actual, and not virtual, tautology becomes a dangerous deficiency, offering the possibility of both sympathy and superstition, and becoming the latter when language is imprinted on reactive minds that are more like spatial surfaces than the temporality of ideas that "succeed each other in accustomed order."[39]

Thus, while Wordsworth fixates on repetition as a way to generate refreshed and regulated feeling, he also locates a pathological repetition of hearsay that hinges upon the materiality of language.⁴⁰ The problem with superstitious chatter is the vagrant slippage we began tracing above between empirical and supernatural arrangements and their tendency toward contiguous contagion and disordering of internal causality. Hearsay would seem to have its effects by means of a use of words that overexcites our "animal sensations" through a sameness of repetition that becomes threatening not because of its redundancy but because of its affecting power.⁴¹ Associated primarily with physiological susceptibility, shared by our indolent narrator and his neighbors, the version of tautology that brings sailor and villagers into relation has more to do with the power of that subsistence arrangement of things than with the meaningless stutter of backward people. Tautology is rooted in the essentially rhetorical problem of the priority of words over reason and of reflexive motion over self-sameness. From the Greek, tautologia combines "auto" and "logos" and is most often read as meaning "the same" plus "speech, word," or as "reason." Tautology can thus most directly be traced back to its meaning as selfsame reason and in this form has been treated as a figure for an innate identity of meaning or ironized as self-undermining meaninglessness. A more marginal tracing would also find roots for a dispersed sense of gleaning in which repetition turns into a gathering of "like it was, merely" (αὐτός) and "to collect, gather" (λέγω),⁴² the first a derivative of "self" and "same" in an adverbial mode, the second the root verb from which "logic" comes to us. This contiguous association of word elements is bound up with the world, unreasonably.⁴³ While difficult, if not impossible, to trace properly, this somewhat vagrant etymology nonetheless persists in Wordsworth's characterization of superstitious imaginations, which "produc[e] *impressive* effects out of simple elements."⁴⁴ This mode of tautology preserves the power of a gathering that does not follow the historical reason claimed by the Witchcraft Act, in which the designation of superstition supposedly neutralizes the power of the supernatural as a thing of the past. While "The Thorn" and its note may set us up to feel sympathy with Martha Ray's misery, it also continually asks us to feel horror at the superstitious hearsay that makes Martha an outsider. In making superstition a problem of such same-saying, Wordsworth cannot help but reproduce the anxiety underlying the Witchcraft Act, that the power of superstition derives from the gathering of ways of living in the present that are inseparable from past violences that created their conditions of becoming. In this sense, what is most worrisome to Wordsworth is a lack of balance of feeling threatened by the superstitious sayers of the poem, in a mode of tautology that takes us back to an uncanny likeness between subsistence, empiricism, and gathering as a way of life.

This recursion to the early modern European witch hunts and their influence upon Wordsworth's poem may risk reinserting us into a temporal movement whereby the threat of superstition in Romantic-era England appears quite isolated from Moseley's concern with the history of sugar, as well as his fascination with Obeah. This is why it is important to recall why, according to Federici, witch hunts were so important to the processes of capital accumulation and to an accounting of the contingency of social relations through which such accumulation emerges and is reproduced. In her view, we cannot explain the history of capitalism without recourse to the social potential for divisions of labor and among workers. Such a process entails an immanent relation between capitalism and the bricolage of the social, and of the continuous and messy remediation of practices and beliefs that mediate the molecularly empirical and forms of knowing the world. Thus, we can only begin grappling with the strangely resonant associations between Wordsworth's sense of tautology, Darwin's and Hegel's taste for sugar and salt, respectively, and Moseley's history of sugar by locating them within the modernity that Rosalind Shaw has described as stretching back to the beginning of the transatlantic slave trade, in which "capitalist modernities took plural forms in different parts of the Atlantic from the very beginning."[45]

As Shaw argues, what was depicted as age-old practices of witchcraft in West Africa by the time of English dominance in the slave trade were already the result of world-historical processes of capitalist and colonial violence, as well as memories of the destruction and remaking of "a trans-Saharan trade that linked three different continents" into the European trade in humans, guns, and credit.[46] Supernatural beliefs and practices offered intricate ways to negotiate an ever-changing landscape in which previously unimaginable accumulations of wealth, tribal consolidations of European guns and weapons, new debt and credit systems, and the destruction of entire tribes and families shaped West Africans' experiences of their worlds. On the part of many West Africans, as Shaw argues, the myriad effects of the slave trade generated an acute sense of a "vampiric modernity" and "occult forces that modernity was supposed to have superseded," thus "fold[ing] together past and present experiences of capitalism, transregional flows, and violence."[47] The best-known example of such "occult forces" within literary studies is likely those numerous attributions of sorcery and magic to white people that Olaudah Equiano / Gustauvus Vassa makes in his *Interesting Narrative*. For instance, upon arriving at the coast and boarding the ship that would take him through the Middle Passage, Equiano says that he "was now persuaded that I had gotten into a world of bad spirits" and describes the ship as "some spell or magic."[48] Such instances demonstrate how the violence and trauma of capture, together with the arrival at slave factories and ports, affected people's conceptions of the supernatural as they were traumatically transformed through the otherwise unimaginable forms of violence they experienced. Indeed, the formation of "African" ethnicity can be seen as undergoing a remediation of the kind we see in historical revisioning of witchcraft. As Alexander X. Byrd argues in regard to European conceptions of Igbo ethnicity, it is possible to see the production of this ethnicity insofar as Europeans understood it in the eighteenth century as the result of the death and rebirth that occurred in the journey from central Africa to the coast. Even the term "Igbo" can be translated in such a way as to register a passage from other worlds, as the "strangers beyond those strangers" of known towns.[49]

Once the enslaved arrived at the plantation colonies, the supernatural was no less a routine force in their lives. As Vincent Brown compellingly argues, the fantastic wealth generated by sugar production in Jamaica came into the world dripping with the supernatural, as the likelihood of death and the pervasiveness of dead bodies were routinely used by plantation owners, magistrates, and the colonial government to terrorize and dominate the enslaved. According to Brown, "supernatural beliefs and the machinery of the colonial state were inextricably enmeshed" in what he can be understood as "a materialist history of the supernatural imagination."[50] Brown's insights remind us that ways of life that are destroyed by dispossession and enslavement are translated into images and memories of the continuous discontinuity of such so-called primitive accumulation. These moments of superstition remind us that the sustained campaign of terror that was the slave trade cannot be reduced to the pastness or historicity of such belief. Similarly, every unfamiliar practice or accusation of witchcraft witnessed by English writers in Jamaica such as Moseley was a contemporary mediation of the war, militarization, relocation, defense, and relations between elites, villagers, and kin through which the slave trade was established and maintained. Something similar is at work in Moseley's depictions of Obeah and Obi objects, which, as many have noted, strive to establish it as an originally African practice rather than as one generated under the pressures of dispossession and enslavement. In presenting Obeah this way, Moseley follows in a long line of English and European writers who styled African cultural and spiritual practices as archaic rather than as forged in the crucible of the extreme violence of murder, kidnapping, the passage through West African hinterlands to port cities, the Middle Passage, and the death drive of slave labor as a mode of production. Superstition, even in these European texts, derives from the knots that were formed in the destruction and remaking of ways of life and systems of knowledge inside and outside of Europe in the Romantic period.

Moving from Moseley to Wordsworth, from witch hunts to the slave trade, and from rural villagers in England to natives of West Africa is not meant to analogize or collapse them as some kind of historical sameness but to gather a tautological modernity governed not by reason but by the destruction and remaking of noncapitalist ways of living as they were and are rooted in material bodies. If, as Shaw and Brown show us, capitalist modernity cannot be extricated from the supernatural—including its own brutal fabulations of equivalence—then we need to begin to ask how Romantic texts do more than banish superstition to the past. The clustering effect of tautology is not only interesting for the etymological connections it evokes with enclosure and the criminalization of gleaning but also for the ways in which it maintains the language of superstition in the empirical body as one of the foundational operations between thingly bodies rather than a residue of the past. Brought together, these texts we have been discussing show how superstition is not reducible to a narrative of past and present, of witchcraft turning into scientific discourse or subsistence into modern labor—even those texts concerned with producing just such narratives. The entanglements of superstition, the body, and subsistence that are rooted in them offer another historical movement of remediation, one in which subsistence is not only a way of meeting needs but ways of knowing that are inseparable from affectable and impressionable embodiment. Attempts to situate superstition in the past are themselves still living and ongoing negotiations with the uncanny likenesses, the adjacent and still affecting, the nonlinear entwinements that constitute this thing called modernity and "connections between world historical processes and 'magical' capacities."[51] In the next two sections, we shall read more tautologically and less progressively, or regressively, in order to see subsistence as it is smuggled into the production of our present.

A Sufficient Commons and a Wretched Thing

For Hegel and Darwin, salt and sugar were things that exemplified the coincidence of sense experiences from which more complex forms emerged. Sensorial archipelagos of a kind, things were empirical coordinates of the unfolding of regulated (Darwin) or self-conscious (Hegel) subjects. The thing that launches so much hearsay in "The Thorn," however, is sensed somewhat differently, as a "wretched thing":

> There is a thorn; it looks so old,
> . . . .
>
> No leaves it has, no thorny points;
> It is a mass of knotted joints,
> A wretched thing forlorn.
> It stands erect, and like a stone
> With lichens it is overgrown.
>
> Like rock or stone, it is o-ergrown
> With lichens to the very top,
> And hung with heavy tufts of moss,
> A melancholy crop;
> Up from the earth these mosses creep[.][52]

What is striking about these first lines is the way in which repetition of sounds and movement is conjoined. Rather than the separate but connected subsistences of salt, sugar, and sensation, the thorn as a thing is depicted in a condition of abjection, with all the intermingling of insides and outsides that the word implies. If the constellated associations of salt and sugar present a dispersed multiplicity, then the overlapped gatherings of the thorn produce a life form "sunk in distress or dejection."[53] In contrast to the accounts of sensations discussed above, the thorn as a thing immediately displays natural history in a wretched form. Our experience of it, given through repetitions of "it, it, it" rather than "also, also, also," is not received "singly," as Darwin wrote of salt sensations. This composition is distinct, however, in its knottedness and accumulations that make separability seem impossible. The first distress we encounter in the poem is not moral or economic but a historical form of "strain, stress, pressure" that accumulates over time. As far as we can tell from these opening lines, this awful affect has to do with the ways in which the thorn is folded in and curled upon its nonself. In the opening stanzas it seems that wretchedness is more a matter of the manifold of directions (overgrown and up-creeping) and positions (hung, standing, and massed) that wind insides and outsides together like Macbethian auguries, without "visible connection or dependency."[54] In contrast to the sensorial immediacy experienced with salt and sugar, the thorn as a thing is rooted in the accumulations of time. Unlike Darwin or Hegel, Wordsworth's "wretched thing" takes on a decidedly historical feel, orienting us toward subsistence relations in a sedimented temporal key. This historicity of subsistence is simultaneously "many-sided" and enfolded in its form, introducing a slightly different perception of the commonality that things carry with them.

The thorn was undoubtedly such a distressed thing, built into the English landscape at the miserable crux of the commons and enclosure. The hawthorn—the tree to which Wordsworth was most likely referring—was one of the main materials used to build the quickset hedges that sprang up all over England at the turn of the eighteenth century. Like the paradoxical associations evoked by the sensation of things mentioned above, the thorn is a historical variation of thingliness that holds a surplus of commonality and the scarcity of enclosure together at the same time. The use of thorn trees in the construction of enclosure hedges signaled multiple transitions in the industry of enclosure—an increased reliance on coal that led to the homogenization of tree species used for hedges that no longer needed to be relied on to provide fuel. The thorn thus went from being common-in-variety with other species of trees, which afforded greater ecological diversity, to a commercially produced commodity, thus bearing a memory of the "sufficiently common" in its wretched accumulations over time.

The term "sufficiently common" comes from Wordsworth's description of his superstitious narrator but also registers an affinity with the thorn itself.[55] Common enough to be widely available, the thorn became a means of measuring sufficiency in entirely new ways, as means of subsistence were converted into units of money. The thorn as a commodity is already stuck in the history of enclosure before we ever hear of the misogynistic exclusion of Martha Ray from her superstitious community. As a thing, however, the thorn is not simply a metaphor for pathological resistance to modernity. Wordsworth produces an especially repetitive phrasing of its thingly inextricability in the phrase "sufficiently common." Emerging through the

Example of a quickset hedge made with thorn. Reprinted with permission from the Isle of Wight History Center.

historical sensibility we have begun to trace, the thorn is caught up in this strange refrain of the mere and the satisfying. It is a sufficiently common thing, evoking the wretchedness of potential scarcity and unnecessary excess at the same time, much in the manner that subsistence ways of living were historically produced through dispossession. Along with its embeddedness in the material markers of enclosure, the thorn as a thing opens up to modern understanding this strange coincidence within the otherwise straightforward narrative of rural ignorance. Entangled with the material objects of enclosure and thingly subsistence, this refrain roots us further in those superstitions that are not markers of the past but images of the messy re-creations of subsistence in the context of so-called primitive accumulation. In this sense, the process through which the common and the shared became a source of mere survival, as what is just enough for meager reproduction, is figured by the sufficiently common.

But if we emphasize the tautology of this phrase, there is also a nonsensical abundance figured that offers a subsistence not through measure but through what is enough in a common way. In its tautological mode, the sufficiently common is an absurd excess, a relation of sharing that is, by definition, unnecessary because it is neither distinct nor defined. Bound up with the surplus of a manifold earth that does not move forward necessarily into successive history or regulated subjects, the sufficiently common can instead hold together heaps and mosses and knots as the shape of heterogeneous ways of meeting needs that persist in their vitalness to the present. The thorn, as both object of enclosure and thing of surplus beyond a meager necessity, registers what Fred Moten calls "a certain thingly resistance to the status of the mere thing," not by being outside the processes of enclosure but by being knotted with them.[56]

In Moseley's treatise we get another variation on this account of the sufficiently common. Moseley's version is contemporaneous with the cropping up of quickset hedges but, in contrast to the homogenization of the thorn, holds out a variety of things that can be used to satisfy a sweet tooth in a common fashion. Coming close to a thing that manifests from the sky, the "saccharine principle" that constitutes sugar in its original form is, according to Moseley, quite sufficiently common: "The maple, the birch, the red beet, the parsnip, the grape, wheat &c. contain it. Margraff extracted it from most vegetables. The petals of many flowers, and the nectariums placed in these organs, elaborate a principle of this kind. The sugarcane, *arundo saccharisera* [sic], contains it in larger quantities, and affords it more readily, than any other plant."[57] In the excessive inclusion by other writers of other plants that have something of a "saccharine principle," we have an overly adhesive history in which there is no palpable difference between certain kinds of salt, the ashes and residue of plants, and the dew that is thought to fall from heaven. On the one hand, Moseley sets out to clear away the confusion around the only commodity that has the historically salutary effects of sugar, while on the other hand, he seems to suggest that sugar is "as like as like can be" to any number of other things.[58] When found in its state as a saccharine principle, it seems to be in excess, a commonplace plant that could be gathered anywhere. Elsewhere Moseley makes clear that the thing that is abundantly available is, in fact, superfluous because sugar is not found in nature and is only produced: "Every kind of sugar whatever is made by art. Native sugar never existed. Ignorant people, even at this day, in our own part of the world, imagine that sugar is found, like pith, in the hollow of the canes; in the state in which it is brought to Europe."[59] This notion of the "sufficiently common," as both speech and tautological sweetener, merits further reflection, especially for the ways in which it holds a transformative, historically determining substance such as sugar in a relation to subsistence, or what Moseley imagines as the getting of something for free.

The history that Moseley gives us is one in which a varied surplus of saccharine principles is made superfluous and the only way to experience sweetness is through the production of sugar as a commodity. He banishes almost all mention of labor to a single footnote in his *Treatise*. After describing the catastrophic cultural and physiological decline in Europe that would result from the end of sugar production, he notes that if Jamaica "were to share the fate of St. *Domingue* . . . a distress would arise, not confined to the present generation, but that would descend to the child unborn.—Of such importance has the agriculture of half a million of Africans, become to Europeans."[60] Here his footnote reads: "The negroes employed in the West Indies, in cultivating the cane, and manufacturing sugar, do not much exceed this number. Altogether there are, in the English colonies about 461,684."[61] Notably, Moseley does not use the word "slavery" but turns enslaved people into laborers and the employed, perhaps attempting to alleviate anxieties over the imminence of a revolution like the one that had taken place in Haiti. Nonetheless, Moseley's history constitutes a defense of slavery as a mode of production, of unfree, brutalized, and deathly labor. As such, of course, it does not fit seamlessly with the capitalist superstition of a world of equivalences at the level of labor but openly seems to defend equivalence only in the sphere of commodities. Sugar will be exported to Europe and, as he notes, consumed for the benefit and health of European workers.

While Moseley makes a slight attempt to mythify slave labor as employment—through a relation of exchange—what is truly significant is the way in which his history is one of universal equivalence, a point that John Stuart Mill would later make in his speculations on the place of plantation colonies within the British empire. Mill argues that the key function of the colonies was not just the expansion of trade but the extension of the money form and a population whose consumption was dependent upon it. In this sense, the colonies were not external but "more resemble[e] the traffic between town and country." What Mill means is that the "tropical commodities" of the West Indies are "not to be exchanged for things exported to the colony and consumed by its inhabitants, but to be sold in England for the benefit of proprietors there."[62] Not a matter of trade in heterogeneous things, the plantation economy ensured the expanding space of debt and dependency on money that changed capitalism in the model of the British Empire. The plantation economy and its brutal reliance on slave labor had far less to do, ultimately, with the profits of any particular planter and far more to do with the British model of capitalism in which production and exchange were internalized through a territorial expansion by which money—not just goods—would circulate. This economic account tells us of the significance of slavery to an economic system that is posited as the progression of universal, free labor in order to achieve the free movement of money.

What such accounts disavow, however, are the other forms of the "sufficiently common" that were remade from within this wretched compression.

That is, the sustaining of an economy that Mill understands as an entirely internal matter is not without its own dependencies upon subsistence, and not only those that were orientalized or relegated to the past. Indeed, Moseley's mythification of subsistence as past superstition was produced under the duress of a plantation system that continued to rely on slaves' subsistence forms of life, which were also associated with the threat of their becoming autonomous. Although still thirty years away from England's termination of the Atlantic slave trade, the early nineteenth century was a time of crisis for the sugar colonies, given the liberation struggles in Haiti, the persistent problem of runaways and rebellions, and the fragile structures of indebtedness that sustained the purchase of slaves.[63] A modernity defined strictly by the internalization of universality, whether of money or paid labor, was never possible here, as subsistence practices remained crucial to the survival of slaves as well as necessary, with the end of slave labor, to a capitalist system. Rather than a successful imposition of binaries posited through the split of nature and history or the successful subsumption of all life and labor by the money form, Moseley was surrounded by present-day examples of subsistence that were simultaneously threatening and necessary to the supposedly internalized plantation economy.

The subsistence practices most visible to Moseley would have been those of slaves and maroons in the West Indies, practices that were necessary to the maintenance of a fragile economy but also constituted a constant threat to it. It was not the (fictionalized) subsistence practices of Arabs that were most visible to Moseley; instead, it was the contemporary practices of slaves in the West Indies, practices that were constant reminders of the limits to their complete subjugation and even, perhaps, of the ways in which maroons survived outside the plantation.[64] In other words, Moseley's historicization of orientalized ignorance disavows the presence of other economies, ones that are not reducible to the contradictions internal to the money form but needed for the plantation economy to work and that surrounded Moseley in Jamaica. Although he relegates things obtained outside the money form to an Arabic past, his actual reference points of remediation are the provision grounds, the markets organized by enslaved peoples to exchange their goods, and the slave habitats outside plantations that he would later associate with Obeah. That is, Moseley's depiction of the coincidence of premodern oriental superstitions about sugar combines a hermeneutic of capitalism and colonialism with a sufficient commons, necessarily remade.

Numerous things of this sort crop up if we move our gaze from the dichotomies of the free and the unfree, the dispossessed and the enslaved, through which we tend to read a binarizing history of enclosure and slave labor. Clearly it is not only slave apologists (and owners) such as Moseley or liberal mediators such as Wordsworth who make use of creation recursions that defy linear narratives. After all, as Diana Paton has so powerfully shown, one of the major achievements of freed peoples in Jamaica was to "resist proletarianization" and make the "large-scale capture" of labor as waged impossible there. Instead, freed people were able to "construct a peasant way of life" and ultimately evade the consolidation of a wage-labor economy that planters immediately tried to impose through a combination of carceral measures that were no different than the brutality of slavery and legislative measures that incorporated the language of free labor.[65] Even prior to emancipation we can find examples of this thingly subsistence. In Robert Wedderburn's description of his grandmother, threads of hearsay, witchcraft, and subsistence through a market coincide. Talkee Amy was this practitioner's name, "signifying a chattering old woman." Amidst the surplus of gossip Amy must have circulated, she was also a part-time sales agent for "all sorts of goods, hard or soft, smuggled or not" that came into Kingston, and even "trafficked in her own account with the goods of other merchants, having... half-a-crown the pound for her trouble." Accused of witchcraft by "a malicious woman-slave," the last we hear of Amy is of the brutal beating she received from a master who was "a believer in the doctrine of witchcraft."[66] Combining trade for goods and money and that sufficiently common speech for which Wordsworth faults his narrator, Wedderburn's depiction of Amy syncretizes the persistence of subsistence with the creation of a side market for female slaves. Wedderburn's recollection of this woman who took care of him after his mother is one clear image we have of what Paton describes as the deliberate cultivation of surplus products to sell at markets, where enslaved people also developed "a strong awareness not only of events in other parts of the island but also of political developments across the Atlantic" and did the work of sustaining themselves and their families.[67]

Moseley cannot help but weave these various pasts and presents together, knotting them into a thorny thing in which the sufficiently common remains everywhere but is plotted as a remainder of an uncivilized past, on the one hand, and as an active threat of subsistence that is required for the fragile plantation economy to remain, on the other. The ways in which these sufficiently common things continue to show up in Romantic texts are significant, both in terms of reading Moseley's justification of slavery and because of the ways in which those things are situated as *more* than unpaid labor at the center of a capitalist present. The sufficiently common points to the superfluous ways of meeting needs that remain central, if ambivalently so, to our modern ways of living.

Not through its poetics of balanced feeling but of a wretched thing, "The Thorn" archives the ongoing accumulations of both capital and a sufficient commons. As Saree Makdisi has argued, the *Lyrical Ballads* were not novel in their content nor were they meant to represent the transhistorical common man to himself. Rather, they were an entirely contemporary project that aimed to reform any existing and radical relations between those in the middle class and the poor. But Wordsworth cannot do this work without defaulting to the superstitious chatter he means to deride, so he indulges it while attempting, in both the poem and the prefatory note, to remediate it as the language of feeling. From the narration by the Captain to the glimpses of village gossip, most of what we know of Martha Ray is circulated through hearsay, by a repetition of sayings that are the same in their superstition promptings.[68] In so doing, it is not only the thorn and heap that appear "as like as like can be," it is also the language of the poem and the language that Wordsworth wants to discipline. In contrast to any straightforward narrative of enlightenment, the necessity of repeating superstitions that hold on to some semblance of subsistence marks the contemporaneity of recursion. The product of modern processes, tautological ways of living and speaking became "as like as like can be" to modernity.

And indeed, the production of superstition of the kind Wordsworth describes was a remarkably knotty affair, part of a history that is knottier than any "going back" in order to step forward. The gossip of the kind presented in "The Thorn" was not only the outcome of a sustained campaign against those genderable as women; it was also a creation of the primitive through contemporary mechanisms. Here in this dialectic of enlightenment, the tautology of superstition becomes a central component of progressive history. Associated by Wordsworth with a debility in one's imagination and a propensity to repeat meaningless things, tautology is also implicated in a repetition that "seems the same" but is not. That is, while an enlightenment narrative of history separates itself from the superstitions of witchcraft, the necessity of witch hunts for the production of reason establishes a strange continuity through difference. This recursive process of so-called primitive accumulation revises our understanding of history not as one of rupture or continuity, discontinuity or progress, but as those uncanny entwinements that form the landscape on which the thorn survives. The precarious proximity of tautological repetition and meaningful repetition creates other kinds of associations as well, in which there is more likeness between the witch hunts and the incredulity of rural superstition than we might suspect. What is important in this connection is that it shows sympathy toward reinforcing a historical narrative of development, while tautological sayings constellate a new mode of resistance to the accumulation of capital, which cannot itself be separated from a melancholy history. What Wordsworth depicts instead is the conversion of a successful campaign of terror into a new set of obstacles for enlisting the poor in the self-regulating habits of the present.

Even the context of post–witch hunt Europe, which for Federici is a context in which "social discipline was restored," demands a different reading of the persistent obstinacies of superstition.[69] Superstition also became a thorn in the side of progress, as we see throughout Moseley and Wordsworth. An overgrowth that could not be anticipated, the tautologies of superstition and chatter hold together a mode of life through which noncapitalist habits are remade. Heaped together through the transformation of hearsay from a social abundance to a weapon of enforced scarcity, the gendered and racialized violence required for capital to accumulate does not occur without contemporaneous practices that function as a resistance to regulation. Such a thorny mode of accumulation is as like the disorderly gathering of tautology as can be. Within this likeness there is an abundance of contingency and constellated histories; there is a history of internecine class divisions and the remaking of the commons in the form of gendered and enslaved labor. As with the thorn, both thing and poem, these histories are entangled, yielding new modes of subsistence together with wretched things. A heap of recursions that are themselves re-creations, the strangeness of likening relations in "The Thorn" tells us something about the entirely nonprimitive nature of primitive accumulation and the ways in which noncapitalist habits come to live alongside capitalist modes of reproduction. "As like as like can be," the processes of accumulation by dispossession, as many others have noted, are repetitions that are never the same; they give capitalism its disavowed center of persistent subsistence and knots of survival otherwise.

This review of the sufficiently common draws out its status as a wretched thing in a historical materialist sense of a history folded in on itself and entangled with both the destruction and the remaking of subsistence. Here we have gnarled and woven repetitions that solidify like stone and provide the ground for other masses to grow, fostering a taut and tender ecology of moss and rock. This thing works its way into our first impressions of the poem, routing repetitions not in gossip but in heaps of words. If we set aside the narrative from superstition to the self, the thorn plots sayings as repetitions that are not straightforward. Instead, like a heap, the sounds of these first few lines grow over and under each other melancholically, bearing a sense of the past that is by no means over and done. This mode of repetition and its workings in an otherwise transitional history offer up a gathering that is ongoing and unfinished in its subsumption of the ways of subsistence. As a thing, the thorn gives us a history in which superstition and progress, subsistence and capital accumulation, become "as like as like can be." That is, there is no separating one from the other, but in this likeness there is a historical and material relation to be found that directs us to syncretic practices of subsistence that are ongoing. It is through this thorn that we can situate Romanticism alongside the things of salt and sugar produced by those dispossessed of personhood without falling back into the overly historical models that separate the residual from the present-day. It reminds us, then, of the need to continue to gather noncapitalist ways of living as they were remade by those undefined by universal equivalence without constituting some kind of pure outside to capitalism. The thorn as a thing that is sufficiently common represents one node of a reminder that these figurative means of subsistence that do not go into measurable or equivalent relations are not for that reason outside a wretched history.

A History of Affectable Things

In 1817, Samuel Taylor Coleridge published "The Three Graves," an unintentionally collaborative poem that was begun by Wordsworth in 1797 and later completed by Coleridge. The poem tells the story of "a widow-woman bordering on her fortieth year" who declares her love to her daughter Mary's fiancé, is humiliated by his rejection, and throughout the poem is implicated in the casting of a spell that leads to the misery—and madness—not only of her daughter and daughter's husband but also of their close friend Ellen. Having completed the poem, Coleridge added a prefatory note with striking similarities to "The Thorn" and its note, expressing, in particular, a concern with the belief in witchcraft as a psychophysiological error, as well as with the poet's own necessary indulgence in the language of superstition. Superstition is similarly presented as a present-day problem of sensation: "The outlines of this Tale are positive Facts, and of no very distant date."[70] In this time of "not very long ago" an uncanny likeness and difference structure maternal, familial, and erotic relations, as mothers pine for daughter's lovers and Mary, Ellen, and Edward live in something like a platonic three-way marriage. The prefatory note to this poem does not address tautology by name, but as we will see, it is composed through that same language of affecting likeness. However, in contrast to Wordsworth's focus on "some village or country town" in England, Coleridge expands superstition to a transatlantic scale that contaminates the rural English, slaves, and Indigenous peoples of America:

> I was led to chuse this story . . . from finding in it a striking proof of the possible effect on the imagination, from an Idea violently and suddenly im-

prest on it. I had been reading Bryan Edwards' account of the effect of the *Oby* Witchcraft on the Negroes in the West-Indies, and Hearne's deeply interesting Anecdotes of similar workings on the imagination of the Copper Indians . . . and I conceived the design of shewing that instances of this kind are not peculiar to savage or barbarous tribes, and of illustrating the mode in which the mind is affected in these cases, and the progress and symptoms of the morbid action on the fancy from the beginning.[71]

In this note, Coleridge converses not only with Wordsworth and Bryan Edwards but also with Edmund Burke's and Immanuel Kant's discourse on common sense. Extending Burke's notion of common sense as a "conformation of . . . organs," Coleridge turns the moral philosopher's discourse of sensibility toward a universal susceptibility to superstition. In contrast to the common sense of sensibility, which hinged on balanced and regulated bodies, Coleridge creates another common sense of morbid fancy that crosses contemporary constructs of race.[72] This common sense disregards the particularizing effects of climate and environment, instead establishing a coexistence of impressionable minds. According to Kant, in his own critique of superstition published in 1766, the supernatural is invalid as a sphere of knowledge because it is uniquely unshareable, remaining in the realm of private experience rather than seeking corroboration by the judgment of others.[73] Coleridge's prefatory note blends Kant and Burke, taking Burke's position on the universality of sensation while also implying that it can indeed be shared beyond the confines of individuated experience.

However, instead of the well-known line "as like as like can be" that was used by Wordsworth to compare a "heap of earth" to an "infant's grave," the Old Sexton narrator of "The Three Graves" declares, "All seem'd the same: all seemed so, Sir! But all was not the same!" This declaration confirms that, despite appearances of likeness between the past and the present, something was fundamentally altered when Mary's mother uttered a curse upon her dear friend Ellen. In "The Three-Graves," this change is marked by Ellen's realization that what ought to have been a superstitious nothing has indeed had effects. Thus, the supposed sameness of Ellen's own past and present has been disordered through the actual continuity between the past and present that the Witchcraft Act was supposed to have terminated. For all its declarative difference of not-sameness, however, this line is not the opposite of Wordsworth's "as like as like can be." When the two are read together, in fact, it becomes hard to parse the difference, as surface-level differences give way to the unsettling possibility that what looks like a repetition of the same is a far more figurative matter—that it is a matter of tautology. Connecting different poets and poems, these lines space out the mere difference between likeness and sameness, elevating the comparative "as" into the nonequivalence of "like." Furthermore, Coleridge's minor modification of likeness into "not the same" intensifies the sense of semblance written into sameness, as that phenomenal appearance that conveys the real and is particularly prone to apparition, vision, or the more mundane discrepancy between what a thing seems to be and what it is. Rather than an oppositional relation, these lines speak across poems to one another, suggesting a tenuous affinity between external thingliness and being, between sensuous appearance and material relations. This off-repetition figures a gathering of what we see above as relations of subsistence, holding together temporalities other than that of future progress: that of associations such as the "fast-linked," of knotted directions, of constellated overgrowth scattered throughout the poem.[74]

This entanglement of likeness as not-sameness through the phenomenality of semblance prompts the most acute sense of horror in "The Three Graves." Alerting us to the unreliability of apparent sameness, "The Three Graves" provokes a feeling of terror when the recognition of a friend's face turns into a likeness of the mother and as Ellen attempts to hold Mary:

> And once when Mary was down-cast,
>   She took her by the hand.
> And gaz'd upon her, and at first
>   She gently press'd her hand;
>
> Then harder, till her grasp at length
>   Did gripe like a convulsion!
> Alas! said she, we ne'er can be
>   Made happy by compulsion!

> And once her both arms suddenly
> Round Mary's neck she flung,
> And her heart panted, and she felt
> The words upon her tongue
>
> She felt them coming, but no power
> Had she the words to smother;
> And with a kind of shriek she cried,
> Oh Christ! you're like your Mother!"[75]

In this moment of the poem, Ellen falls under the sway of a supernatural power in which she'd previously expressed a glib disbelief and sees in Mary's face the physiognomy of Mary's mother, who has cursed Ellen. Upon looking into Mary's face, Ellen, "with a kind of shriek," cried, "'Oh Christ! you're like your Mother!'"[76] In this moment, we watch an instantaneous recognition of a transient likeness as Ellen recognizes the witch-mother in her friend Mary. This recognition of inheritance remade as the passage of superstition through motherhood horrifies Ellen. It causes her to see not a pure repetition but a physiognomic tautology in which all is not the same but is as like as like could be. The likeness crystallized in Mary's face finally shows Ellen that what she had chalked up to superstitious chatter has indeed had real effects. The horror of this moment does not derive simply from the likeness of friend and mother but also from the transience by which the past enters the present and the ways in which superstition takes on a new face. Reproduction, impressed in the figure of the mother, entwines this past and present inescapably, as new relations, separations, and ways of meeting needs carry a historical violence into the creation of the next day, the next meal, the next gossip session. The power once imputed to those women charged as witches may be gone, but the enclosure and differentiation of the necessary and the unnecessary, the surplus and the superfluous, as it passed through gender lines is as present as ever. The entanglement of likeness and unsameness in the reappearance of Mary's mother offers an image of the forms of so-called primitive accumulation we have been tracking, as the destruction and remaking of reproduction, labor, and gender through the European witch hunts and then through the historical reconstruction of the Witchcraft Act. So-called primitive accumulation, as we've seen, fosters a repetition that is never the same, inasmuch as capitalism repeatedly originates through the destruction and remaking of noncapitalist social relations and means of subsistence. Coupled together, Coleridge's and Wordsworth's lines, and their own reproduction of tales in the present that cannot stop making recourse to the past as violence, introduce a syncretism of subsistence that is rooted in the manifold knots of bodies, things, and their shared sensations.

This horrific syncretism of subsistence modes of social reproduction remade is the "idea violently and suddenly impressed on" Ellen in this moment that is "of no very distant date."[77] But as Coleridge's prefatory note indicates, the persisting threat of other arrangements of history through contiguity rather than causality, through transience rather than ruptures, is not restricted to the English countryside: it encompasses the global space of the so-called Caribbean, America, and Africa. Such a history is also the "soil of capital accumulation" in the Caribbean, the ground of racialized reproduction constituted through the matrilineal lines of "free" and unfree labor. Hilary Beckles uses this language of the soil to refer to the becoming-woman of whiteness, which is also the becoming-white of motherhood on the Caribbean plantation that began roughly in the mid-seventeenth century and continued on throughout the eighteenth and nineteenth centuries. As Beckles describes it, the remaking of maternality through race made colonial white women in the West Indies "not the same as" enslaved women. In the sixteenth and seventeenth centuries,

> manual labor, slave trading, and domesticity were not considered locked in a contradictory orbit during the formative stages of gender representation. In fact, these practices were *held together* in determining the elements that constituted the images of the colonial white woman.... These [images] are to be found in the early narratives, histories, travel accounts, and biographies. In them, laboring white women are described variously as 'loose wenches,' 'whores,' 'sluts' and 'white nig . . . ,' and designated as suited mainly to field labor.[78]

One only has to turn to Daniel Defoe's *Moll Flanders* to see a cleaned-up version of what Beckles describes. Early in the settling of colonies, the rampant demands for cheap labor to expropriate and accumulate wealth meant that the separation between production of commodities and reproduction of the social was not yet mapped essentially through racial difference. The pre-Romantic image Beckles gives is one in which ungendered bodies shared a space of degraded labor but also one in which the wretched enclosure of reproduction as unproductive labor was not yet divided between the unpaid labor of a slave mode of production and that of the domestic "free" labor of white women. After the creation of laws that differentiated free from unfree children on the basis of the mother's status, what had been the largely deracinated population of enslaved and indentured female workers in the colonies was slowly transformed into white mothers and Black slave labor. The otherwise indistinct laboring capacities of women here began to undergo a separation, between the ungendered labor performed by enslaved women and the gendered, deracinated nonlabor of white and creole women who (re)produced "free" labor. Through these conversions of "elements" once "held together" rather than in opposition, the unpaid labor performed by previously indistinct bodies was converted into a hierarchy of gendered domesticity and what Hortense Spillers famously designated as a process of ungendering that had already begun in the Middle Passage.[79] What had been held together in the loose space of likeness was codified—legally and then socially—through the difference between the free and the unfree products of reproduction.

This processual impressing of racialized difference also does work on the base nature of need, desynonymizing the foundational and the degraded that are associated in that term and separating whiteness out from the epithets of violent use that Beckles finds in sixteenth-century references to European women. What is most essential to the biopolitical reproduction of population on the plantation economy is split off from the essential and debased labor of the necropolitical reproduction of slave labor for the plantation. Such labors are not fully comprehensible either through the units of commodities or through those of labor power. We require the language of subsistence and its rhetorical relating of the necessary and the superfluous, or the rooting of the essential and the sexualized, the reproductive and the ungendered. Such language takes the necessary subsistence labor of reproduction, so dire within the plantation context of constant death, and pulls it underground, where a visceral abjection of what is needed but not differentiated, of what is useful but not equivalent, crops up, showing sugarcane to be soiled by the sufficiently common. This language is important because it tracks the transportation of the violence of the witch hunts and the hunt for slaves into the social reproduction of the plantation system, which is far more than the biological reproduction of species. It is, rather, the "soil of capital accumulation" that maintains the meeting of needs outside relations of equivalence through the abjection of need itself. This excess of social reproduction—not just unpaid labor but the historical process of ungendering desire, of violently sexualized use value, of the global reproduction of that wretched thing of the plantation—is rewoven, compressed, and objectified in the body of the ungendered slave. In other words, what happens here is not a simple split, say, between one form of unpaid labor and another but an intensification of the abjection of base needs in the body of enslaved women, women who by the eighteenth century were often imputed to be in "possession of satanic powers that lured white men away from association with their virtuous white females."[80] What Beckles tracks in the racialization of labor is no straightforward separation, but rather a recomposition of the means of subsistence that can never be separated from the social if production is to take place. While the racialization of gender points us toward further enclosures that render differences as racial taxonomies, the persistent reliance of the plantation economy on remediated modes of subsistence fills that uncanny space of what passes from past to present with a new face. The semblance of witchcraft reproduced in Wordsworth's and Coleridge's poems gives us a way to read that process of accumulation through social reproduction as a global one in which "we cannot unravel one female's narrative from the others, cannot decipher one without tripping over the other."[81] It is this accumulation through a social reproduction caught up in more than the commodity form that is captured, I argue, in Ellen's horrified response to Mary. That moment of misrecognition in which difference is marked but uncertain, both outside and inside, offers a sense of the uncanny semblance of subsistence that is like but not the same as that of exchange relations.

I do not want to suggest that Coleridge's poetic instance is analogous to the social process that Beckles describes. More useful than analogy here is the more tautological illogic of what Alexander G. Weheliye has described as "the refusal to compare" in favor of a "'process of bringing-into-relation' [that] eschew[s] the traces of calculability."[82] That is, the image of horrific reproduction captured in "The Three Graves" offers us an instance in which to see a passage that is not a rupture and in which the superfluity of the social is redistributed. Instead of a calculable resemblance passed down from mother to daughter, what is transferred in Coleridge's poem is that likeness of an affectable commons, gathering present-day associations in women in whom unmeasurable and heterogeneous needs and unpaid labor have been enclosed through significantly different social relations. More than the straightforward hierarchization of a previously existing and abject bricolage, these horrific reorganizations of subsistence relations figure an intensified abjection of the excess of needs and ways of meeting them that could never be satisfied by capital but of which it certainly makes vampiric use.

Moseley's treatise writes this recomposition of a global commons through a momentarily masculinized but quickly ungendered European working class and Caribbean enslaved population, which maintains the horror of base bodies and needs across these geographies. In contrast to those metropolitan workers nourished by sugar, Moseley depicts the rural European working poor as particularly visible examples of the way in which "the formation of the body, and more of the inclination of the mind . . . depends on the nature and quality of our food." He continues: "This is indeed so strongly distinguished among the lower classes, in some countries, that one would almost conclude, a man is but a walking vegetable—or an hieroglyphic—importing the food of which he is a compound."[83] Those bodies untouched by the blinding enlightenment of the "art" of sugar-white substance remain metonymic compositions, a farrago of plant and image-language that appears much like an Obi object. Strangely, the "lower classes" are not only compounds of the most common of living matter, the vegetable, they are also signs of the most archaic kind, the hieroglyph.[84] The horror of the poor's susceptibility is only intensified in Moseley's treatise as he tries to account for the phenomenon of Obeah in Jamaica, in a discourse that is simultaneously scientific and hysterical. Much like Ellen's horror at the reappearance of the supernatural in her friend's face, Moseley is at a fever pitch of fantasy when he explains how Obeah makes its way from Africa through the susceptibility of slave bodies at the periphery of the plantation:

> When a negro was attacked with [yaws], [it was then custom] to separate him from the rest, and send him to some lonely place by the sea side, to bathe; or into the mountains to some Provision Ground, or Plantain Walk . . . until he was well. . . . A cold, damp, smoky hut for his habitation; snakes and lizards his companions; crude, viscid food, and bad water, his only support; and shunned as a leper,—he usually sunk from the land of the living. . . . Some of these abandoned exiles lived, in spite of the common law of nature, and survived a general mutation of their muscles, ligaments, and osteology . . . with their noses, like the beaks of old eagles—starving the creatures, by obstructing the passage to their mouths—and their limbs and bodies twisted and turned, by the force of distemper into shocking grotesque figures, resembling woody excrescences, or stumps of trees; or old Egyptian figures.[85]

This paragraph holds together an astonishing cluster of the knots we have been gathering throughout this chapter. It articulates slave bodies at once with the thorns of enclosure (woody excrescences, or stumps of trees) and with the horrifying transience of history in the hieroglyphics of the European poor (old Egyptian figures). Moseley draws a likeness between England and Jamaica while also reaching back to his mockery of Arabic peoples, abjectified rural, not yet white workers and sick African slaves on the outskirts of commodity consumption. His likening of bodies occurs less through analogy and more through the shared affectability of their unformed bodies, decomposed simultaneously as archaic sign systems and enduringly plastic physiognomies. Gathered together much like the metonymic arrangement of Obi objects, this global commons is not only prehistorical; it coexists with the world of commodified sugar, living threateningly alongside it. While many have played up Moseley's and others' obsession with identifying the origins of Obeah in Africa, thus retrojecting it to a mythic past, it is just as much a material syncretism that seems to horrify Moseley here.

Indeed, it is in the hovels of these yaws-stricken slaves that Moseley thinks Obeah is reproduced. The connective tissue of their habitats on the margins of the plantation is always open to "wayward visitors . . . deeply skilled in magic . . . which they had brought with them from Africa."[86] This production of Obi men is linked to origins in Africa, but through origins that circulate as wandering bodies that force themselves onto the isolated slaves as hosts: "In their banishment, their huts oftentimes became the receptacles of robbers and fugitive negroes; and . . . they had no power to resist any who chose to take shelter in their hovels."[87] Here Obeah is not attributed solely to Africa but to a combination of forces that takes the form of contiguity and susceptibility. Arranged in a proximate relation, associated like the architecture of sense experience, yaws-stricken slaves, fugitive Negroes, and decaying habitats become conduits of the supernatural. It is not pure origins but the (il)logic of magic and its laws of contiguity that hold this scene together, contaminating the present with a power that continues to act from Africa on escaped slaves or maroons. The horror Moseley has for this mode of survival that, as Darwin wrote of sugar, never arrives singly is linked to the transmission, the passage, of ways of living that surround him in the present.

Taking immense descriptive license with his fantasies of degeneration, Moseley's depiction of the process of becoming Obeah creates a pathological abjection of survival on the outskirts of the plantation. Here Moseley taps into what Spillers calls the "Eternity" of ethnicity that "has no movement in the field of signification."[88] But there is also the transmission of a set of associations that does not adhere to the order of historical signification but rather to what Denise Ferreira da Silva has referred to as the science that "addresses human beings and social configurations as phenomena . . . [,] as 'empirical' things."[89] The metonymic relations Moseley offers here—from rural workers to vegetable hieroglyphs to slave body to tree to Egyptian figure to damp habitat to wayward guests—continue to pass along a different ordering of causality through contagion and endorse, however abjectly, those laws of magic in which "objects which have been in contact, but since ceased to be so, continue to act on each other at a distance."[90] Moseley preserves the thingliness of these bodies as a definitive feature of the simultaneous existence in the present, where slaves and the rural poor are the surfaces on which such things are inscribed, inhabiting a global commons populated by living "compounds" susceptible to impression.

Wordsworth's, Coleridge's, and Moseley's global commons of susceptibility holds something other than remnants of a prehistoric past or a repetition of sameness from European spaces to its others. These thingly arrangements and arrangements of things gather together like but not the same ways of living alongside those of equivalence that structure Moseley's world of European progress through the commodity form. Like Darwin's and Hegel's own contamination by the language of magic, Coleridge's, Wordsworth's, and Moseley's configurations of the supernatural are not entirely other to the movements of progress through the balanced feeling of liberal-minded reformers or the sugar production of plantocratic defenders of slavery. They are abjectified accounts of the excess of labors, practices, and relations that must subsist in order for capital to accumulate. More than the internalization of all space by relations of exchange, or the dialectic between Labor and Capital, these representations of the supernatural reveal an industrializing England predicated on the unpaid labor of enslaved men and women as well as "free" women but also on the continual labors, imaginatively material, of their reconstituting of worlds of nonequivalence over and over again. What is rendered as the superstitious here is the continued effects of the supernatural, those sensuous relations that are as "like as like can be" to the accumulations of equivalence but in which "all is not the same." It is the mereness, the semblance of this distinction, that makes it easy to miss amidst the horror of abjection that is attendant upon so-called primitive accumulation and our tendency to separate the production of commodities from ways of meeting our always more than base needs.

It is not enough to write off Moseley's or Coleridge's engagement with witchcraft as pure mystification. They too get caught up in an order of things that is not a repetition of the past but a gathering in like but not the same fashion. As we have seen above, the so-called primitive accumulation of the European witch hunt, the hunting of and trade in African people, and the subsequent histories that arose retroactively to structure them as progressive narratives all seized upon existing social relations and the differences that compose them. But this seizure could never be completed, in part because the reproduction of the working poor and enslaved people alike relied on the maintenance of means of subsistence that are not subsumed within the sphere of money and the commodity form. Those relations imputed to superstitious beliefs were never eclipsed; they reappear in the language of sense experience in scientific and phenomenological accounts of subjects and history. Across these manifold gatherings, the repetition of dispossession yields differentiated syncretisms of subsistence from which capitalism is not immune or entirely other. Rather, its development as a constitutively racialized and gendered system is an effect of this contamination and of capital's dependency on the exploitation and fixing of difference, which is also a separation and fixing of needs as what does and does not pass through the money form.

Cedric Robinson and others have argued that the divisions fostered throughout the eighteenth century led to a failure in unity among workers and slaves.[91] However, we might also take our gleanings from this chapter as a way to shift from the narrative of the failure of the working class to the reproductions of subsistence at different scales and through other modes of association. The knotty remakings of a subsistence we have followed here cannot be reduced to the abjection of mere need or the universality of labor in a straightforward sense. Constellated together, images of motherhood, erotic friendship, taboo desire, disease, ecological enmeshment, nonautonomous entanglement, and the extensive capacity of dependency take embodied form in a differentiated but relational flesh, in radically sensational empirical entities that join the work of survival together with the connective tissue of slave rebellion. Building upon Spillers and Silvia Wynter, Weheliye presents the flesh as counter to bare life and its capture of need through meager measure. Instead of such calculability and a perspective of life rationed out by the state, the flesh signifies through a hieroglyphics in which bodies and need are not forced into the conceptual unity of signification. Such a sensibility does not aspire to the modes of representation available to subjects as the bearers of rights ensured by universal equivalence but draws instead from the deep and mossy mass of those practices of subsistence that are transiently passed down as the abject persistence of unmeasurable needs and their meeting. That is to say, the sense of flesh that Weheliye suggests would be located in spaces of reproduction that are continually targeted for destruction and necessarily revivified in order for there to be any other movement from one day to the next.[92]

This more jointed and mossy way of reading situates tautology as an ambivalently structuring trope of so-called primitive accumulation, as seen in the transmission of witch hunts from England to West Africa to Jamaica in the varieties of superstition we have tracked here. In the similarities between tautology and repetition we find a figure of disorderly history in which repetition occurs through that contingent subsistence of gathering, through those thingly relations "in which the many properties subsist apart from one another" as, to borrow from David Lloyd, "the elemental form of those forms of life, the 'non-capitalist social units,' that, as Rosa Luxemburg grasped, capital and the colonial state *repeatedly* come to destroy."[93] Tautology's supposed sameness in Wordsworth's account helps us follow the ceaseless repetitions of enclosing the commons in such a way that it supports both subsistence and commodity production. It is not just the transmission of witchcraft and witch hunts, whether in England, Africa, or Jamaica, that comes down to us through these texts; it is the remediation of our own means of subsistence as it has been produced through that "way of life losing its life" through capital's violent enforcement of needs as they are recognized only through the form of exchange—that form of repetition that most characterizes capital accumulation. This is a remediation not of the oral into the written but of means of subsistence that flow over into poetry.

CHAPTER 4

Figure, Space, and Race between 1769 and 1985

> Overcoming the concept of "progress" and overcoming the concept of "period of decline" are two sides of the same thing.
> Walter Benjamin, The Arcades Project

IN 1985, THE BLACK AUDIO FILM COLLECTIVE (BAFC) released *Handsworth Songs*, a controversial montage-style documentary that splices images of the 1985 and 1981 riots in Handsworth and Brixton in the United Kingdom with scenes of (de)industrialization, state violence, and the social life of diaspora.[1] *Handsworth Songs* suggests that the riots, and their metonymic relation to Blackness, were a matter of neither a lag in progress or a decline in the economy but of a history constituted by gaps, absences, cuts, and leaps that we tend to associate with an avant-garde stylistics. Outside of *Handsworth Songs* and in mainstream media, the riots were cast through an entirely sociological lens of crime, on both conservative and leftist sides, both of which rushed to make claims about their transparency of meaning. Black bodies were either self-evidently criminal or entirely responsive to economic conditions. But the BAFC was more interested in undoing the historically accumulated ways of seeing, hearing, and feeling Blackness through the montage form, in which race and capitalism are presented by means of an accumulation that resists transparency in favor of an essentially fractured materiality. Refusing both a representational politics that would seek to reveal the "truth" of Black subjectivity and the state's attempts to depict the Windrush generation, Afro-Caribbeans who immigrated between the 1940s and 1970s, and other immigrants as nefarious others, *Handsworth Songs* instead splices the past into a still-colonial present. Arranging images in a way that was misread by many at the time as elitist, the BAFC sought to "articulat[e] spatial and temporal states of belonging and displacement differently," outside a binaristic framework of a positive and negative representational aesthetics.[2] In contrast, they used montage as a technique that they call "straightforward," one in which race is not presented through a logic of exclusion or stereotyping but as central to the production of modern history.[3] This was no merely aesthetic or formal matter but an engagement with a historical material record composed through a method of cutting that makes it "difficult to tell whether a given cut signals a flashback, a flashforward, or simply an ellipsis,"[4] thus calling into question the extent to which montage is a *critical* form of history or, more simply, the form that history takes. We shall see how the montage form deployed in *Handsworth Songs* helps us to begin grappling with the racial as a signifier of what Denise Ferreira da Silva has designated exteriority, spatiality, and affectability.

But if *Handsworth Songs* is an experimental response to the violent experiments of empire, then why do two early Romantic figures of industrialization and scientific progress appear on-screen in the first minute and a half of the film? What are James Watt and Joseph Priestley, two members of a group once labeled "the Industrial Revolution writ small" and "one of the most potent agents of economic progress in its time," doing spliced into a montage meant to undo the conventional order of things?[5]

In order to answer this question and to approach a more generally nondichotomizing arrangement of the British Empire and industrial capitalism, we shall go back to the beginning of the film and then turn to Priestley's own image of universal history. In comparing Priestley's *A New Chart of History* (1769) and the BAFC's *Handsworth Songs* (1985), race can be taken as most fundamental to imagining universal history in the early Romantic

Statues of James Watt and Joseph Priestley in Birmingham, UK. Black Audio Film Collective, *Handsworth Songs* [film], 1986; LUX, 2012, 0:1:30 and 0:1:36.

period, not through classificatory or taxonomizing logics but through the racializing association between figural sensation, spatialized affectability, and subsistence ways of living. Here I do not mean to reject the significance of either the industrializing logics of abstraction and measurement or the racist scientific classifications that were both emergent in the mid- to late eighteenth century so much as to consider how they depend upon a certain spatialization and phenomenalization of material needs and affects in order to determine history as a progressive movement.

The first image to appear onscreen in *Handsworth Songs* is a large factory wheel, looming as large as the scale of industrial progress but sonically surrounded by a heavily synthesized looping of mechanical sounds that turn into a dystopian echo chamber. As the camera gets closer and closer to the wheel, a Black worker becomes more visually distinct from the mechanical apparatus. Not an industrial worker himself, this man seems to be a security guard or watchman, responsible for watching the machine as we watch him through a machine. As we watch him watching it, this man slowly turns forty-five degrees, making most of his face visible to us but casting his eyes upward, skyward, and never looking toward us. In this moment our own gaze becomes uncomfortably exposed while at the same time limited to what we can see through the camera that is trained on machine and man. These first few seconds establish a disjunctive relationship between images that persists throughout. The man's eyes are turned toward an off-screen space; then the scene cuts to a scene of birds in cacophonous choreography. The "splits and unevennesses" of collaged images are held together by the figure recollected by La Mettrie, that of a bird perched on the edge of flight. Their flits and leaps disjoin the smooth, forward motion of the industrial wheel, and their relationship with the man's eyes, looking away, uncannily recalls La Mettrie's not quite mechanical figuration of the imagination, in which mechanistic imagination is like a bird that is "always ready to fly away" if the mind does not "quickly seize and nail [the imagination, the bird] down." Escaping La Mettrie's seizure by the soul, our eyes are moved from this man's to the birds and then to the blue backdrop of the sky, which blurs into a screen saturated with colors from an out-of-focus camera, displacing us back into a documentary image.[6] Mocking any attempt to fix or focus our view, an automated clown encased in glass then appears on-screen with a fixed and mechanical smile, pivoting on the ironic axis of 180 degrees. Next, a black screen specked with white dots turns into the faces of a small crowd of reporters, looking at a scene occluded from our vision. The montage form of the film removes any sense of history as a series of events, instead opting for an arrangement of images that emphasizes metonymic contiguity and sensation struggling to get free of the successive ordering of the mind. It levels the often proscribed eventfulness of the riot through the relations of constrained views, manifold gazes, and an emphasis on the sensational. "Poeticizing every image," as they would later write, the BAFC contaminate history with a constitutive dispossession in which linear and causal order must be abandoned in favor of the discontinuous recursions of dispossession, immigration, and police violence that are held in the "nervous reflexes . . . and sensibilities of those forever 30 years voiceless," which had previously been "encapsulated and imprisoned" in sound bites of BBC and other television interviews.[7]

The relationships between images do not consist in an internal continuity that evades the materiality of form but rather are constructed with an eye toward framing, constraint, and delimitation. Instead of a continuity that makes us forget that we are seeing an arrangement of images, the organizing schema of *Handsworth Songs* operates through a radical distribution of the materiality of images that are both seen and impressed upon our senses, and through the gaps that necessarily enable this nonreciprocal process. Here the relation between images and the entities enclosed within them is configured in spatial terms of contiguity and proximity—of man and machine, of eyes and screen—rather than through the metaphorics of transparency. In the first few seconds of the film, space, sound, and sensation are spliced in such a way that there is already something "felt, viscerally and intellectually. . . . There [is] a gap between official discourses of race and what we [know]."[8] This gap is not brought about by the absence of what was but through the sensational materiality of archival images, through an experience of the past and the present via the historical manifold of phenomena and affect. Here seeing is offered as a curated constellation of spatialized sensations unsynthesized by successive time. This archive is

Stills from *Handsworth Songs*.

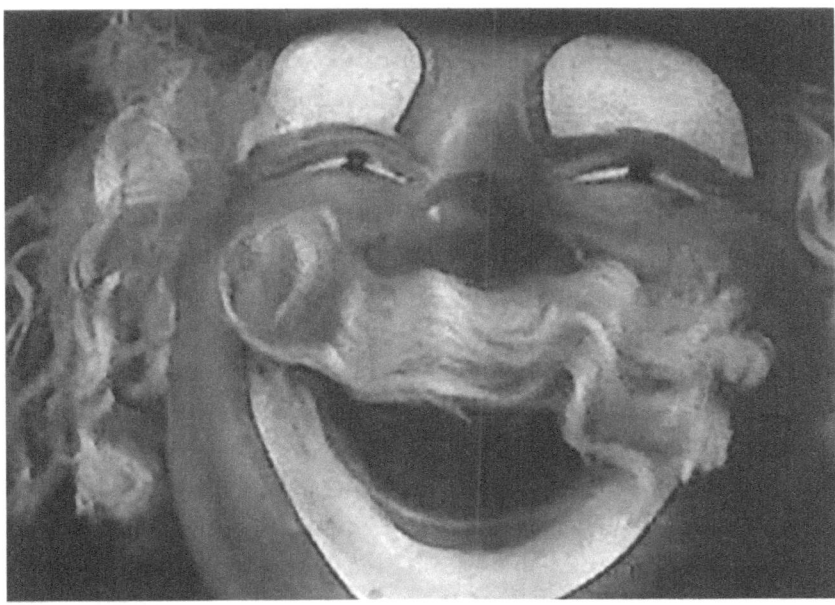

structured through what Ferreira da Silva calls exteriority, or knowledge derived from the senses' phenomenal experience, which in *Handsworth Songs* is presented as a site of historical accumulation.

This arrangement gives us a sense of what the figural history of dispossession might be like—a history more fundamentally bound up with the relations often confined to space rather than time and affect rather than reason. Figure provides a way to hold these reflexes and sensibilities together rather than nailing them down as stories, through its peculiar capacity to make oppositional entities "coincide with, rather than exclude one another" in instances of direct indirection that take the visual form of montage.[9] Rather than making an appeal to set time right, *Handsworth Songs* instead recovers the figural origins of a history dispossessed of either progress or decline, as Walter Benjamin once put it, presenting the relation between past and present through the flash of images.

But why then turn to Priestley and Watt? What is the effect of embedding these two proponents of labor discipline and the techno-fetishism of their day within this series? Certainly there is reason to read this strange inclusion as owing to the BAFC's radical commitment to a nondichotomous approach to history, in which "the Western gaze can never regain its privileged position as the ultimate arbiter of symbolic meaning and representation."[10] What better way to do this than to cast the memorials to Western imperial and capitalist progress within a form that makes it "difficult to tell whether a given cut signals a flashback, a flashforward, or simply an ellipsis"?[11] But there is more than meets the dichotomizing eye in this inclusion. As with any constellation that survives into the present, this arrangement of images remains useful in presenting a history we think we know. This is an order in which the racial—in these sensational and spatialized arrangements—also serves to reconstitute the past. As Kodwo Eshun puts it, scenes from *Handsworth Songs* force a recognition that the technical is "a racialized problem that immediately becomes a spatial question."[12] More than three hundred years after the inauguration of the slave trade and Indigenous genocide on the part of the Spanish Empire, we still need to be reminded by a film from 1985 that the Lunar Society's widely criticized investments in industrializing technology and science were already racialized, which is to say, along with *Handsworth Songs* and the work of critical race theorist Denise Ferreira da Silva, were always a spatial and phenomenal matter. Such a reminder is also needed in our recent context of recuperative readings of Priestley and Darwin, which have tended to elide the relationship between the figural and the racial that is explored here. The BAFC's attempt to "pry open" dichotomies through a figural arrangement presents us with an altogether different spatiotemporal framework for a history, one in which Priestley, Darwin, and Watt, along with "the Industrial Revolution writ small," are displaced and do not stand outside the simultaneity of industrialization and that primitive accumulation of differences being tracked through this book. *Handsworth Songs* invites us to reconfigure our binarized and dichotomized frames of the early Romantic period, leaving us without the comfort of a critique of progress or the absolute alterity of figure.

By following the associative schema in the science of Lunar Society members Joseph Priestley and Erasmus Darwin, Ferreira da Silva's racial analytics of affectability and exteriority, and the BAFC's "straightforward" cuts, it will become clear how the simultaneity of sensation and space play an essential role in Priestley's own visualization of modern, global history in his 1769 *New Chart of History* and how the racial logic of such simultaneity "pries open a negative/positive dichotomy" of race, showing how very Romantic our modern logic of race continues to be.[13] Dispossession provides a spatiotemporal framework rather than constituting a historical or empirical event, which highlights the heterogeneously material constitution of racial capitalism that has been occluded by the framing of the Industrial Revolution through the vocabulary of progress, linearity, and standardization. The subsistence practices discussed by Priestley, and later on by the empirically minded scientist Alexander von Humboldt, become racialized not through the nineteenth century's biological essentialisms but through the necessary simultaneity of subsistence-style living and modernity.

Universal History and Simultaneous Figures

Like Erasmus Darwin, who has been our constant companion, Joseph Priestley was a theorist of industrialization as well as a scientist whose practice contributed directly to it. Involved through personal investments, friendships, and a zeal for the messianic possibilities of perfected knowledge and heightened productivity, Priestley's astonishing number of published texts are impossible to separate from the strange fusion of utopianism, technology, and capitalism particular to the Lunar Society. While James Watt and Michael Boulton, partners in the Boulton & Watt engineering and manufacturing firm, worked on the actual implementation of new mining technologies, free market legislation, and labor disciplining, Darwin and Priestley developed ideas and projects that might never have been as directly applicable but endowed liberal doctrines of progress and improvement with an almost religious fervor. Priestley's writing spans an impressive array of topics, including religion, language, conjectural history, philosophy, science, and abolition. Here we take up his *New Chart of History*, which was meant to accompany his wildly successful *Chart of Biography*, in order to consider previous readings of it through an entirely industrialized frame and to understand the supplementary text as part of that entanglement of the technical, racial, and spatial we began developing above.

Priestley's *New Chart of History* was first published in 1769 and went through as many as twenty editions.[14] As Priestley tells us, it is meant to prevent "error[s] being impressed upon the mind more forcibly by means of sensible images in the brain" caused by maps "crowded with figures and explanations" and "different scales of time." Here Priestley makes clear that our understanding of history hinges upon the proportionality of an impression, which, when once made, takes an immense amount of time and labor to undo if, as he says, it imposes too much upon the imagination. What one is after in the production of images and external stimuli is not representational accuracy but rather a feeling in which human history corresponds with the regulatory laws of nature, which Priestley understands to be happily and habitually leading toward "the extremely favourable . . . progress of knowledge, virtue, and happiness." Earlier charts of history had been unable to produce sufficient affective balance on account of the mass of data they presented, leading to an imbalance between external stimulation and sense-based understanding and thus an unnecessarily disfigured face of history.[15] In Priestley's chart, by contrast, "time here flows uniformly from the beginning to the end of the tablet. It is also represented as flowing laterally, like a river, and not as falling in a perpendicular stream." According to Daniel Rosenberg, Priestley's chronography is part of the first Western attempts to organize time and events using the figure of the line.[16] Approaching the representation of time and the inclusion of text on the chart with an understanding that "we have no distinct idea of length of time, till we have conceived it in the form of some sensible thing that has length, as of a *line*," Priestley emphasizes the linearity of time and uniformity of space over the mass of information that would accrue from histories organized through multiple different chronologies or that dictate historical significance through subjectively determined events.[17] By means of the linearity of time and the uniformity of space Priestley generates the conditions for sensing history as an economic affair of "conveniences that could not have been had without the inconveniences [and] the pleasures and advantages of society that could not have been had without the disadvantages."[18]

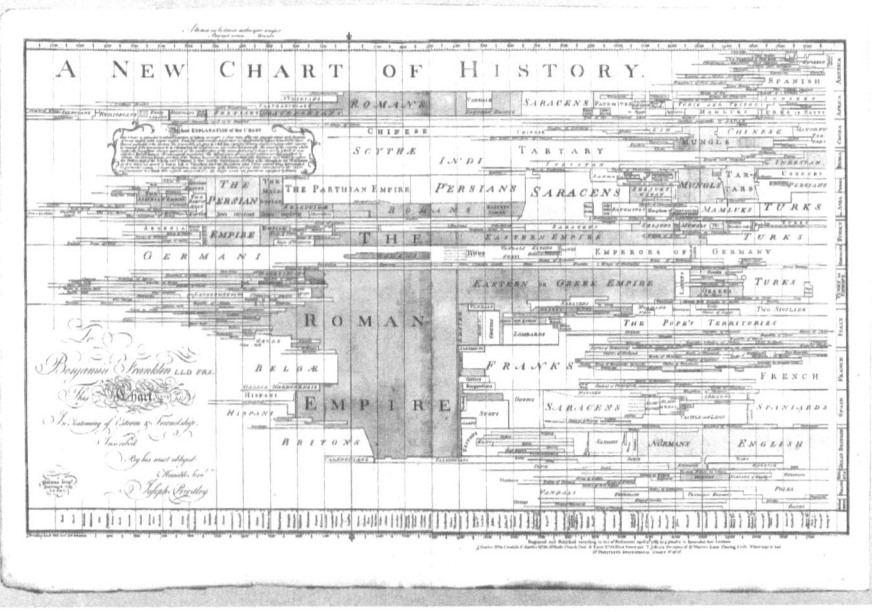

Color version of Joseph Priestley's *A New Chart of History*, 7th ed. (London: Printed for J. Johnson, No. 72, St. Paul's Church Yard, 1789). Reprinted, in black and white, with permission from The Library Company of Philadelphia.

Present-day readers of Priestley's chart such as Jonathan Sachs and Daniel Rosenberg have emphasized the innovations of its abstraction of time and uniformity of space. Sachs situates the chart in the context of "a widespread sense of time speeding up that made it more difficult for those living in the eighteenth century to imagine the future."[19] Here Priestley's universal chart is mirrored by a universal viewer, "those living in the eighteenth century," for whom the future had been made uncertain by a proliferation of print media, the effects of the French Revolution, and a developing free market economy. The abstraction of the chart offered a stable depiction of the future for what Priestley and his present-day readers treat as its universally overwhelmed eighteenth-century subjects and for their new sense of nonteleological progress. This technical intervention, operating with greater temporal regularity than previous charts of its kind, was a precursor to later technical innovations of biopolitical capitalism such as statistics, aggregation, and "the standardization and repetition of events and episodes."[20] Similarly, according to Rosenberg, Priestley's primary contribution was his shifting "the emphasis of chronography away from representation of events and towards the representation of historical time as such."[21] This allowed for both a production of the "uniformity of historical time" and for "time-saving devices" that aided in the acquisition of the "rapid expansion in the field of knowledge."[22] Priestley's manipulation of space rendered it less concrete and immediate and more generalized, forgoing incommensurable experiences of time in favor of a uniform abstraction of space and linear abstraction of time. From this perspective, his chart appears to be exemplary of a universalizing spatiotemporality in which everything that was solid melts into air, subsumed by the capitalist relations of abstraction, surplus value, and modern subjects calmed by an experience of history as the commodity form.

But in focusing solely on the "innovation" of abstraction and uniformity, such readings of the chart take for granted that history has been determined by a capitalist modernity that turns everything into homogeneous, selfsame relations. As Sachs notes, Priestley's chart essentially cartographizes Adam Smith's fantasy in *The Wealth of Nations* of universal progress that implies impending doom for any particular nation. For Sachs, the apparent decline seen and felt in the immediate can "be recognized as part of a quantified pattern ... in order to observe changes over longer and more significant spans of time," in a visualization that registers progress at a different scale.²³ All that was certain in this fantasy was that the division of labor would lead to heightened productivity and the world of commodities that would launch Marx's *Capital*. Moving to a "longer timescale of 'a little more than a century,'" progress comes to exceed any particular nation, empire, or fixed site.²⁴ Such representations of transience, emergence, and decline made "abstract time something that can be imagined and visualized concretely as a continuous linear progression."²⁵ When nonteleological time is spaced out through uniformly divided plots, the anxieties of eighteenth-century viewers can be felt as universal progress, transforming temporal uncertainty into smooth space.

While the chart indeed aims to produce such an abstract representation of history, we fall into the trap of reproducing the self-declared claims of capitalist modernity as a purely abstracting and homogenizing system if we read only these aspects of Priestley's image. Considered alongside Eshun's remark that *Handsworth Songs* shows the technical to be racial and the racial to be spatial, Priestley's chart and its technical innovations also need to be read through their entanglement with the features of affectability and exteriority that show up in the accompanying text. These features carry another account of history with them, an account of originary violence that is accumulated in the discourse of the senses. While these features appear distinctly unmodern from the perspective of capitalist abstraction, they may help us to revise our own cartographies of a deracinated modernity and avoid the reinscription of what Walter Benjamin terms the "narcotic historicism" induced by mechanism.²⁶ Ultimately, we shall see that such assessments of modern, capitalist ideology only reproduce what Ferreira da Silva has called the post-Enlightenment transparency thesis, which "presuppose[s] that the racial is extraneous to modern thought" rather than constitutive of its technical, aesthetic, and time-saving innovations.²⁷

We must also consider Priestley's accompanying text, "Description of a New Chart of History," in order to see that the chart is not only a straightforward abstraction of history but also an image that depends upon the sensational dimensions of knowledge to produce a feeling of history. The figure of the line produces our sense of history through its sensible form, impressing upon viewers the movement of progress over the accumulation of data that is present on the vertical axis of the chart. Along with the line, Priestley tells us that he "[makes] use of the same scale through the whole. By this means, the imagination will never be imposed upon by the eye."[28] At first glance, the "Description" shows that Priestley's project of abstraction cannot be separated from the more general physiological aim of many Romantic-era scientists and poets to produce what Tim Fulford describes as a desirable "state of normal excitement produced by all the stimuli that affect the body," thus "restor[ing] over- and under-excited beings to a healthy level of excitement."[29] Priestley's concern with the risk that the viewer's imagination will be overtaken erroneously by an excess of "figures and explanations" thus aims not only to abstract but to create a regulated level of excitement in the viewing of history. Following David Hartley's associationist principles, Priestley is particularly attentive to the effects of stimulation upon how we perceive the correspondence between nature and second nature, between natural history and human history. While this analogy between the body and knowledge certainly has a proto-biopolitical bent that can be heard in Sachs's projection of the chart into a future of statistics—"the standardization and repetition of events and episodes"—I am more interested in the onto-epistemological role that the "excitement [and] stimuli that affect the body" play in the production of a history that is uniform and time-saving.[30]

On the one hand, Priestley's chart is designed with an eye toward the sense of regulation that is made upon the eye by the perception of phenomena. The effect of regulation depends upon a curated equilibrium that Priestley strives to produce through the uniformity and linearity that we've already discussed. At the same time, he also assumes the task of making all of history available "at one view." As Rosenberg states, it was this feature of the chart that distinguished it from "other sorts of chronological reference material."[31] Along with the desire to generate a sense of stability in a context of accelerated history, the novelty of Priestley's chart also lay in his ability to "keep the chart to a single, synoptic image and *at the same time* to maintain a uniform representation of time."³² The aim of the chart as described by Rosenberg is not a homogenizing one but a coinciding, simultaneizing one. Priestley wants bodies to be more regulated and faster, tasks that cannot be collapsed into each other but must be produced "at the same time." These demands for simultaneous but different states of being produce a far more complex sense of what is involved in the production of modern history: the production of a "single, synoptic image" of history retains a crucial difference from "a uniform representation of time," and it is in that difference that something in excess of abstraction appears.

The immediate and comprehensive impression of universal history to which the chart aspires is, of course, part of its labor-saving project. If all of history could be seen "in one view," then a more perfect knowledge of this kind of history might be gained by an hour's inspection of the chart than by reading for several weeks. As Priestley writes, "All the revolutions that have taken place in any particular country" can be learned "in much less time, than it could have been done by reading." In designing a pedagogical technique analogous to the discipline of capitalist labor, Priestley's stated aims accord with capital's own ideology of a self-valorizing system that transforms all labor into a form from which surplus value can be extracted. But this speeding up of the labor of learning history is not free from the requirement to produce different states of being at the same time. The reduction of labor time is not identical to the experience of history in a single image. Where the former implies a production of sameness, the latter implies a rhetorical relation, the coincidence of difference at the same time. Where others have imputed an identical version of modernity to these multiple tasks, I see instead an association of heterogeneous temporalities and affects that must be held together in the figural relations we have taken note of in previous chapters. And it is to figural, rather than standardizing, means that Priestley turns to accomplish the production of modern history.

Here Priestley must make use of the figural capacities we saw in Chapter 3, in Darwin's description of the empirical experience of sugar.³³ The term for this simultaneous series of impressions, as Darwin states in *Zoonomia*, is "figure": "Hence, when we acquire the idea of solidity, we acquire at the same time the idea of FIGURE; and this idea of figure, or motion of a part of the organ of touch, exactly resembles in *its figure* the figure of the body that occasions it."[34] What Darwin means here is that we have no concept of a thing (solidity) without first having been touched by something solid, which leaves a resemblance, something like a negative impression, of *its* body on *our* body. Like the idea of history as a line, "figure" denotes the simultaneous relation of an idea and a sensible thing without reducing them to the same thing. Simultaneous sensations are exterior associations, such as when "*a part* of the organ of touch" (e.g., the eye) is associated with "the body that occasions it" (e.g., the image of the chart).[35] They gesture toward the reliance of knowledge and reason upon "extended things."[36] In this sense, figure for Darwin is very much the figure of Greek etymology, that form or shape which makes it innately a bodily matter. In other words, ideas about the external world are conveyed only through the simultaneous association of a quality (solidity) with the shape or figure that generates a sensation of it. Figural association holds together the differences of bodies as they impress each other at the same time at the repeated origin point of accumulating knowledge. The figural origins of knowledge are necessary to Priestley's production of a history that can be viewed in an instant; the spatialized, phenomenal thing of figure facilitates such a history, involving the chart in an experience irreducible to uniformity.

The phenomenal and affectable dimensions of knowledge themselves get distributed spatially, even once the successive habits of thought are achieved. Thus, as Darwin writes, when we read the letters that make up the word "printing press," we do not "attend" to their shape or size but only associate the words with ideas of progress and innovation; the impingement of figure is eclipsed by development. Figure functions as an ambivalent point of articulation in a mechanistic sense, a joint between phenomenal bodies and the trains and tribes of thought that order them in the successive time of progress. Elsewhere, though, Darwin describes this process less as an erasure and more as the distribution of external phenomena. He gives the example of "walking through [a] grove before my window" without "run[ning] against the trees or the benches, though my thoughts are strenuously exerted on some other subject." While "the tree or bench, which I avoid, exists on my retina ... neither itself nor the actions of those muscles engage my attention."³⁷ Figural entities continue to coexist with the thinking subject, distributed now as irritating phenomena rather than origins of knowledge. Resonant with Priestley's concern for the imposed-upon eye, Darwin's description of those sensations that rise to the level of successive trains of thought cartographizes sensations by distributing the exterior (what is impressed on the retina) and the interior (what we attend to in strenuous thought). Those exterior sensations are not erased but occluded from thought by way of a distribution that maintains them as simultaneous to successive trains of thought. In wanting to balance bodies and reduce labor time, Priestley and Darwin default to a material and sensational assemblage that requires the difference of other spatiotemporal configurations.

It is not only in his attempts at time-saving that Priestley turns back to the figural; he also does so in order to produce a feeling of history. While it is on the horizontal axis that the viewer can follow temporal uniformity, flowing like a river in the transition from one empire to the next, Priestley locates pleasure on the vertical axis. On the progressive line, we see the successive rise and fall of empires in a continuous movement that separates noncoincident empires and nations. It is on this axis that a "a more perfect knowledge of this kind of history may be gained by an hour's inspection of this chart." Turning to the vertical axis, "the reader ... will see the contemporary state of all the empires subsisting in the world, at any particular time."³⁸ On this axis of contemporary and subsisting empires, viewers experience the simultaneous coincidence of empires and territories that are depicted "as falling in a perpendicular stream" and not as time that "flows uniformly from the beginning to the end." And it is on this axis of the chart that Priestley locates pleasure and efficiency: "This view is particularly pleasing, at the time that we are studying any particular history, for when we are contemplating what was doing in any one part of the world, we cannot help wishing to know what was carrying on in other parts at the same time; and by no other means can this knowledge be gained so completely, and in so short a time."³⁹ Typically pleasure tends to be understood as a symptom of a regulated system, as the physiological effect of "internal organization [and] constituent parts" in harmony.⁴⁰ Pleasure ought to indicate a system in equilibrium, a balance between stimulation and habit, as discussed in previous chapters. But here an accumulation of simultaneous phenomena generates that feeling; indeed, it is the axis of the chart most crowded with figures and text that is associated with the feeling of progress. The experience of seeing "other parts [of the world] at the same time" provokes an economic affect. Figure reappears here as the mechanism of pleasure; the feeling of simultaneous and coinciding phenomena generates Priestley's desired affect equilibrium. Rosenberg describes this dynamic between the vertical and horizontal as a "productive tension" created by Priestley's desire to "establish [a] relationship between place and time."[41] But it is perhaps more than the simple tension of opposites here and rather a recourse to the spatiality of experience that is incommensurate with the reduction of history to the line. As we saw above, figure—that instant of the impression of bodies upon one another—affords an experience of simultaneous association of manifold sensations. This fundamentally exteriorized arrangement of figure is also the arrangement of the vertical, spatial axis of the chart, where figure becomes a means of arranging global space, in a pleasant way. The feeling of a "just image" comes not simply from a time that "flows laterally like a river" but also from the impression of different spaces as they pile up perpendicularly on our retina in an instant. Space becomes the place for a certain kind of arrangement in which the empirical figure is extended beyond any well-regulated psychology of an individual viewer and into an onto-epistemology that consistently defaults to figure in order to accomplish its heterogeneous tasks simultaneously while also separating the figural out from history.[42]

The last figural aspect of the chart that we shall discuss here counters the experience of contemporary and uneven elsewheres as pleasure, instead drawing a visual connection between what Priestley designates as the prehistorical and the future that bears with it a tinge of fear. Two segments of the chart are left blank. The first has been artificially truncated, because, "if a proportionable width were allowed for other regions, barren of events, as Tartary, Siberia, and America, the chart would have been immoderately large, and the face of it would have exhibited little more than an [sic] uniform blank." This barren space takes up what is now called America between 1100 BC and 1200 AD, the point at which the empires of what are now called Mexico and Peru are founded, and before which is taken up by

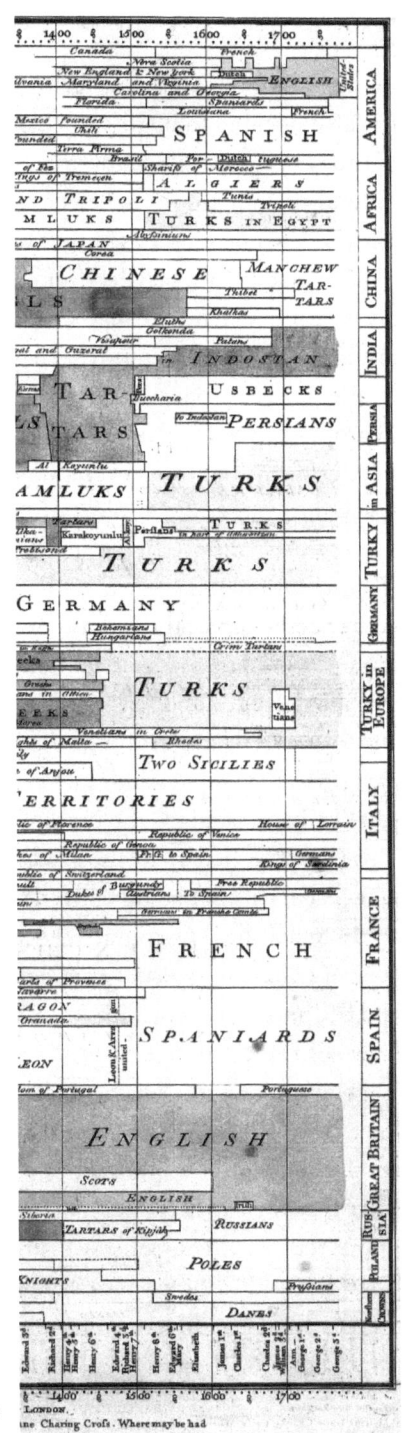

Vertical section of *A New Chart of History*, from 1400 to 1700 AD.

the title, "A New Chart of History." In addition to the erasures, Priestley has also decided to begin the chart at 1100 AD instead of at the beginning of time because, as Rosenberg puts it, "if a chart were to begin at the beginning of time, it would either have to include a large amount of *unutilized space* or it would have to sacrifice temporal regularity."[43] If it were to depict a history that did not privilege human empires characterized by a linear, progressive movement, the map would be dominated by the empty space-time of a universe without empires. To prevent this realistic consumption of man by the "barren" space of what came before, Priestley distributes blankness in proportion to the desired affect of equilibrium.[44]

Certainly, the transformation of such vast and immeasurable "barren" space into the uniform plots of the future goes some way in settling the perception of "those living in the eighteenth century" through a colonial representation of history in which actual places inhabited by actual people are rendered as vacant and unpopulated.[45] But I am more interested in the minor flash of formal association created between this barren and disproportionate space and the open-endedness of the future that renders past and future in relation through visual impression. With the emptiness of the past, Priestley also includes a vacant future; this second absence is much smaller, beginning in "the present year 1769," running up to the year 1800. This is "to be filled up by those who purchase the chart, as the changes shall take place, without being obliged to erase anything."[46]

In including these putatively empty spaces, however, Priestley also creates an instance of visual connection between "empty" spaces of the past and the potentiality of a future as yet unrealized by empire. That is, "at one view" of the chart, the future is most visibly impressed upon us through association with the "uniform blank" of prehistorical space, creating a nonlinear leap of centuries. While it is certainly the case that the blank spaces on the chart are the product of a conjectural orientation toward history, what is less clear is the temporality the conjectural creates. According to Frank Palmieri, conjectural histories are a "kind of historical narrative [that] traces the origins of society back to a time before the existence of documents and other remains."[47] We have already seen, however, that Priestley is more than willing to abandon narrative in favor of producing a figure of

Section from *A New Chart of History* showing the "barren" space of what would become America.

Section from *A New Chart of History* showing the "space to be filled up" in the future.

history.[48] Palmieri also writes that "unlike natural law theory, conjectural narratives aim to provide plausible narratives of slow historical developments, not thought experiments focused on a single founding moment of contract.[49]

Maureen McLane, however, has challenged such a sense of the conjectural as either primarily narrativized or gradual, suggesting that a Malthusian "foreclosing of possibility" and a Godwinian optimism in which "human progress would continue asymptotically into the future" created conditions in which "whether considering primitive or prospective man [writers] gave themselves over . . . to the conjectural."[50] For McLane, a Romantic version of conjectural history disrupted the stagism of the conjectural, replacing it with a more performative and poetic uncertainty of past and future, primitive and prospective, alike. What McLane considers poetic uncertainty is for me another version of the figural dimensions of capital accumulation, an indication of the constitutive aspects of modernity that are not "plausible narratives of slow historical developments" but visualized as single moments, as the constellation of instants that remain imposed on the retina even of a writer of universal history such as Priestley. In other words, with what Priestley calls barren and empty spaces the chart impresses an image of the future upon viewers with a leap backward in a striking spatiotemporal recursion that threatens to overtake all of history. While we are accustomed to thinking of such leaps, cuts, and flashes as immanently utopic or radical, these coincidental associations between the past and present actually present a far more uncertain scenario of what Benjamin has called "an image which flashes up at the moment of its recognizability, and is never seen again."[51] Rather than being determined toward any particular ends, this flash records the immanently contingent structure of history that, as Benjamin tells us, the ruling classes work to turn toward their own self-preservation. Priestley's attempt to institute a new universal history conjecturally writes the prehistory of European empire as empty, but in so doing it also introduces a visual relation that preserves a violence to the self-identical origins of "slow historical development." In this sense, modernity is never as indebted to the linear as is often claimed but is instead caught up in mythifying, fictionalizing, theorizing, and fantasizing about the phenomenal and manifold others it brings into being through the processes of capital accumulation.

Whether we are looking at the vertical or horizontal axis of Priestley's chart, we are reminded that the different arrangements enabled by spatiality are just as much a part of the map as the reliance on uniform scale and linear time. Along with the narratives of uniformity and abstraction propagated by proponents of capitalism, Priestley's production of universal history continues to rely upon the difference of an epistemology based on the primarily affectable and exterior origins of knowledge. Here the spatiality of figure is key, unfolding a historical material relation between sensation and global space. In order to produce a chart that generates both a uniform feeling of history and a sped-up time of learning it, Priestley relies on the capacities of the figural, which are irreducible to linear time and uniform history. The chart's ability to produce the feeling of a progressive and uniform history ultimately hinges upon Priestley's account of the senses as a site of simultaneous and spatialized relations.[52] Paradoxically, the chart responds to the sense that time was passing rapidly by making it possible to visualize history almost instantaneously, not through a lack of mediation but through the figural mediations of sensation, touch, impression, and excitement.[53]

We began this chapter by noting Kodwo Eshun's remark about *Handsworth Songs* that the technical is at once a racial and a spatial problem, meaning that for the BAFC there were no questions of "colour correction, filtering, lighting, the whole field of what is called sensitometry" that were not questions about the accumulated history of perceiving difference. We cannot approach something like Priestley's chart without asking similar questions about the overdetermined relationships among affect, spatiality, and the function of the senses upon which he reflects in his "Description." As posited by Ferreira da Silva , this accumulated history of perception reaches back to Francis Bacon and a pre-Kantian "stage of exteriority" in which "[reason] operates as the exterior ruler of affectable things," and the universality of secular reason remains dependent upon unreliable phenomenal relations that Priestley worried might lead to an erroneous impression of history.[54] The unstable reliance of the thinking subject upon phenomenal things, of universal reason upon extended bodies, is at the center of what Ferreira da Silva calls the racial, and it is also central to Priestley's representation of universal history. Repurposing Derrida's notion of the trace, Ferreira da Silva posits the racial as that groundless link between the signifier and the signified in which declarations of transparent selves and universal subjects necessarily inaugurated "'being and meaning'... in exteriority and violence," in the absence of a preceding metaphysical identity. Prior to any proclaimed science of race, the racial is an always spatializing relation in which the movements of reason and the mind are only ever effects of phenomenal coexistence and relationality. While Ferreira da Silva is engaging with a deeply philosophical genealogy in making this claim, our beginning in *Handsworth Songs* shows us that such a conceptualization of the racial is also worked out "in the ways in which the technical, the formal, and the spatial entangle each other in a way that is difficult to pull apart and resolve."[55] Something else clings to the abstraction of space and time, then, and that something else is in excess of the enclosure of history by the selfsame capital that is the underlying assumption on the part of readers who see only the innovation of abstraction as determining of modernity.

Working back from the appearance of Priestley's statue in the first few minutes of *Handsworth Songs*, we might begin to see a long-standing genealogy for the figural and phenomenal, which Priestley and Darwin treat as occluded origin points of knowledge as well as a phenomenal phase that becomes the irritating surrounding of a thinking subject. Functioning as the organizing schema of colonial pasts and presents, the montage form of *Handsworth Songs* reminds us that how we read the cuts, leaps, and senses of history also dictates what we think we know of it. To avoid these same aspects of the chart is to reproduce a deracinated account of modern history at the level of our own affectability and to dismiss the possible histories that such affectability holds. According to the BAFC, the work of decentering a Western hegemony of meaning requires an approach to archival images that does not diagnose them as positive or negative but works to develop "new cartographies of presence while rethinking the old."[56] If we focus only on the innovations in abstraction developed for those in the eighteenth-century, then we would most certainly miss the "old" epistemologies of the chart that rely on Ferreira da Silva's "stage of exteriority." We would also miss a reading of the central role played by the distribution and stimulation of phenomena, the significance of a system of reason dependent upon exteriority, and the paradox of an abstraction generated by affectability. While these features of the chart can easily be set aside if we decide in advance that the technological innovation of abstraction is the only relevant feature in reading history as shorthand for British or European subjects only, such a reading will be harder to come by if we understand the history of capitalism not as enclosed in its own industrial logic but originating in the leap of dispossession and so-called primitive accumulation that is the focus of this book.

Referring us to the numerous differentiations that are the condition of possibility for the measured time and efficient production of Priestley's history of empire, figure provides a better account of how linear time and labor-saving techniques are produced through what Ferreira da Silva calls a racial analytics. The absences, occlusions, and blank spaces on the chart hold open sensorial accumulations of what Benjamin has called the "compelling—the drastic experience" of history that reverses and refutes gradual and developmental temporalities and, only if grasped in a perilous and critical instance of reading, "is an awakening from a dream."[57] The chart relies on that sense of dispossession as constitutively figurative, as an arrangement of elements enmeshed with one another, rather than linear time.

Priestley's chart does not so much work against uneven and competing senses as it works through them, generating a temporal trajectory of progress via figures of spatial multiplicity. With this schema in mind, let us turn to the racialization of subsistence using a global Romantic frame, taking up the productive nature of the incoherent, the superfluous and the spatialized that clings to a modernity that is not reducible to historical time. More than just repression, the consistent emergence of a modernity that accommodates subsistence shows us a figural production of history through flashes and leaps of space. These are conditions of subsistence ways of living that span England and what was known as the New Kingdom of Spain, and more generally to a modernity that continues to incoherently require needs and ways of meeting them that are not subsumed by "the assumption of temporal uniformity and naturaliz[ing] the regular, measured time of calendar and clock."[58]

Racializing Subsistence

Priestley's chart has been recognized as particularly novel for its representation of a nonteleological version of universal history in which progress is not enclosed within any particular empire but is presented as cycles of progress and decline. But what is occluded by such narratives of novelty and innovation is the preexisting model of nonteleological history provided by the stagist racial theories that were still dominant in Priestley's time.[59] As Roxanne Wheeler describes it, the four-stages theory proposed that the "progress and perfectibility of society" was possible but only through a version of history that "should not be mistaken for a *teleological* theory." Instead, "progress was usually perceived as *part of a cycle* in which eminence characteristically preceded decline."[60] So while one of the chart's innovations may have been in abstraction, it was not in the introduction of a new mode of progress that was nonlinear and cyclical: such a model was already on offer in existing theories of racial variety. Existing accounts of capitalist modernity in Romantic literary criticism are too often marred by a severe inattention to the ways in which the racial structures not only capital accumulation but also our narratives of the history of capitalism. The rhetorical reading of Priestley's chart offered above provides important tools for beginning to center the constitutively racial origins of capital accumulation and what Jairus Banaji has called "the simultaneity of capitalism and primitive accumulation."[61]

European stagist theories of racial variety, which still dominated European versions of natural history in the eighteenth century, depended heavily upon the exterior determination of affectable bodies discussed in this chapter, thus implicating the figural epistemology of theorists such as Priestley and Darwin in a certain account of racial difference. The susceptibility of any body to exterior impressions that generated knowledge of the world was also a feature of bodies that supposedly exemplified their place within civilizational development. According to stagist accounts, racial variety was determined by geography and the reciprocal interplay of environmental forces and the susceptibility of bodies in developing what tended to be referred to as "modes of life," including dress, habits and mannerisms, facial features, commerce, culture, and skin color. The variety of the human species was thus classified and represented through geographic association and on a continuum from barbarous to civilized modes of life. As others have shown, the European capacity for self-regulation became the causal mechanism for their civilizational superiority over the hypersensational or else insensible others of African, Indigenous, and sometimes even settler-colonial bodies in places such as the West Indies.

In creating a chart meant to facilitate the correspondence between self-regulation and universal history, Priestley rewrites some of these features of a stagist account of human variety on the vertical axis. For one thing, the association between geographic space and affectability remains, as does the exteriorized accumulation of an excess of lines and texts upon the senses that threatens to overwhelm the imagination. In addition, it is on this spatial axis that the simultaneity of "elsewhere" makes it possible to glimpse history "at one view" and, paradoxically, produces pleasure. The visual organization of different modes of life that could be seen simultaneously returns in the form of elsewhere spaces. The cultural signs that were the effect of physiological affectability are recomposed along its spatial axis, in which the visual of racial variety remains in the coincidence of different spaces—some imperial, some national, and some vacant. Beyond its reliance on a nonteleological representation of history, the chart also seems to retain other features of stagist racialization in terms of the simultaneous coexistence of difference and its association between spatialized phenomena and physiological affectability. The surface of impressionability does not capture difference as variety here but depicts it as the coincidence of global space within a modernity that is *not* plotted along the linear temporal axis. Here the racial, as relations of coexisting simultaneity and phenomenal affectability, are converted into the abstraction of space. But this abstraction is not reducible to the uniform or the homogeneous; it accompanies such abstraction but persists, necessarily, as a difference through which the temporal trajectory of progress is narrativized. What in the four-stages theory were the signifying cues of gradual, epigenetic varia-

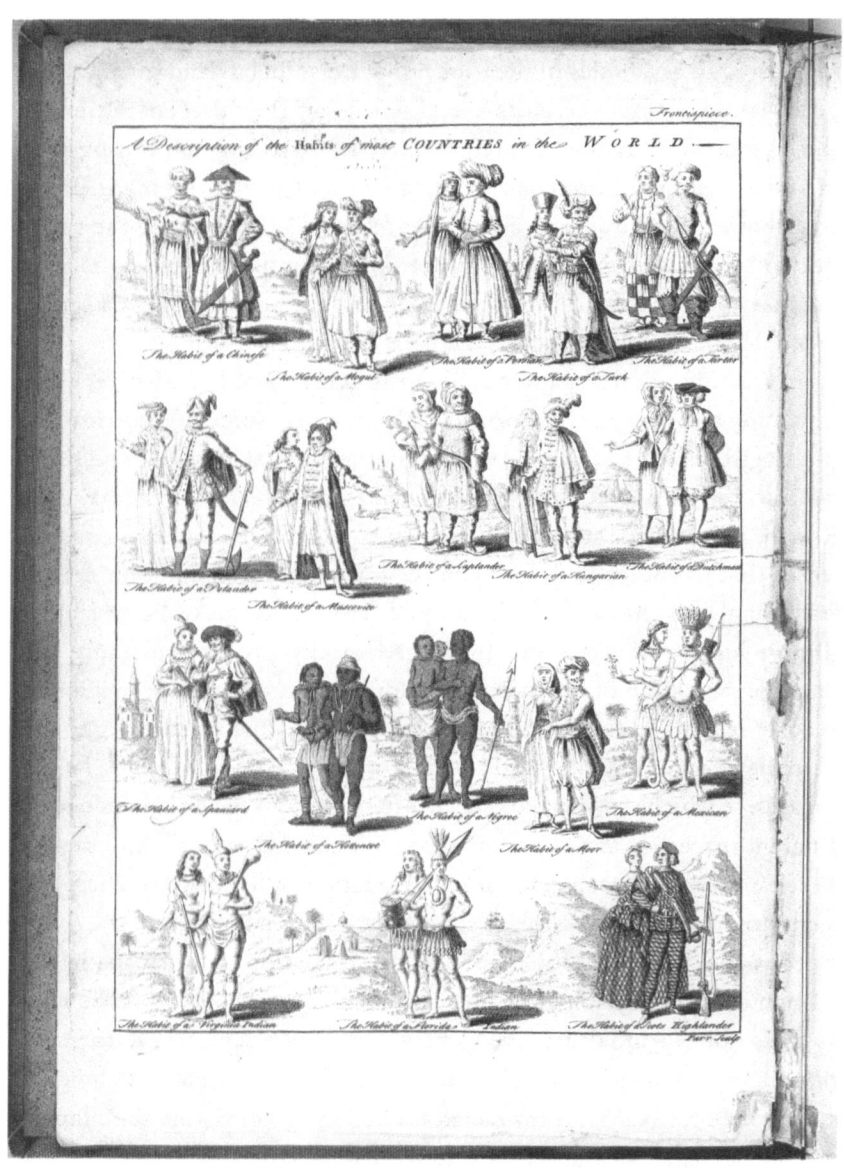

Thomas Osborne, *A Description of the Habits of the Many Countries of the World*. From *A Collection of Voyages and Travels* (London: printed by Thomas Osborne, 1745), 1. Reprinted with permission from the Columbia University Rare Book and Manuscript Library.

tion appear along one axis of the chart as the reversal of the instantaneous, the "one view."

Along with the translation of nonteleological history, these features of affectability and simultaneous difference are impressed upon the architecture of the chart. The reappearance there of these features of racial variety is not a matter of intention or an explicitly racist project but rather an effect of the persistent structuring of temporal progress through the difference of figural and exteriorized relationality, of a racializing knowledge production that operates by establishing the superfluity of the phenomenal. As Ferreira da Silva makes clear, this is distinctly not an exclusionary logic but a productive one. It puts race at the center of the production of modern history in an onto-epistemological project that renders being through the knowledge of others. The translation to the chart of the features of the stagist theory of race still dominant in the eighteenth century are part of what Marlon B. Ross calls the "subliminally exposed structure" of "the very places we inhabit or pass through" of the racial, of an ongoing negotiation between sovereign minds and sensational bodies that structures Western epistemologies through a historical materialist process.[62] Another way of saying this is that the abstraction of Priestley's chart relies as much on the reconfiguration of difference into the hierarchy of the temporal over the spatial and self-regulating affectability over dependency on an exterior force as it does on the uniformity of abstraction.[63] In addition, the translation—whether intentional or not—of the coexisting differences of racial variety in a stagist theory of race into the relations of simultaneous elsewheres on the chart reminds us that the eighteenth-century discourse of modes of life is written as the coexistence of abstract but still heterogeneous space.

It is through the sublimation of such phenomenal and figural infrastructures that the racial comes to appear as an effect of, or as epiphenomenal to, the progress narrative of capitalism that is depicted as a homogenizing drive toward measured time. The features through which we often identify industrial modes of production—measured time, extended work days, standardized rates of production, and the linear, progressive ideologies of history that buttress them—are secured through the distribution of the phenomenal, the spatial, and the exterior as the matter through which self-valorizing capital moves, reflecting a now long-standing privileging of temporality and self-reflection over the dependency of the body upon the "outside" world. Even if we read Priestley's chart critically as a representation of linear history, we still miss the ways in which it is structured through what Ferreira da Silva reminds us is the racial "at the center of the critique of modern representation."[64] In other words, we cannot narrate the history of modernity and capitalism as one primarily of abstraction and uniformity without reproducing a racial logic.

How might we begin to read such seemingly transparent scenes of progress otherwise? In what ways does Ferreira da Silva's long trajectory of a racial analytics and the necessary persistence of those phenomenalized and affectable modes of life within racial capitalism allow us to reapproach modernity through the simultaneity of capitalism and a primitive accumulation that has never stopped working upon noncapitalist ways of meeting needs?

Priestley's 1787 *An Account of a Society for Encouraging the Industrious Poor* provides a useful point of entry into locating the global racialization of subsistence through its spatial coincidence with progressive history and modern capitalism.[65] This text is one of many that documents the problem of workers' irregular and inconsistent work habits as a persistent obstacle to industrial capitalism throughout the British Romantic period. In *An Account of Society*, Priestley describes the problem of work discipline as having been created by the system of Poor Laws, leaving men in a "wretched and dependent state." Men have been reduced to a level below the brutes; their natural condition, in which they would work longer hours to secure the surplus resources that would allow them to "look to the future," has deteriorated. As conditions stand, "if the greater part of workmen can earn enough in three or four days to maintain themselves and their families for the week, they will never work anymore."[66] Instead of securing the future through more work than is necessary for the present, the working poor as presented by Priestley happily measure their needs and satisfaction by a unit of three to four days. The way to produce a history predicated upon foresight, then, would be to extend the working day, enacting by law what Marx would later call formal subsumption.[67] Such extension was to be accomplished by a version of legalized wage theft, the forced investment of a part of workers' wages in an investment fund, requiring them to work beyond what a day's labor could satisfy.[68] Standing in the way of this endeavor was the preference of the working poor for a way of living in which waged labor was a partial and even inconsistent means of reproduction; from their perspective, there was nothing insufficient about subsistence ways of living. Indeed, Priestley freely attests to the fact that inconsistent waged work, the mode preferred by workers, is actually sufficient to satisfy their needs and to "maintain their families for the week";[69] it is only insufficient in times of accident or illness. And even in this dismissal of what is spent extravagantly outside the time of labor, a sufficiency that does meet needs without any more work and a surplus beyond what work provides is still visible.

The disciplining of workers' habits was crucial to their forced dependency on wages for their reproduction. This was also a significant and much-discussed need for the industrial and scientific endeavors of the Lunar Society, especially for members such as Priestley's close friends James Watt and Michael Boulton. As Robert Schofield notes, they often complained of difficulty in "acquiring workmen sufficiently skilled to perform the more exacting work demanded by machine parts" and "finding men of regular work habits."[70] From the perspective of a certain history of modern capitalism, such workers were needed in order to produce surplus commodities for consumption, a condition that itself presupposed the reliance of the vast majority of workers on the consumption of exchange values. According to certain Marxist as well as non-Marxist accounts, it was the process of enclosure that led to the dependency of a certain segment of European workers on the wage form. Enclosure and the dispossession of noncapitalist means of subsistence for the vast majority of the English working class became the crucial mechanism for guaranteeing the extension of the working day and of producing the appearance for such workers that all necessities of life were provided for by money.

Work on racial capitalism has shown that the dependency of the English working class upon the wage form is inseparable from cycles of capital accumulation that fostered the conditions in which those workers' means of subsistence could be provided for by a global market. In other words, as work by Cedric Robinson has shown, the "freedom" of the wage laborer in England required the surplus commodity production of slave labor, together with the consumption of the plantation colonies, in order for the European worker to be made independent from the soil.[71] Slavery and its prestructuring conditions of financial capital and colonialism going back to the fourteenth century have to be integrated into our telling of the destruction of the English working class's subsistence ways of living and dependency on the commodity form. What otherwise readily appears as a drive toward standardization is an always global matter of a capitalism in which the English enclosures and industrialization are simultaneous with other forms of accumulation. As Ruth Wilson Gilmore has argued, capitalism is rooted in a kind of abstraction that does not take the form of uniformity but is a "death-dealing displacement of difference into hierarchies . . . that pushes disproportionate costs of participating in an increasingly monetized and profit-driven world" onto those without the means of alleviating such costs.[72] In this sense, what is significant about the previous cycles of accumulation Robinson and others track is not really their pastness or their historical origins, in which, for instance, slave labor becomes a phenomenon of the past, but rather that so-called primitive accumulation is simultaneous to the capitalist present of *any* present. This has become increasingly clear in recent years, as uprisings and riots across the so-called United States, or what many Indigenous people and scholars refer to as Turtle Island, make present for others the continuous discontinuity of indebtedness and state violence that feeds disproportionately off gendered and transgendered Black bodies.[73] What this means, as we have seen throughout this book, is that it was not strictly dispossession from the resource of land that launched the movements of industrial capitalism or the complete destruction of noncapitalist ways of living; it was also a deathly fixation on the contingent discovery of sugarcane that Robinson narrates as the catalyst for the transformation from the slave trade to the mass market in slave labor and the horrifyingly fluid transformation of captured labor from across Europe and Africa into the hierarchy of Black, creole, and white bodies. And it is simultaneously the forms of subsistence that were reconstituted by enslaved and Indigenous peoples, whether in maroon colonies and provision grounds, for the survival of their families, or, as discussed in Chapter 3, in postemancipation Jamaica. It is only through such cycles that we can understand the English context, not through the event of dispossession but as an interwoven dependency upon what Fred Moten has described as "the historical reality of commodities who spoke—of laborers who were commodities before, as it were, the abstraction of labor power."[74]

This crucial aspect of racialized accumulation is, admittedly, not the central concern of this book. I bring up this history of humans as things and survival beyond exchange in order to show what is erased if we read representations of universal history only as symptoms of one mode of abstraction. Processes other than "the abstraction of labor power" come to the fore in work on capitalism as always racial capitalism and confront us with the staggering challenge of de-centering what Reece Auguiste has described as "the privileged position [of the Western gaze] as the ultimate arbiter of symbolic meaning and representation" in Priestley's chart.[75] Interventions by scholars of racial capitalism and Black studies do far more than demand our attention to slavery as the history we think we know—they compel an onto-epistemological reckoning with our entire approach to Romantic materialism, ideologies of progress and modernity, figuration, and, particularly at this moment, the recuperation of Lunar Society members Darwin and Priestley.

One way of reading Priestley's racialized characterization of the English working class as less even than brutes would be through the telos of industrialization and the consolidation of more essentializing forms of race in the Victorian period. Indeed, many narratives of the transition from eighteenth- to nineteenth-century Britain follow along these lines, in which, to borrow Saree Makdisi's language, England finally became Western in the late nineteenth century. Such narratives of completion, however, reinstitute the very terms of a self-valorizing and homogeneous history of capital that I have been working to undo throughout this book, and render the processes of so-called primitive accumulation as a thing of the past rather than simultaneous to capitalism's own reproduction. Even in critical narratives of the emergence of the British working class as one that becomes white and Western, we fail to heed Ferreira da Silva's call to "relinquish self-determination" not only as a racist, capitalist ideal but also as an idea we accidentally reproduce when we presume that any nation-state in a modern context actually follows a developmentalist trajectory.[76] As Moten suggests, we must work to undo our own fantasies of the uniform and universal abstract as both the beginning and end of capitalism, looking instead for all of the catachrestic historical realities that accumulate over the time of capital accumulation.

Alongside the more traditional depiction of a proto-industrial workforce in Priestley's account, there are also peculiar moments that situate workers' preference for unwaged means of reproduction as conditions that coincide with practices across the Atlantic rather than being prehistorical. As with the chart, in his *Account of a Society for Encouraging the Industrious Poor*, Priestley fashions subsistence-style living using the same spatial logic. Rather than a purely residual way of life, subsistence is portrayed as a way of living that coincides with speculations about the progressive movement of time. According to Priestley, well-meaning interventions into the productive nature of man has "in effect debased him to a condition below that of any brutes; who, without having the capacity of man never fail to provide for their real wants." That is, workers' preference for as little waged labor as required is not a primitive holdover from a premodern era; for Priestley, it is a result of the exterior conditions set by the Poor Laws and of the working poor's susceptibility to such forces, conditions which, as Maureen McNeil has argued, were of direct concern to the Lunar Society.[77] Here subsistence is rendered as the product of figural impressionability, in a kind of socio-climatological misstep that is contiguous but not identical to the movement of history. This has left men in a state of dependency rather than bringing them into the "humanity of individuals." We must, according to Priestley, rewrite history and its present-day overaccumulation of regress, and "und[o] as fast as we can, all that we have hitherto done, and ge[t] back into the plain path of nature," "revert[ing] to that natural condition of man from which we have departed."[78]

Subsistence here sits in relation to capitalist work time in much the same way as global space is distributed on an axis with linear history. The working poor live in conditions that are characterized as spatial rather than temporal, as "below [those] of brutes," and as coexisting with the speculative

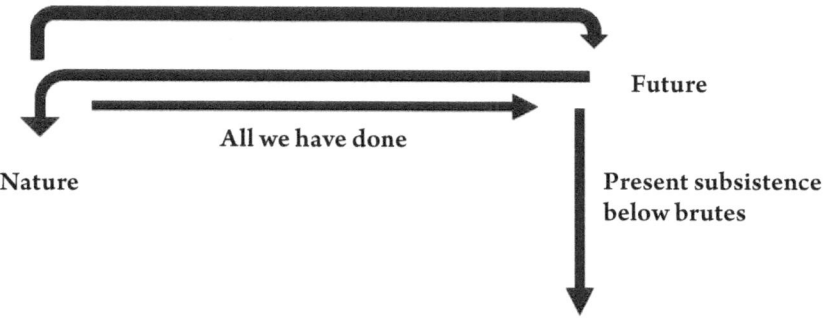

Visualization of Priestley's description of the process of reverting to nature in the future and the temporal location of subsistence. Author.

movement of the "humanity of individuals" in the future. As with the chart, the conjectural movement into the future is associated with a leap into the past, as a reversion to the productive nature of man that, like the vacant spaces of past and future on the chart, writes a temporal leap into the speculative production of linear time. What has put them in this relation to the future movement of history is not a historical problem, per se, in the sense of their being historicized in the past but a problem of coincidence, in which the empirical materiality of bodies remains simultaneous with but arranged elsewhere than the historical. In presenting the problem of subsistence in this way, Priestley's *Account* offers subsistence as a set of associations that assist productively in the determination of progressive history through a continuous contemporaneity rather than as a time frozen in the past.

All of these peculiar phrasings of subsistence as spatialized and progress as backward-looking might easily be dismissed as superfluous if we were to remain committed to an account of modernity subsumed by homogenizing abstraction and the extraction of surplus value through standardized labor. But to set such an accumulation of details aside would be to reproduce a sense of history as transparent. Rather than a symptom of capitalism that abstracts everything through standardization and uniformity, our reading of Priestley's work suggests that even the strongest proponents of capitalism as a socially progressive force are impressed by a racializing arrangement in which noncapitalist means of meeting needs remain structuring. Priestley's narrative of subsistence as a contemporary effect of social conditions upon affectable bodies reproduces a figural association between phenomena, space, and exteriority to legitimate an otherwise entirely fictional and fantastical account of the future. Here a discourse of modes of life shows up from eighteenth-century accounts of racial variety, remaining crucial to speculations on universal history through an abstraction that is not reducible to uniformity. As I read it, difference according to Ferreira da Silva is the descriptor of the irreducibly material and exterior conditions of our existence and it is the relevance of such conditions as they continue to do racializing work with which we shall conclude this chapter, in order to challenge our tendency toward narratives of rupture in the shifting accounts of race in eighteenth- and nineteenth-century British studies as well as to push us toward a better understanding of the constitutively racializing work of so-called primitive accumulation.

The point in addressing Priestley's chart and his wage-theft proposal here is not to re-center the English working class but instead to de-center the conceptual telos that has tended to structure the accounts of the working class that emerged post-enclosure, as well as to make plain the global coincidences of differential remakings of subsistence and the racialization of need, thereby taking up Ferreira da Silva's notion of the centrality of the racial in producing the onto-epistemology of modernity. The process of so-called primitive accumulation discussed throughout this book shows the relevance of an accumulation of differences to noncapitalist ways of meeting needs, a process from which a vast number of white workers are by no means free. Along with attending to the global cycles of accumulation to which thinkers like Robinson, Wilson Gilmore, and others draw our attention, we must also be aware of our tendency to lightly pass over the phenomenalization of need and use that Ferreira da Silva highlights in her account of the racial as "the necessity of satisfying needs rather than the freedom of will"—not as an origin point of history but as the conditions of the ongoing emergence of capitalism.

The translation of the variety of forms of life that had defined eighteenth-century stagist accounts of race reappears here in Priestley's paradoxical account of the simultaneously foreign and Indigenous modes of reproduction of the working poor, and these elements continue to structure the production of the racial until today. Without rejecting important work on the becoming-white of the British working class, we must also keep in mind that the hierarchies produced by ongoing so-called primitive accumulation continued to ensure the limited and even provincial nature of that designation. Reading through the figural and affectable form of the racial developed here through a constellation of the *Handsworth Songs*, Ferreira da Silva, and Priestley may be helpful not only by complicating our tendency to binarize the history of race and capitalism but also by prompting us to search for global connections among persistent noncapitalist forms of living, thus revealing genealogies that would otherwise be foreclosed by more teleological accounts of race and class.

Let us turn to such a coincidence in the work of Alexander von Humboldt, who is perhaps best known as the author of *Cosmos*. In a traditional schema of histories of science there is little that would suggest connections between Priestley and Humboldt, given the tendency to put Priestley in a mechanist and Humboldt in a materialist camp. But some scholars have begun troubling these divisions, with Monique Allewaert going so far as to posit a direct philosophical connection between the two through their shared belief in a world composed of "motile, flexible matter that contributed to a world in which movement and change were continual."[79] They shared other beliefs as well, one of which was in the development of civilization through a disciplined and waged workforce. Thus, along with what Allewaert calls Humboldt's "nonidentitarian natural history," which resonates with recent claims for Priestley's nonidentitarian ontology, Humboldt spends quite a bit of time analyzing the relative progress of a productive labor force in his *Political Essay on the Kingdom of New Spain*. This text covered his time from 1799 to 1804 in what is today known as Mexico, when Charles IV granted Humboldt much-coveted access to traveling in Spanish America. As Daniel Nemser notes, however, "Humboldt did not travel extensively in New Spain, opting instead to base his work on statistical data provided to him by the Spanish authorities."[80] In the *Political Essay*, Humboldt lodges a complaint against the persistence of subsistence, distinguishing between "mulatto artisans and free negros, who, by their industry alone, procure much more than the necessaries of life,"

> [and] the swarm [of] twenty to thirty thousand wretches (*Saragates, Guachinangos*), of whom the greatest number pass the night *sub dio*, and stretch themselves out to the sun during the day.... These dregs of people bear much analogy to the Lazaroni of Naples.... If they work one or two days in the week, they earn as much as will purchase their pulque, or some of the ducks with which the Mexican lakes are covered.[81]

Immediately noticeable here is the extended and phenomenal language by which Humboldt describes these "wretches" who seem to differ entirely from the industrious subjects whom he wants to cast as part of a productively liberal nation-state. He reproduces the framework Priestley sets out for subsistence and history, rendering it more recognizably racialized. Constellating Priestley's brutish subsisters with the "wretches" of Mexico and Italy, Humboldt's swarm are situated outside the more recognizably racial taxonomies of "negro" and "mulatto" and associated with one another through their excessive pleasures and excessively meager work time. In contrast to subjects regulated by the more than necessary length of working days, the "swarms" and "dregs" of "wretches" that are lumped together across the ocean from so-called Mexico to Naples are, quite literally, figures of another measure of time and necessity that coincides with progress. The lines of distinction here are drawn not only through racial taxonomy but through the sedimented base of the social body who depend on natural resources (the sun, the lake, ducks) for their subsistence and pleasure. Here we can see a "double vision" of race at work that does not map along the lines of classification but rather demarcates a population through the practice of subsistence outside a waged economy. Distinguishing between "mulatto artisans" and "free negros" who are industrious, on the one hand, and an amorphous and indigent mass of "wretches," on the other, Humboldt demonstrates how a certain kind of fluidity or transferability built into the resistance to work was translated into the racial difference of subsistence living. This exteriority associates the surface sensation of sun on skin with a space unbounded by national lines. What was a problem of local labor for Priestley and his Lunar Society collaborators here becomes apparent as a global logic, in which the phenomenal and figural nature of bodies was always already scalable because spatialized, associated with surface rather than individuation.

As another instance in the essay suggests, subsistence-style populations become so firmly entangled with the successive structuring of progressive history that it is easy to miss their coexistence. It is with this scene that we shall move toward a conclusion, denaturalizing the explicit progress narrative available in the scene and returning to the BAFT's sense that the most straightforward presentation of the history of racial capitalism cannot be presented in linear terms. In this passage, Humboldt describes

> a traveler who sets out from a great town where the social state has attained to perfection, traverses *successively* all degrees of civilization and industry, which keep diminishing till he arrives in a few days at the rude and unseemly hut formed of the trunks of trees newly cut down. . . . We set out from the most complicated union to arrive at the most simple elements; we travel in retrogression the history of the progress of the human mind; *and we find in space what is due only to the succession of time*.[82]

On the one hand, this passage attests to a transparent form of progress through the exclusion of the savage's space from civilized time. Indeed, as Humboldt puts it, space is the *effect* of successive time, or in other words, successive time is the causal force of spatial arrangement. It is clear that our traveler moves "retrogressively" in this scene from a perfected civilization to "the most simple elements" of primitive man. This motion clearly seems to be structured as narrative, or that "operation elicited by . . . succession *and* time." But if we read more closely, we will also find a scene that is constructed along Priestley's axis of succession and simultaneity, where succession is structured only by the "human mind" and unsupported by the "simple elements" of space. For instance, notice how this immense temporal distinction is traveled in the span of a few days, thus shrinking the spatial distance between the social state and the "simple elements" of man. Similarly, Humboldt tells us that we have traveled eons, but the actual space of the paragraph holds the time of travel and the space of the present together. And while the contrast with a "social state that has attained to perfection" marks the rude hut as primitive, this hut is no relic from the past but "formed of the trunks of trees newly cut down." What marks Humboldt's passage holds together "retrogression [in] the history of progress" and the "most simple elements" of hut and trees. These elements bring us back to figure as described by Darwin, when different bodies are bound in the instant of impression. It is only in the travel that takes place in "the human mind" that this paragraph can assert the power of successive and progressive history, as Darwin also shows in his distinction between successive ideas and simultaneous phenomena. This elemental space functions for both as the origin and the phenomena through which a representation of progress is composed. In a paragraph that comes as close as possible to Priestley's accelerated visual of history, Humboldt's text asserts the constitutive role of subsistence-style living alongside his narrative of liberal capitalist progress. What we learn from this image is meant to be a story of succession, and yet the passage in which it is given has more of a simultaneous effect; in other words, our passage through time is a more figural passage than standard accounts of progress would allow. This passage is no mere forward motion: it is also an accumulation, a piling up, of spaces and "simple elements." Such an intermingling of time and space, succession and simultaneity, is part of the empirical tradition in which figure is elemental. Although framed as if plotted on a linear timeline, the "simple elements" of this passage stand out as examples of "the simultaneity of, rather than the lag between different moments of social formation; more precisely, they represent the interpenetration of the most advanced capitalism with those other recalcitrant formations."[83]

If we read carefully, the impressions of such figural relations upon history can be found throughout our archives, opening up ways of understanding the foregrounding of spatial and sensational relations that are so central to the history that *Handsworth Songs* offers us. It is through the persistent centrality of such relations—which since the eighteenth century have only been subject to intensified forms of state, patriarchal, and speculative violence—

that genealogies of survival and evasions of becoming-white appear. Constellations of the difference of material existence—of subsistence—show up across our Romantic archives if we begin reading through the language of simultaneity and spatiality that Darwin and Priestley push off to the periphery of the thinking and historical subject. But as the montage form of *Handsworth Songs* reminds us, race is "a formation which exists both on the margins at certain points, and at the center of English social life."[84] In discussing the contextual impetus for *Handsworth Songs*, Okwui Enwezor says that "in the aftermath of the protests in Handsworth, the film inhabits a different order of things: it is as much about Britain as it is elsewhere. That elsewhere is the broader postcolonial world. This feeling of disjuncture is reflected not only in the jump cuts of the film's narrative—moving between archival photographs, newsreel fragments, media reportage, and on-site aural pulse, the disjunctive syncopation of the snare drum, the mournful reverb of the dub score that sustains a quiet rage."[85] What would it mean for us to take up this "different order of things" that is "as much about Britain as . . . elsewhere" in our readings of the Romantics as our contemporaries? To attend as much to the irreducible disjunction of sensational archives and ways of living that "pr[y] open a negative/positive dichotomy" and leave us with more questions than answers about our material conditions of existence as reproduced through difference?[86]

This is by no means to say that either Priestley or Humboldt pushes such a disjunction to the fore but rather that their fantasies of a universal history in which all space is the effect of time still retains the trace—not in a historical but a signifying sense—of the necessary coincidence of subsistence ways of living, which are themselves more structuring of the spatiotemporality of late capitalism than we tend to admit. As the BAFC put it, images of Britain are just as much images of elsewhere, and such elsewheres are crucial to our histories of the British Empire as more than the telos of industrialization. They are necessary to any contemporary effort to put race, as Ferreira da Silva tells us we must do, at the center of modernity rather than locating it as a peripheral or epiphenomenal elsewhere.[87] Ferreira da Silva's ontoepistemological account of race—involving the production of the racial as a way of knowing that constitutes universal history and its subjects—shakes the foundations of our event-based narratives of enclosure and the production of labor and the commodity-form as purely homogenizing. Positioning the racial at the center of our accounts of modernity means that many of us have to start our work over again, looking for the structuring effects of difference as it produces conditions of existence, whether we are looking at the British context or our own. This entails a serious reconsideration of the different modes of living that continue to crop up throughout Romanticism and the ordering of such ways as necessary and subordinate to progress.

Humboldt and Priestley both provide an image of the more than historical work of dispossession, as noncapitalist ways of living are targeted and remade in the ongoing process of primitive accumulation. Out of step with history and the temporalizing freedom of the will but in step with the anachronism of subsistence and the satisfaction of material needs, these images of obstinate populations are held together by a nonchronological space-time. Romantic texts such as Priestley's are not significant for the rupture they mark between Romantic-era theories of race and later ones, still grounded in climatology, but rather for the ways in which needs, dependencies, and certain means of satisfaction and pleasure come to constitute the malleable enclosures of the racial that formed and continue to form capital accumulation as it coexists with the death-dealing abstractions of so-called primitive accumulation. The racialization of such features of material bodies necessarily draw our attention to other structures and mechanisms of tenuous differentiation that may be messier and more incoherent than those that have tended to structure Romantic literary criticism. The image of past and present offered by both Priestley and Humboldt does not relegate spaces and subjects to a purely prehistorical position but rather assembles them within modernity and adjacent to such history. Such configurations demonstrate the extreme significance of the maintenance of times that are not those of capitalism but that it cannot do without, in which "racial essences... are made up not of a fictively fixed and finite set of features but of an essentialized malleable and substitutable range."[88]

This is why it is significant that Priestley's production of temporal uniformity works through, rather than against, the unevenness and layering of affectable bodies and simultaneous elsewheres. From this perspective, it is all the more important to understand Priestley's chart within a "single visual frame," as Sachs suggests, but in the figural sense that allows, to paraphrase Guyer, for the coincidence rather than exclusion of otherwise oppositional space-times. Yet just as figure holds oppositional states and scenes together, the scenes of the everyday to which Priestley and Humboldt refer offer another side of ambivalence—that is, when Priestley and Humboldt warn against the drag of subsistence on the progress of history, they negatively index not only a resistance to wage labor but also a creative and vagrant constitution of other modes of life and mutual aid that can help us begin to create constellations of antiracist, anticapitalist ways of living and forms of pleasure worth recovering and finding in the present. The centrality of need to those ways of living opens the science of race—of empirical, sensational, and affectable beings—to possibilities encoded in subsistence once we understand that they necessarily cling to the present rather than remaining locked in a long-lost past. While always at risk of remaining unremembered, as Walter Benjamin would argue, and being told as chronological histories enclosed in the past, these figures can point us to the politics of need rather than will and of subsistence rather than progress so long as we continue, again, to learn how to read beyond the binaries and dichotomies of capital and race, of history and rhetoric, of abstraction and figuration.

Coda

Rhetorical Reading toward a Global Romanticism

THIS BOOK IS INDIRECTLY INDEBTED to the psychoanalytic notion of the unconscious as collective, cross-generational, and palimpsestic. In *The Arcades Project*, Walter Benjamin gives us a moving image of this embodied, collective consciousness in the shape of internal organs we travel through in our sleep, somatically recalling the historical forces that leave their imprint on our vital infrastructures.[1] If understood as embodied and material, as connective tissue formed in the accumulation of nonlinear time and unknown/unknowable experience, then the unconscious provides an important way of approaching history as a passing of time always rooted in a past that is not over, as well as in a present in which repressed potentialities remain. But it is not Benjamin's intestinal traveler to which we shall turn in this coda but to the psychoanalyst Sabina Spielrein, a lesser-known theorist of the collective unconscious, and to the dreamlike scene she describes of a girl playing with her doll. This scene unfolds as an account of the deep and inherited past that makes the experiential present meaningful: "A young girl reads stories of witches with great joy; as a child, she often played at being a witch; analysis shows that the witch in the girl's fantasies represents the mother with whom the girl identifies."[2] The girl's past experience of her mother invisibly fills the space between her mother and her games in the present. She restages her identification with her mother with this object, this plaything, that becomes her substitute attachment in her mother's absence. This association of the witch with both daughter and mother remains largely unanalyzed by Spielrein, but it is one that this book can help us to unpack further.

Here multiple pasts are held together in an instant of activity and reading, a moment that exceeds its immediacy or the particular relation between this girl and this mother. The past accumulations that give the mother this significance overflow this particular relation, evinced by the strangeness of the figure of the witch, rather than a doll, in the scene. As Spielrein goes on to explain, the mother is not just a site of this girl's memories; she is also symbolic of the unconscious and its collective accumulations, which remain actively structuring albeit forgotten. For Spielrein, the relation to the mother was a point of entry into the unconscious because of the species drive of biological reproduction, and an archive of unremembered and primal pasts.[3] As such, she is a reservoir of the past and its repressions, as well as an active conduit for its reproduction in the present. She is a figure that holds together accumulated experiences that must be restaged repeatedly because they are the experiences that give the present its meaning. Spielrein's unaccounted-for reference here to the witch tells us that we are dealing with a displaced repetition, a sign of past traumas that have not been worked through but are held in a constellation of times rather than in continuous memory. Such an arrangement gives us an opening for analysis into the seemingly peripheral or incidental associations that provide the conditions for our attachment to the immediate. In order to feel the fullness of the scenes we inhabit today, we have to look beyond the psychoanalytic primacy of the family and toward the processes of accumulation through which social reproduction has been transformed, along with the noncapitalist means of subsistence often reproduced by women.[4] In this Coda, we shall explore the implications of the figure of the witch as a flash of history that presents the possibility of grasping constellations between Romanticism and the figure of the mother in Rojava, an autonomous region of Syria, the figure of the teacher in Federici's Nigerian diaries, and finally, the struggle for justice in Palestine as it demands a rhetorical reading of exactly what we are reproducing under the sign of the literary as a professional mode of reading.

There are other reasons for this coincidence of daughter, mother, and witch, thanks to which the unconscious becomes an exceptionally useful model for history. This coincidence and repetition over punctuated restagings has something to do with the nonlinear and contingent accumulation of history and the activity of reproduction—of day-to-day subsistence—of which the mother has been made into both the central producer and a symbol. What Spielrein retrieves in this scene is not just the paradox of the fact that "we psychically experience very little in the present" but also that the relations of reproduction in our present can only be understood through a restaging of dispossession through which the present finds its context.[5] In other words, the witch remains a charged and contemporary figure here because the girl's own condition of being, her own trajectory in life, will be lived out through a relation to the past that is repeated in the day-to-day configuration of labor, social relations, gendered shame, care work, and an unconscious memory of noncapitalist and non-, or at least less, patriarchal ways of living. In this sense, the witch is still a useful figure for our present because she is rooted in a past that moves forward through repetitions that are never quite the same.

This figure of the witch is a flash of history; it holds the sensational impression of experiences that are still alive because of their operative iteration through the gendered persistence of subsistence labors. It is also a superfluous figure; in excess of memory and as an extraneous detail of the mother-daughter relation, the witch stands out as an unanswered question in this set of associations. In a framework that crosses the Marxist with the psychoanalytic, we might say that it is an image of trauma, an origin, that remains structuring and has the potential for redemption through remembrance. If we take this as a primary principle of reading, not in order to pursue a hermeneutics of suspicion but because we know that certain histories can only be remembered in the dreamlike form of constellations, then we will already be indebted to a reading in which history begins in trauma, in which origins are not unified bodies but open wounds. Such accumulated experience, registered in discontinuous figures still needed in the present, is no mere source of absence but rather a vital resource for the present.

This approach through the unconscious as a site of accumulated constellations rather than successive memories offers a model for the historical vicissitudes of so-called primitive accumulation and the coordinates of the necessarily speculative connections to be drawn between Romanticism and present-day enclosures. The "origins" of capitalism in nonsuccessive repetitions that produce new asymmetrical hierarchies by drawing from existing differences has been one of the most difficult problems introduced by Marx's notion of so-called primitive accumulation. The possibility of a transmission that is nonidentical yet uncanny in its effects, as well as the creation of capitalist modes of production through noncapitalist relations, has proved quite resistant to analysis through narrativization. Often attempts to narrativize this process cannot help but fall back into a dialectics of rupture and continuity, and of contingent events that are assimilated into progressive time. As one critic puts it, a consequence of "any endeavor to narrativize the phenomenon of so-called primitive accumulation is that any attempt at its representation . . . must deal with both a specific, irreducible historical trauma and a structural repetition built into the horrific consistency with which 'accumulation by dispossession' subjects whole populations to abject vulnerability or death."[6] In other words, narrativization, which aims to represent, struggles to maintain both the difference and the repetition of a vast array of techniques of dispossession. This phrasing of accumulation by dispossession suggests that what exceeds the capacities of narrative is the uncanny simultaneity built into that process, a relation through which otherwise oppositional processes—specific, irreducible historical trauma and structural repetition—coincide in history, in the reproduction of means of subsistence and of capital. This illegibility has to do with the contiguity of origin and trauma, where both are routed through a force or eruption that exceeds successive memory and narrativization. Spielrein's daughter-mother-witch and its significance as an association of an overflowing past gives us a striking image of repetitions beyond the confines of succession and linearity. And it bears its own unconscious association with the remaking of subsistence we have tracked throughout this book, in the accumulations of dispossession that destroy, divide, and reorganize the noncapitalist activities that are effects of capitalism's constitutive trauma.

This is a mode of association not formed through habit or through an equilibrium between subject and world but one in which simultaneous affections and manifold experiences accumulate to the side of the subject. These associations have their roots, like a child, in need and its unmeasurable, relational nature that is targeted by the "entry of forces, their eruption" in the reproduction of capitalism.[7] And they provide histories that look nothing like linear narratives of either progress or decline. Indeed, it was the force of needs that gave associationist theories their explanatory power and proved too much for an ideal subject to contain. As Lorraine Daston describes it, the death blow to associationism came in Condillac's charge that "the pressure of needs and interests" was a more powerful force in understanding than the regularity of repeated experience. The other insuperable limit was "the illusions perpetrated by imagination." Paired together, the excess of needs and an "overwrought imagination" overflowed the explanatory capacities of that theory as far as a reasonable, predictable subject could go.[8] But it left an excess of material relations that fits neither into mechanistic nor strong Romanticist paradigms. The imbalance of need was there at the outset of associationism, however, in the repetition of rhetorical figure and scenes of subsistence that we have discussed. Such figural beginnings give us a different way to approach the imagination, not as autonomous from material needs but as conjoined with them from the outset. Needs are originally figural and in that sense can be neither absolutely bare nor separated from the vagaries of the imagination.

This is why associationism shows up as a genealogical weaving together of riots, dreams, and witchcraft, because needs and imagination conspire from the outset to be both more and less than the austerity of reason. This materiality of association is incapable of giving us a proper history, either of domination or resistance, but it does provide some tools for reading the fractured and improper history of an accumulation entwined with the demands of the everyday. It is through the flashes of history impressed in this material relation that the enclosure of mother-daughter-witch can be, in the weak and practical sense of struggle redeemed for a present from the narcotic mythologies of the past. Associationism's rootedness in the accumulation of such relations alongside the subject remains a valuable Romantic threshold for contemporary conversations about the potentiality of the past, especially of those pasts located structurally outside subject identifications, as well as the practices through which people refused such identities in favor of subaltern and antirepresentational relations.

There is a fraught immanence between figuration, the originary operations of capital accumulation, and the rhetorical methods of reading that have given Romanticism its relevance as a contemporary formation. Though not a relation of identity or causality, there is nonetheless an indispensable relation between the target of so-called primitive accumulation and the deviations that define a subsistence beyond historical scarcity. The entwinement of figure and dispossession is historical, but in such a way that demands a different reading of history than those often used to account for capitalism or enclosure in literary studies. What drives the Romanticism formed at the crux of dispossession and subsistence is not the immaterial, ahistorical surplus of the subject that Romantic ideology offers nor the immanent reserve of the subject's impossibility offered by certain deconstructive and more recent materialist turns in Romanticism. Of interest here are the simultaneity of capital's traumatic origins and the messy practice of living at its thresholds.

The figure of the constellation is apt here but requires that something first be said about its status within Romantic criticism. Whether glossed over or seriously engaged, references to this Benjaminian figure often leave to one side an analysis of history as the accumulated violence of capitalism and dissipate into an always available but never seized potentiality. Too often, the constellation is used to refer to a radical and alternative history that conflates the immanently material structure of history with its redemption. Most recently, the Romantic constellation has been described as a frame for a vague and dark unproductivity that is "immanent to itself" and permeates Romanticism.[9] Such versions of Benjamin's constellation render the leaps and fractures that are the matter of history as always available for discovery. What we risk in treating the constellation as such a purely radical force is forgetting that what is unproductive in the constellation is also meant to be a weapon and that what is unseen there is meant to point us to the struggle for remembrance. As Benjamin notes in "On the Concept of History," the essay most famous for its invocation of the constellation, there is a threat built into the flash of memory—namely, "the danger of becoming a tool of the ruling classes." In other words, the constellation does not have innate transformative value; rather, we must "strive anew to wrest tradition away from the conformism that is working to overpower it" if it is to remain of use rather than fading into a historical traditionalism that is by no means unique to historicist modes of reading.[10]

More often than not, the material accumulations of violence that made the constellation both a critical tool and a model of immanence for Benjamin are forgotten. Preferring a more abstract and infinite disruption of linearity as a positively tinged or radically enacting force, we have left another, crucial aspect of Benjamin's historical materialist work aside as if it were inconsequential to the power of constelled pasts and presents. We have often failed to take seriously that the potentiality of the constellation comes in the recovery of forms of struggle and memories of loss that are kept in those "most acute manifestations" of historical discontinuity.[11] Such memories are impressed at the crux of historical violence and unmeasurable experience. And there is no using a constellation without a reading of the forces through which their potentiality is sedimented in the memory of noncapitalist ways of living that remain vital and necessary in the present. It is with this danger in mind that this book has worked to locate potentiality in the repetitions of dispossession and in conditions that are always at risk of turning into the naturalized and neutralizing histories of intraclass divisions, racial and gendered identities that are transhistorically divided, and bourgeois property. It is at these impure, messy, and ultimately materialist intersections that we continue to find those recalcitrant ways of living that are needed in the present. Remembering the connections between present-day and Romantic-era struggles over subsistence and those necessarily noncapitalist means of survival and reproduction is a project that remains to be taken up. This is especially true if we are interested in wresting history away from ruling class traditions that are reinvented all the time, such as the reinvention of gossip, superstition, theft, spontaneity, and the many other examples shown throughout this book. Doing so will require returning to history as a problem in the sense that Benjamin presents it, one that is simultaneously weakly messianic and in constant danger of being lost to traditions that seek to anesthetize it. It is our task as critics now to catch up to those remembrances and learn how to find them today.

Spielrein's association of mother-daughter-witch offers a flash in which a "secret agreement" between the past and the present appears with Mary Robinson's lines and life, discussed in Chapter 2, which will also be useful in moving us toward possibilities of rhetorical reading in the present. Robinson strikes me as a figure, in the sense of coinciding oppositions, because of her ambivalent status as a subject through which to recover Romanticism under the sign of woman. Despite being part of the more general recovery work in British Romanticism, Robinson is entirely irrecoverable as a "good" subject, either for progressive or for critical ends. While she was at times an advocate of women's rights to education and intellectual equality, Robinson also writes in her auto/biography of the animosity she feels toward women. She clearly sides with Marie Antoinette and the aristocracy in the matter of the French Revolution, worrying that "the illiterate, unsteady, factious multitude, [are] actuated by principles of interest and too often led on by private resentment, or public temerity, to the commission of crimes too horrible to contemplate."[12] And Robinson's infantilization of and identification with Black domestic workers displays the kind of racializing empathy of which Saidiya Hartman has written at length.[13] As a subject, we can categorize her at best as a reactionary formed in the oscillating fortunes of the bourgeois merchant class, as a white woman who was able to make some kind of a living in a developing industry of sympathy for white women. The daughter of a declined and dispossessed "respectable family" in Ireland on her mother's side and of an emergent bourgeois class of merchants on her father's side, Robinson was a notorious celebrity and consort by the age of twenty-two, who financially supported two men through her work in the theater and through poetry and editorial work; she died at forty-three, indebted and in poverty.

Robinson is thus a blemished subject for the purposes of representation aimed at recuperating a quasi-universal Woman in the Romantic period. She is also a source of dream documents that provide a language of surplus experience that recalls the dispossessed history of subsistence relations. I will approach Robinson's writing here as a Spielreinian scene in which the past is encoded in immediate sensations and subsistence appears in the doubled condition of gendered vulnerability (motherhood) and its refusal (witch). In her auto/biography, Robinson leads us further into the entanglement of capital accumulation and the remaking of subsistence relations through the figuration of three women who appear at the cross section of gendered labor, a colonial debt machine, and the persistence of anticapitalist ways of life. Robinson's auto/biography, begun by her but edited and completed by her daughter, is a kind of dream document, a text that cannot help but attest to the coincidence of the reproduction of capital and the social in the late eighteenth century. In it, Robinson's life, that of her mother, and that of her beloved and abjectified instructor are woven together through repetitions of abandonment and vulnerability, and through the still-ongoing past of dispossession, speculation, colonialism, and acceptable forms of dependency. It is a dream space caught up in dislocations that can be neither collapsed nor separated.

Three women become sites of a figural repetition—Robinson's mother, Robinson, and Robinson's teacher—of the expansion of a debt-based economy, the destruction of former communal relations of care, and the internalized and reproduced shame of vulnerability. In the auto/biography, we hear how Robinson's father loses the family's home and ruins their financial security after gambling on a speculative land grab in so-called Canada. The success of this debt scheme depended upon the dispossession and enslavement of native peoples, and its failure meant the abandonment of Robinson's mother by her father and all the later "accumulated vicissitudes" of their lives.[14] Robinson depicts this as a scene during which "a potent witchery possessed his [Robinson's father's] brain, and all the persuasive powers of reason shrunk before its magic."[15] Here the witchery that possesses Robinson's father is not that cast by an overly sexualized or demonically depicted woman but the fetishized effect of unpaid, expropriated labor transformed into a magical source of wealth that comes from nowhere and is simply waiting to be discovered. The speculation that supported this failed colonial endeavor unleashes the "epocha [that] date[s] the sorrow of my family" as a series of debt-ridden vulnerabilities that structure Robinson's life.[16] Later, her father absent and her mother desperate after the severe illness of two of her children, Robinson is married by her mother her at the age of sixteen to a Mr. Robinson. "Only three months before I became a wife I had dressed a doll," Robinson tells us.[17] Her performance as a mother in that scene of doll-dressing is also repeated throughout Robinson's life, as she becomes responsible for taking care of a family constantly indebted by her husband's dreams of wealth. Robinson's entire auto/biography develops under the sign of speculation that is only possible because of repeated cycles of dispossession in Ireland, England, and America. And one of its structural requirements is the routine exposure of women to abandonment and violence, which also imposes the demands of care and labor in reproducing the family. The third reenactment of this figure and its "accumulated vicissitudes" comes in the peripheral story of Robinson's beloved instructor, Meribah Lorrington, at her school in Chelsea. Mrs. Lorrington was "an extraordinary woman" who "delight[ed] in the task of instructing" Robinson and from whom she declares she learned all she ever knew, but who also had a deep and abiding addiction to opium.[18] Mrs. Lorrington returns to the story later, at the extreme end of the continuum on which Robinson and her mother also reside, wandering in front of their home in a "deplorable situation," "filthy" and "almost naked."[19] Robinson cares for Meribah that night and gives her the little money she has but later learns that she has died in a Chelsea workhouse in a "premature decay, brought on by the indulgence of her propensity to intoxication."[20] Mrs. Lorrington's failure at self-regulation becomes a marker of both difference and similarity with Robinson, who by virtue of writing her own story displays more capacity for self-discipline but at the same time writes her own story in an attempt to salvage her reputation as a fallen and sexually deviant woman. While superficially juxtaposed as good mother, smeared mother, and fallen mother, these figures are organized in the auto/biography in close proximity to one another and differentially caught within the shared conditions of neglect, vulnerability, and excessive visibility. Along with mother, daughter, and witch, Robinson adds teacher and addict to Spielrein's constellation.

Robinson's own "deplorable situation" comes via her work in the theater, where she is employed out of long-deferred desire as well as desperation in the face of her need to pay off her husband's debts. The theater also serves as the first scene of encounter with the Prince of Wales, for whom she ultimately leaves this source of subsistence after promises of financial security from him that are never to be fulfilled. It is in the theater that Robinson, for a short while, both procures the means of subsistence for her family and exposes the vulnerability of her own "deplorable situation." Humiliating her father in the same way her mother had, when the latter opened a school to provide financial support, Robinson's place on the stage is one scene of that "leap from the wings to the center stage" of so-called primitive accumulation.[21] A related leap finds Spielrein's witch in the case files of Erasmus Darwin, which we have already reviewed in Chapter 3. He too uses the trope of the stage to tell of a woman dispossessed and without adequate means of subsistence who appears "like a witch on the stage" when she lifts some wood from the local farmer's property.[22] This example, of course, is the one that inspires Wordsworth's "Goody Blake and Harry Gill." This leap between Robinson's scenes and Darwin's anonymous "witch" is associated through the emergence of capitalism in its own improper history, holding these two women together in the separability of enclosure. Not enclosed within the scenography of self-representation that makes a subject possible, both appear more as side stories or digressions—either desperate or primitive, improper or ignorant, women.[23] The scene in which these figures are staged is that of capital's continual emergence, which does not generate straightforward connections or proper subjects but instead leaves a trace of the centrality of subsistence through substitutions, coincidences, displacements, and leaps of a figural nature. This association moves us away from Robinson's status as an individual subject who gained celebrity, as well as infamy, through the theater and points instead to the reverberations of a more dispersed and decentralized scene of others living in the "deplorable situation" of differential dispossessions, finding ways of living that fit neither the family nor its metonymic relation to the state. This leap from Robinson to Darwin constellates a loose multitude of women who do not fit into the schema of representation but do provide a series of associations through the work of reproduction. As an improper means of reproduction that accords with other, often criminalized means of reproduction, the stage becomes a site that we can follow to the expansive margins, peripheries, and exogeneities that constituted the English nation at the time. Emerging through layers of sedimentation constrained by the violent demands of making, hiding, punishing, and killing a labor force and its superfluous needs, these figures of reproduction signal our need for messier, nonbinaristic readings of the coupling of subsistence and accumulation. They also remind us of the ongoing need to understand the contours of violence that make such figures useful for the study of struggle and survival against it.

Mother. Daughter. Doll. Teacher. Witch. Addict. While the available archive of those living against or outside the emergent state/empire is minimal, these kinds of association provide layers of sedimentation that can be followed to a dispossessed Romanticism. We do know of certain writers in the emergent lumpenproletariat of the vagrant and the underemployed, former slaves, and those who moved between these categories, a crucial assemblage that was necessarily global, immigrant, and diasporic. Written work from this undercommons is sparse, but this is all the more reason for developing the practice of close reading that follows dispossessed histories. Each chapter of this book has tried to show the excessive presence of bodies, relations, and movements that were not just remnants of a premodern or feudal era but already at the threshold of what one critic calls the "not yet fully realized and yet already mutilated project of the nation state."[24] The unnamed populations that understand food riots as a kind of divine violence against a monarchical monopoly of mythic violence, the numerous bodies of those who prefer reappropriation to the disciplining of their labor for exploitative ends, the manifold hands that compose notes turning subsistence into an eschatological matter, those differential relations of vulnerability and care experienced by women and surplus populations, the enclosures of constitutive exclusions that also provide the conditions of survival for others, and the coincidences through which spatial elsewheres provide the constellations of global interrelation—these relations do not transcend the nation-state or capitalist relations. To borrow from Spielrein, these are "allegories . . . that seek analogues in the present,"[25] allegories not only of unconscious processes at work but also of the passage of historical processes through which certain figures become conduits and reservoirs of the unconscious, of the accumulated experiences that overflow the immediate. Read alongside one another, as figures ask to be read, this composite mother-daughter-witch-teacher-addict holds together multiple temporalities with the co-constitution of violences and endurances, of surplus and poverty.

But in what associations with the present do we find such analogues? We find them in the associations that sediment around dispossession in its ongoing and heterogeneous modes. Such analogues will necessarily be found at the limits of the state and its reiteration of authority through the erasure of the direct violence of originary accumulation. As Brian Whitener writes, "liberalism, whether in its imperial or democratic formulations, has a compulsion to hide the violence on which its social order depends. Capitalism requires violence and coercion, and liberalism is at pains to distract from, diminish, and deflect the centrality of capitalist violence and the state violence needed to sustain accumulation and impose order."[26] A certain tendency of Romantic literary criticism has been to look for ways to inhabit the immanent paradoxes created by the nation-state and citizen, orienting toward a politics of expansive inclusion or an investment in failure that provides only a very abstract sense of living at the thresholds. For far too long the rhetorical attunement of Romantic readers has been on the failures and (im)possibilities built into a modernity defined by the subsumption of liberal states and represented subjects. Such repetitions have led to the critical presumption that there was nothing of value left outside such states and that the failures of liberal governance could only be changed by an expansion of its structures. These tendencies, shared by historicist and theoretical Romanticisms alike, produce the sense that there are no ongoing enclosures in which liberal states continue to depend upon the simultaneous reproduction and destruction of noncapitalist ways of living and practices that are found globally at different scales and intensities. In contrast, this book approaches Romanticism as significant for the ways in which the destruction and remaking of subsistence involves, but is by no means accounted for by, the liberal constructs of the human, cosmopolitanism, the subject, and democratic representation.

A Romanticism useful for living today will be rooted in the work of remembering the many in ways in which the expropriation and exogenization of noncapitalist means of subsistence can be followed into the present. Romanticism is a good tool for creative recollection that enables our refusal to grant pure origins or identity to enclosures in favor of a motley susceptibility to indigence, vagrancy, superstition, nonequivalent exchange, riots, affectability, and uncountable needs and the overwrought imagination that accompanies them.

Here Robinson's status as a figure both at the center and to the side of the state-building requirements of capital suggests surprising likenesses and connections between Romanticism and present-day global struggles over subsistence. Such a figure will necessarily be messy and enmeshed. She will not be extricated from the colonial project that made a family's wealth and then ruined it; her family's ability to live for long periods of time by accumulating debt will be entwined with the enclosures and dispossessions that opened up new forms of speculative accumulation that fueled colonial projects; and her own personal exhaustion, misery, and poverty will not be separable from the colonial and capitalist endeavors that made England a state with a global composition of industrial and enslaved workers. But the dreamlike arrangement through which this figure casts her own life as a site compressed by dispossession and impressed by coincident ways of living is useful precisely because of its impure and enmeshed making. It embodies layers of sedimentation that are possible to follow if we are willing to abandon an investment in recuperating subjects and instead ask how lives at the thresholds of state and capital were lived. If we follow the constellation of mother, daughter, witch, teacher, and addict she sets up, we will find passageways to other threshold spaces of reproduction that travel alongside but are necessarily kept in a place of strategic subjection within the processes of capital accumulation.

Such spaces, what Foucault calls "the concrete body of a development, with its moments of intensity, its lapses, its extended periods of feverish agitation, its fainting spells," offers coordinates for remembering the differential dispossessions that link Romanticism with the present.[27] Ways of living that are contiguous to the flows of capital and subject to enclosures of land, labor, and relations are compressed at the center and periphery, as both the day-to-day practices of subsistence and the manifold labors of social reproduction. Robinson, her mother, her teacher, and an old wood thief are figures of a dispossession in its ongoing mode and the simultaneous reproduction of heterogeneous ways of improper reproduction. Reading backward and forward, we can begin to construct the constellations that are generated by dispossession and the sedimentation of certain figures that emerge and are reproduced by that imprecise schema of so-called primitive accumulation, in which noncapitalist means of subsistence are always at the front line of the violences of capital accumulation.

The simultaneities that have been tracked here specifically and in the book more generally find creative, Spielreinian associations with conditions of global indebtedness, state violence, and noncapitalist means of subsistence, as well as distinctive ways of living at that central threshold of state and capital in the contemporary cases of Nigeria, Rojava, and Palestine. Forming flashes with Romanticism that are significant in both their similarities and their differences, these examples provide a sketch of possible ways to move in a globally concerned Romanticism, in tandem with excellent work already ongoing in the interventions of Indigenous and Black studies. In keeping with the methodology exemplified in this book, these layers of sedimentation are nonhistorical, if we define the historical through continuity, succession, and/or movements that progress toward self-representation. Instead, they are leaps made through unsettling substitutions, resonances, and displacements created by the interplay of so-called primitive accumulation and remade means of subsistence.

As already suggested, the figure of the mother is an unstable pivot point between the reproduction of the state and capital as well as a limit to them because of the necessarily abject position that reproductive and domestic labor hold in systems of wages or citizenship: "she plays the role of assimilation and 'betrays' the community while also remaining inassimilable by the state, capitalism, and patriarchy."[28] The figure of the mother is a distinctly nondialectical one that is central to the possibility of a different world and to the reproduction of the present one. According to Nazan Üstündağ, the mother has to be defeated in her role as a reproducer of docile subjects and of the family, both extensions of the state; but her constitutive exclusion from state institutions and development projects means that she remains a repository of language, memories, and histories that cannot be expunged from that place of exclusion. Üstündağ writes in the context of the Kurdish struggle for autonomy and survival in Rojava, against both the Islamic State and Turkey. The Kurds, as Bülent Kücük and Ceren Özselçuk write, are "the world's largest stateless people, dispersed across four nation-states," and in their struggle to maintain autonomous and democratic control of the northeastern region's autonomy, Rojava has become "a metaphor for liberation (especially women's liberation)."[29] Üstündağ understands the mother as a figure that holds multiple contradictory positions and possibilities together at the same time. She is at once a subject of the state, an archive of subaltern memories, and the threshold for the guerilla revolutionary; she is an accumulation of the continuous discontinuities that enable the production of subjects. As such, her unassimilability is not a pure ontological potentiality but a potential resource for struggle that is developed at the crux of dispossession and reproduction. The figure of the mother is significant for Üstündağ precisely because she sits outside any binaristic telling of the state and capital. Because of her figural position, the mother is only outside in a relational way, doing the work of reproduction that has been made exogenous to the state because it was, at some point, a resource of insurgency. Such a figure creates possibilities for other ways of living if the violence that has gone into making reproduction into a resource of state violence can be turned against it.

This status of constitutive exclusion, which is necessary and productive for those structures, is a shifting and recombinatory position accumulated over a disjointed and imprecise process of so-called primitive accumulation that takes place both inside and outside capital accumulation through state violence. Üstündağ's point, however, is not only, perhaps not even mostly, a critical one; rather, her reading of the mother as a figure is a simultaneously genealogical and strategic one, in which the most extreme coincidences of difference become the most significant sites of accumulated potentiality. This is not quite the same thing as a recuperative reading of the figure of the mother, in which it is in the reading that recuperation occurs, nor is it straightforwardly intersectional, in the sense that vast amounts of time and the shifting constructions of exclusion come into view here and disrupt stable claims of identities that intersect in their autonomy. Rather, this is a rhetorically charged reading of the mother that raises the messy and unresolved question of how to make these shifted and shifting associations useful, such that the simultaneous positions of the mother become active threshold spaces, spaces in which the disciplinary function of the mother can be "defeated." For Üstündağ, the simultaneities of the mother are transformed—not canceled out—most concretely in the guerilla fighter, who is both hidden and pervasive in Kurdish life and who "unleashes violence, destruction, sadness, longing, worry, pride, and love all at once." She develops the conditions in which the dispossession of "the means of production, reproduction, knowledge, and defense" is transformed into new collective practices against the interpenetration of patriarchy and the modern state.[30] Joining a significant body of work on the psychic necessity of freedom struggles that makes a break with struggles aimed primarily at state recognition and inclusion, Üstündağ's association of mother and guerilla further extends and complicates that break through the necessity of subsistence and day-to-day reproduction in such struggles. This coincidence undercuts the fantasy of a pure break from the material deviations and entanglements that make possible the continuation of any community that carries on such a struggle.

Üstündağ's discussion of the figure of the mother and the guerilla is one example of the potential ways of wandering available to Romanticists if our focus is shifted from the strong historical fixity of the past and the purely linguistic concern with the figural to the genealogies that are waiting to be constructed, rigorously, through what Benjamin called the working class's hatred, which could be enflamed by the memory of "enslaved ancestors" in the present.[31] Any written accounts of eighteenth-century and Romantic-era guerilla fighters (wood thieves, female food rioters, slaves, maroons, insurrectionary workers) will necessarily remain few and far between, more often than not given in secondhand accounts of the kind we see in state reports on urban and colonial communities. Nonetheless, we can make use of the paradox Üstündağ isolates in present-day Rojava to reflect back on the tense relations construed in the figures of mothers in texts such as Robinson's auto/biography, the need to turn to other sources and speculations to "defeat" the disciplining mother, as well as to the horizon of what could not be written there. The association between Rojava and Romanticism may seem like a leap, and it is: a leap in keeping with the formation through which those constitutively excluded from history remain central to the production of a modernity that is quite long in duration. This constellation of figures that we can follow through the simultaneities held together in the mother point us in the direction of a politics of survival that has been through as many iterations as have the processes of dispossession that destroy means of survival.

Locating such constellations will entail reading for the oscillations between day-to-day reproduction and its place in the globality of capital accumulation. In her recently published "Nigerian Fragments," notes and journals written during her time in exile teaching in Nigeria, anticapitalist and feminist theorist Silvia Federici extends her writing on the European witch hunts to the financialized restructuring of the postcolonial nation-state through the intimacy between gendered violence and national debt. Reading Federici's own exhaustion brought on by the demands of daily reproduction in a context where there is never enough and what seem like "petty victories" provide "a true sense of social accomplishment" makes Robinson's auto/biography feel all the more contemporary. One can almost imagine Robinson, partially paralyzed toward the end of her life and working feverishly as poetry editor for the *Morning Chronicle* to make ends meet, writing with some relief that she has finally procured "matches and oranges, key to my reproduction because they mean cigarettes and drink. By the time I have assembled all the basics for my sustenance, my soul has left, my brain is sleepy, not to mention my legs, and my funguses are thriving."[32]

Federici pairs these reflections on her physiological limits and expenditures with an on-the-ground analysis of the disciplining effects of national debt on women. These glimpses into day-to-day reproduction shift back and forth, with reflections on informal labor markets populated primarily by women, the effects of the postcolonial state debt that induces the intensified criminalization and demonization of women, and the ongoing destruction of communal practices through their interpenetration with capital. These moments refract an uncanny sensibility of social divisions and relations that accumulate from the past and are remade over and over again in the conversion of heterogeneous means of subsistence into proper histories of origins and the deserving, working subjects that women are meant to reproduce. The function of gendered vulnerability and dependency as a buffer to absorb the shocks of capitalist-driven indebtedness is repeated in Robinson's and Federici's texts in a way that eludes narrative. The gendered figures associated here carry the fraught entwinement of what is beyond capital's relations of equivalence and the spaces that absorb nonequivalent circulations. Constellating Italy, New York, and Nigeria in Federici's own life, these spaces find themselves in strange simultaneity with the England, Ireland, Wales, and Canada of Robinson's auto/biography.

The condition of being caught in social reproduction's inseparability from capital's colonial drives, which are fueled by enclosures and speculation and secured by debt and inconstant means of subsistence, is new neither for populations that suffer the most brutal force of dispossession nor for those who hover in the mediated field of commodified labor. That condition is, rather, the messy materiality of many of our everyday lives of teaching, writing, researching, paying bills, and caring for kin and family, and of our own superfluous needs, some of which I hope are uncannily felt in the texts constellated here. Robinson, too, was a member of a heterogeneous mix of debt-reliant, inconsistently employed workers who fall in and out of poverty. Her auto/biography documents the effects and reiterations of enclosure and the massive speculative economy that opened up to launch a capitalist empire through a figural arrangement of women and the largely obscured demands of noncapitalist means of subsistence at the threshold of development. Debt is both an instrument of colonial expansion and a means of subsistence for those fluctuating needs for which capital refuses to bear the costs. In both Robinson and Federici, we can see the way in which women come to bear that cost and find themselves at the exogenous center of a society organized around exchange. This intersection of debt as a mechanism of accumulation and means of survival with gender difference as a mechanism of accumulation and means of survival develops as one crux of the so-called primitive nature of capital accumulation.

The figures such accumulation weaves together and holds for the present provide a lesson in reading the repetitions of dispossession in a way that cannot be fixed to a continuous history. Instead of continuity, we find an accumulation of experiences that overflow the present, making pure repetition impossible as a tool of domination. Because dispossession is a process that works on ways of living, it is necessarily an imprecise schema, in which association remains open, punctuated, and nonidentical. Indeed, seeing an undifferentiated repetition would mean foreclosing the possibility of reading here in favor of securing a precise and proper schema of the universal subject of woman as a source of reproduction that is given or originary. If we fail to read these repetitions as never identical and always figural ways in which life is remade outside universal equivalence, we will only repeat the myth of origins that erases the originary violence of dispossession that shatters any such universality. Instead of reproducing this bourgeois myth through which Marx first taught us about so-called primitive accumulation, our task as readers is to follow associations through the noncontinuous, nonidentical accumulations of noncapitalist ways of living that such a myth seeks to cover over.

Romanticism here is unreadable without the relations of dispossession, divisions of labor, and structural effects of debt that bring past and present together in a way that dispels essence but exhibits the "substitutions, displacements, disguised conquests, and systematic reversals" that render history not just as genealogical but also rhetorical.[33] These figures of mother-daughter-witch do not offer an identity that has been constructed over centuries, in which gender becomes the new metaphysics of labor, but rather constitute a set of associations made in the ongoing remaking of subsistence within and alongside capital accumulation. A rhetorical reading of dispossession necessarily centers questions of property and self-possession in literary studies, not only to see how a European subject "behave[s] in a potentially violent and authoritarian way" because "this is the only way it can constitute its own existence," but also to look for the pressure of needs and interests that accumulate all around it.[34] At these heterogeneous points of association covered up by the authoritarianism of privative identity we will find other ways of living in the present. It is in this sense that I understand Fred Moten's use of dispossession, not simply as a term for the historic event of theft of what was originally possessed but also as a continual reminder of a constitutive superfluity of relations that comes in advance and continues to circulate vagrantly through and around possession.[35]

Rojava and Nigeria, Üstündağ and Federici, come into relation with Romanticism in their figuration of the coincident accumulations of gendered reproduction that encompass exhaustion, destruction, discipline, love, and memory. This Romanticism produces such figures as if in a dream, where Robinson's exhausted body shares a space with Federici's exhausted body, which shares a space with Üstündağ's defeated mother-turned-guerilla. While never sharing an identity, which dreams disrupt, such a coincidence would hold together the repetitions of so-called primitive accumulation and hold open the reiterations of subsistence through which these figures remain in association today. This dream analysis would necessarily undo the historical periodization of Romanticism as a bounded literary period while opening it up to the nonequivalent relations through which people continue to subsist in ways that are not originary to but have emerged with capitalism. These reverberations can become the terms for a Romanticism formed around "decentered, lateral connections" that were always already global instead of "those formed around a teleology of origin/return" that remain confined to the nation-state.[36]

Following accumulation by dispossession as it emerges through such figures raises the question of whether there can be a proper site of study in Romanticism as it begins in dispossession. Our passage from Robinson to Üstündağ to Federici holds together a repetition without sameness that hinges on the persistence and remaking of creative modes of subsistence. If dispossession is central to our present, then we may also have to ask if there is anything delimitable about Romanticism. If there is not, Romanticism would be caught in the reemergence, again and again, of dispossessions aimed at destroying noncapitalist means of subsistence and in which they are revised as contemporary practices in the present. Such a Romanticism would not be a specific body of texts or a historical period but a way of reading and study that dispossesses us of the enclosures that separate struggles over subsistence from literature and language.

In recent years, however, literary studies scholars have proven to be largely unprepared for such a task, often preferring to reproduce a metaphysics of proper subjects and statist study. Notwithstanding the antiracist work being done by students and workers around the Black Lives Matter movement, constitutive exclusions of those whose beginnings continue to dispossess historical origins remain the limit point of the cynical expropriation of identity in higher education.[37] In the current instrumentalization of identity politics, the discipline of literary studies continues to demand historically continuous narratives and proper subjects of representation in order for difference to matter. The question of Palestine is particularly significant here, given the ongoing refusal of literary and language scholars in the Modern Language Association (MLA) to respond to the Palestinian call for an academic and political boycott of Israel. In this refusal there was also a failure of reading, a failure to follow the genealogy of rhetoric and subsistence that I have called Romanticism throughout this book. In 2017, this demand and its enclosures became eminently visible in literary studies in the MLA's vote at its delegate assembly that year to "refrain from endorsing the [Palestinian Campaign for the Academic and Cultural] boycott" of Israel on the basis that "it contradicts the MLA's purpose to promote teaching and research on language and literature."[38] The Palestinian Campaign for the Academic and Cultural Boycott of Israel is a nonviolent tactic to end Israeli settler colonialism in Palestine; it is modeled on the use of boycotts during the South African anti-apartheid struggles.[39] It strategically uses Israel's need for US cultural and academic institutions to recognize Israel as a liberal democracy against it and works to educate educators on the reality of the colonial conditions under which Palestinians learn, study, speak, and live.

Jeffrey Sacks has offered a stunning analysis of the MLA vote as a failure of reading, if by this term we are referring to a practice that "disorganizes sanctioned notions of sense, relation, and being." The vote is a matter of reading because reading demands that we call into question the naturalized and neutralized distinctions between insides and outsides, history and figure, that we have been articulating above. It is only as a failure of reading, together with the reinstitution of mythically preexisting borders, that "the call for the boycott of Israeli academic institutions" appeared to "come to the MLA from an *outside*," as an invasion of the proper "inheritance" of literature and language. In a phrasing that emphasizes the constitutive dispossession of origins that reading entails, Sacks writes that the resistance to the boycott of Israel was, in fact, "a resistance to the foundation of illegibility, and the ruptured and split foundation (for example, inside/outside), of what we continue to call 'literature.'"[40] In other words, separating the Palestinian call for an academic and cultural boycott from an unquestionable category of language and literature was a decision to preserve the enclosure of literature rather than pursue the Benjaminian task of reading as a "striv[ing] anew to wrest tradition away from the conformism that is working to overpower it."[41] In voting against the academic and cultural boycott on the basis that it had no relation to language and literature, the largest body of humanities scholars in so-called North America disavowed the ongoing nature of dispossession that we have been tracking here as Romanticism. In contrast to a continued reading of the substitutions, coincidences, anachronisms, and so forth that make Romanticism a problem of and for the present, the vote reaffirmed dispossession as a purely historical problem whose only proper ground is a foreclosed past.

This vote cannot be separated from the arguments and methods of reading developed in this book. Beyond this analysis of the MLA resolution as an endorsement of the resistance to reading, we should also see it as a resistance to an understanding of the continuation of a Romanticism in which dispossession and enclosure are not yet finished with remaking the globe.[42] In this sense, it was a decision in favor of the enclosure of subjects who can be represented by states and against the dispossession of subjects through which the present can be constelled with Romanticism in the first place. What Edward Said referred to as the "question of Palestine" necessarily brings our practice of reading into a crisis in which we must decide whether dispossession is only of the past or whether it continues to require reading. It is a matter of ongoing land and resource dispossession, to be sure; but it is also a matter of the ongoing reproduction of figures upon which dispossession depends: it is a living archive of creative modes of collective endurance and of the insecure and securitized statist claims of origins. As many Palestinians have always declared and as scholars of Palestine are now actively remembering, Palestine is a space beyond borders and as such is a question of reading. As Hamid Dabashi puts it, "'Palestine beyond borders' may be a new theoretical speculation, but it has been a time-honored practice from the very conception of Palestinian struggle."[43] We might also say, then, that Palestine beyond borders is a call to continue reading by making a life on a "ruptured and split foundation." The practice of making a life on such foundations is simultaneously a practice of subsistence and one of reading, in the refusal of myths that cover over the violence of the secure origins of the past. Palestine is crucial to a genealogy of subsistence that is inseparable from the figural, in which struggles over survival are always too minimal and always too much in relation to insides and outsides, borders, and so-called equivalent exchanges. Palestinian struggles stand as a powerful inheritor of a Romanticism that would move beyond the nation-state as the paradigm of modernity and encounter forms of collective living that are decentered, lateral, contiguous, and coinciding.

The refrain of Palestine beyond borders is, then, also a call to remember and read noncapitalist, nonstatist forms of survival as they persisted, were destroyed, and were remade in the spaces now known as England, the Caribbean West Indies, Ireland, Wales, Nicaragua, Canada, the United States, Australia, New Zealand, Guyana, Sierra Leone, South Africa, and India during the Romantic period. While we have tended to read those forms through the containment of and elimination by the nation-state, recent work on Palestine that understands indigeneity and collective identity as established through "bottom-up and nonheroic daily resistance" to "dislocation and depopulation" presents another possible perspective on the subsistence associations that might be made in a global Romanticism.[44] Indeed, it may be the case that these more figural assessments of material struggles in Palestine provide a way for us to begin reworking Romanticism by approaching the dispossession of identity without forgetting that concrete heterogeneities are forged through "constantly asymmetrical relations of power" that condition the figures that must be struggled over in the present. This would mean, of course, respatializing collective identities outside the frame of the state and beginning to locate them instead in the speculative ways that Robert Wedderburn does when he addresses the urban, multiracial lumpenproletariat in London and enslaved people in Jamaica simultaneously. Palestinian struggles are rooted in dispossession and enclosure, creating a constelled entry point with Romanticism and possibilities for understanding transmission—poetic, political, and otherwise—that works backward and forward at the same time. These leaps can be followed through the uncanny repetition of so-called primitive accumulation, allowing us to grapple with relations formed through heterogeneous beginnings rather than homogeneous origins, providing a much-needed memory of an Romanticism inhabited by Robinson, Robert Wedderburn, Thomas Spence, Mary Prince, and others rather than by always already naturalized or yet-to-be citizens. The active, grounded work going on in Palestine offers a place from which to chart such constellations with Romanticism outside the frame of the nation while also demanding that we remain rooted in that Benjaminian sense of struggle over history and the ever-present risk of its becoming a weapon that securitizes the past.

In these rhetorically ruptured foundations of subsistence, "subaltern class memories" that have been pushed out of nationalist narratives can be remembered, enabling a creative practice of indigeneity forged over the time of survival and resistance.[45] As Ruba Salih and Sophie Richter-Devroe have suggested, the current conditions of Palestine have reactivated such remembrance.[46] Thus, the question of Palestine opens up the possibility of remembering a Romanticism rooted in nonidentical but relational ways of living. Constellations such as these that can be unfolded and constructed here are not identifiable with the mechanisms of representation that tend to function as the telos of literary criticism. They are simultaneously beyond and below, in excess of and too minimal to be put to work for representational ends.

As Ann Laura Stoler has argued, we cannot understand colonialism as a project either in the past or the present without attending to the question of Palestine, because the forms of settler colonialism there make visible the use of camps, surveillance, and securitization that have been neglected in more hegemonic accounts of colonialism.[47] This argument provides a powerful framework by means of which to refocus Romanticism around histories that are woven throughout this book, such as the reliance on transportation in the project of settler colonialism, the surveilling of immigrants by the Home Office in London, the inauguration of prisons for slaves in the West Indies during slavery, and numerous other examples that provide new contexts through which to study Romanticism. But we also cannot understand the concepts of most concern to rhetorical readers of Romanticism without these global coincidences that require engagement with Palestine. Attention to those struggles over survival that were and continue to be formed in the emergence of the Israeli state, which Hamid Dibashi describes as the most direct effect of European settler colonialism, can help us understand something about struggles over survival in the past, struggles that necessarily have connections with the present if we begin from a global perspective rooted in noncapitalist modes of subsistence. The question of Palestine has revitalized the potentiality of a collectivity formed by refugees, exiles, and immigrants, a formation with transient and heterogeneous roots in its beginning. If we want to do more than rehearse the ideology of the nation-state as the end of history or reproduce the failures of the liberal subject as the horizon of possibility, then the present-day practices of survival by Palestinians need to take a more central place in our thinking about Romanticism.

In this sense, the current struggle for Palestinian survival is deeply continuous with a Romanticism concerned with the figurality and nonlinearity of history. These associated spaces, brought together through iterations of dispossession, are flashes of an ongoing war against subsistence that builds on previous wars and relies on preexisting social relations to emerge anew. These various iterations of dispossession do not lend themselves to national identities, but they can encourage us to look for those "subaltern class memories" that are forced out of nationalist narratives. Romanticism cannot have relevance if we only engage with colonialism and the accumulation of capital in events locked away in the past and kept in that place by our own writing and positions in the present. A practice and study more attuned to the continuous discontinuity of so-called primitive accumulation will be necessary to a Romanticism that resists falling back into a discourse of subjects and representation that can only reaffirm nation-states and their subjects, and that deems certain movements against state-sanctioned dispossessions legible and others as unimaginable. Indeed, only by evading legibility and continually undoing the ground or origin of Romanticism will we be able to draw meaningful connections between it and the present, through that "which gives and takes away the given in and as differentiation without beginning or end."[48] Recent articulations of the Palestinian struggle as a struggle over survival and subsistence, and not through the state-based language of recognition or sovereignty, provide an important site by which to revisit the bodies, movements, and potentialities of a Romanticism to the side of the subject.[49]

We must, of course, remain vigilant against falling into the trap of treating Palestine as "a theoretical proposition," in which its history becomes an expropriated resource for the renewal of a Romantic scholarly imagination. But we *can* say that Palestine is a rhetorical matter in the terms this book has offered. Following the affiliation between subsistence and rhetoric throughout Romanticism means that rhetoric takes on a history of struggle and that subsistence is always more than a premodern way of life that sits outside reading and language. For this reason the MLA resolution is an appropriate way to conclude this book, because it holds together the ways in which dispossession requires the repeated affirmation of origin myths such as the state while also demonstrating that subsistence and endurance will always require a struggle over figural ways of living. Such are the relations that the question of Palestine beyond the nation-state poses, a question that, if we let it, will find roots in a Romantic coincidence of needs and imagination.

The way of rhetorical reading I have begun developing in this coda opens Romanticism up as a "Red Round Globe Burning Hot," the figure Peter Linebaugh has recently recalled from William Blake.[50] In the shocking contemporaneity of that figure, where global warming and burning police cars are both conjured, it becomes very clear that subsistence is far more than a historically confined mode of production through which bare needs are satisfied.[51] Subsistence has always been a global coincidence of ways of living that are illegible within conventional histories of equivalent exchange and through representable subjects. Through the protopsychoanalytic language of associationism, we might begin to think more about the nonhistoricist correspondences of means of subsistence in the spaces of the working-class home, the debate club, the theater, the debtor's prison, the transportation ship, the slave ship, the maroon colony, and the provision ground. The possibility of memories embedded in the peripheries of association seems to me to suggest an exciting genealogy of relations composed otherwise than as identities in and beyond the Romantic period. If we consider such relations as they scale up from instances of sensation to entire social processes of reproduction, then we might have an entirely different idea of our Romantic archive, as an archive of both pasts and presents. In other words, alongside the important work of recovery and renarrativization that has taken place in Romanticism, a more rhetorically oriented study of Romanticism makes possible the locating and creation of alliances with less chronologically driven modes of dispossession—including the dispossessions of identity mobilized by the nonstatist and subsistence-based desires of present-day mothers, daughters, teachers, guerillas, and witches.

Notes

Introduction

1. See Brigette Keegan, *British Labouring-Class Nature Poetry: 1730–1837* (London: Palgrave Macmillan, 2008), 10–36; Helen Pownell, "Syntax and World-View in John Clare's Fen Poems," *John Clare Society* 34 (2015): 36–49; Jonathan Bate, *Romantic Ecology: Wordsworth and the Environmental Tradition*, 2nd ed. (Abingdon, UK: Routledge, 2013), 56–57; Anne Janowitz, *Lyric and Labour in the Romantic Tradition* (Cambridge: Cambridge University Press, 1998), 71–79; David Simpson, *Wordsworth, Commodification and Social Concern: The Poetics of Modernity* (Cambridge: Cambridge University Press, 2009), 18–21; and Celeste Langan, *Romantic Vagrancy: Wordsworth and the Simulation of Freedom* (Cambridge: Cambridge University Press, 1995), 11. For a fuller treatment of enclosure beyond such contextual reference, see Carolyn Lesjack, "1750 to the Present: Acts of Enclosure and Their Afterlife," *BRANCH: Britain, Representation and Nineteenth Century History*, ed. Dino Felluga, Jan. 26, 2021; and Sara Guyer's reading of John Clare in *Reading with John Clare: Biopoetics, Sovereignty, Romanticism* (New York: Fordham University Press, 2015), 82–83, 88–91.

2. See Jacques Khalip, *Anonymous Life: Romanticism and Dispossession* (Stanford, CA: Stanford University Press, 2008), 1–17; Patrick Greaney, *Untimely Beggar: Poverty and Power from Baudelaire to Benjamin* (Minneapolis: University

of Minnesota Press, 2008), 26–48; and Sara Guyer, *Romanticism after Auschwitz* (Stanford, CA: Stanford University Press, 2007), 46–71.

3. Anna Kornbluh, *Realizing Capital: Financial and Psychic Economies in Victorian Form* (New York: Fordham University Press, 2013), 128.

4. John Clare, "The Eternity of Nature," in *I Am: The Selected Poetry of John Clare*, ed. Jonathan Bate (New York: Farrar, Straus & Giroux, 2003), 38.

5. Karl Marx, *Capital: A Critique of Political Economy*, vol. 1, trans. Ben Fowkes (London: Penguin Books, 1976), 885.

6. Gregory Pierrot, "A Collaborative Review of Francis Botkin's *Thieving Three-Fingered Jack* and Cedric Robinson's *Black Marxism*," with Gabriella I. Johnson, Romantic Circles Reviews and Receptions, Jan. 4, 2021.

7. Federici writes: "Primitive accumulation, then, was not simply an accumulation and concentration of exploitable workers and capital. It was *also an accumulation of differences and divisions within the working* class, whereby hierarchies built upon gender, as well as 'race' and age, become constitutive of class tool and the formation of the modern proletariat." Federici, *Caliban and the Witch* (New York: Autonomedia, 2004), 63–64. Along with Federici, see Jordy Rosenberg, "Original Sin," in *The Bloomsbury Companion to Marx*, ed. Andrew Pendakis, Jeff Diamanti, and Imre Szeman (London: Bloomsbury Academic, 2018), 363–369.

8. *Oxford English Dictionary*, s.v. "Subsistence," https://www-oed-com.proxy.library.nyu.edu/view/Entry/193020?redirectedFrom=subsistence#eid.

9. Clare, "The Mores," in *I Am*, 78.

10. There are surprising coincidences between Marx's tracking of substitution as the defining force of history and certain deconstructive critiques of history that bring us back to Romanticism and the centrality of figure to history. For de Man, "figuration is the element in language that allows for the reiteration of meaning by substitution," and history is nothing if not the imposition of meaning on otherwise arbitrary events. It is, in other words, the singular capacity of figure to generate equivalence between incommensurate things. And history is a "method of reading" that recuperates time as the substitution of movement for monuments. It is the ideology of development that works through relations of equivalence, of succession shaped into forward movement. It is through such an equivalence that a sense of history as meaning is recovered. This relation of substitution makes figure into a universal equivalent in which, in de Man's own words, "everything can be substituted for everything else" within an exchange economy of mind and world, thought and language. Tropes, then, are the medium of exchange, the material form through which the universals of history and knowledge can be established. For more on this economizing relation, see de Man, "The Epistemology of Metaphor," in *Aesthetic Ideology*, ed. Andrejz Warminksi (Minneapolis: University of

Minnesota Press, 1996). See also de Man's description of the imagination and understanding in Kant as "an economy of loss and gain [that] is put in place ... though only within certain well-defined limits. The exchange from part to whole generates wholes that turn out to be only parts" (77); of the sublime in Wordsworth as "an instance of the constant exchange between mind and nature, of the chiasmic transfer of properties between the sensory and the intellectual world that characterizes his figural diction" (82); of the Kantian faculties as "the story of an exchange, of a negotiation in which powers are lost and gained in an economy of sacrifice and recuperation" (87); of Schiller's distinction between the imaginary and the concrete as "a purely structural code of tropological exchange, symmetrical, like all tropes, and as such masterable" (144); of the mutual interdependency of matter and form in Schiller as an "exchange" rather than as a dialectic; and finally, of his description of play in Schiller as "equilibrium, harmony, on the level of principles, between, on the one hand, necessity, rule, *Gesetz*, and, on the other hand, chance, what is arbitrary." De Man continues: "Play, games are a good example of that. They have laws ... on the one hand, and, on the other hand, there is something deeply arbitrary about those laws. . . . It's an absolutely arbitrary decision, but which taken within itself is the principle of law, and which functions as a law" (152).

11. Robert Wedderburn, *The Horrors of Slavery and Other Writings*, ed. Iain McCalman (Princeton, NJ: Markus Wiener, 1991), 82.

12. Joseph Priestley, *An Account of a Society for Encouraging the Industrious Poor* (Birmingham, UK: Printed by Pearson and Rollason, 1787), 7.

13. Or, as Jacques Khalip writes, figurally attentive approaches to dispossession resist the tendency of New Historicism "to return to the lost body of history" that "invokes a historical closure ... resembling the Hegelian concept of totality," thus juxtaposing the material to the abstract, the present to the absent. Khalip, *Anonymous Life*, 12.

14. By "Eurocentric" I do not mean a certain geographic area but rather a conceptual map of the kind that coexists with other, non-European ways of being both inside and outside geographic boundaries. In this sense, my use is akin to that of Denise Ferreira da Silva or Boaventura de Sousa Santos, who proposes the existence of a "non-occidentalist West" as well as a sense of the Global South not as a geographic concept but as "a metaphor of the human suffering caused by capitalism and colonialism at the global level, and a metaphor as well of the resistance to overcome or minimise such suffering" (51). De Sousa Santos, "Public Sphere and Epistemologies of the South," *Africa Development* 37, no. 1 (2012): 43–67.

15. Guyer, *Reading with John Clare*, 5.

16. S. T. Coleridge, *Biographia Literaria*, in *Samuel Taylor Coleridge: The Major Works*, ed. H. J. Jackson (Oxford: Oxford University Press, 2008), 220.

17. Fred Moten, *Black and Blur*, vol. 1 of *consent not to be a single being* (Durham, NC: Duke University Press, 2017), 154.

18. Theories of apostrophe have been formative for our concepts of subjectivity, agency, and ideology in Romanticism, as they have enabled readings of the noncontradiction of presence and absence, of persons and nonpersons, of voice and "mere sound." See Jonathan Culler, "Apostrophe," *Diacritics* 7, no. 4 (Winter 1977): 59–69; Barbara Johnson, "Apostrophe, Animation, and Abortion," *Diacritics* 16, no. 1 (Spring 1986): 28–47, and *Persons and Things* (Cambridge, MA: Harvard University Press, 2008), 3–27; and Guyer, *Romanticism after Auschwitz*, 46–71.

19. Peter Linebaugh, *Red Round Globe Burning Hot: A Tale at the Crossroads of Commons and Closure, of Love and Terror, of Race and Class, and of Kate and Ned Despard* (Oakland: University of California Press, 2019), 11, emphasis added; Moten, *Black and Blur*, 162.

20. Tithi Bhattacharya, "Introduction: Mapping Social Reproduction Theory," in *Social Reproduction Theory: Remapping Class, Recentering Oppression*, ed. Bhattacharya (London: Pluto Press, 2017), 19.

21. Joseph Priestley, *A Course of Lectures on the Theory of Language, and Universal Grammar* (Warrington, UK: Printed by W. Eyres, 1762), 50.

22. Kyla Schuller has distinguished between the terms "impression" and "impressibility" as a way to differentiate a material relation from the scientific discourse of racialized civilization that designates some bodies as progressively malleable and others as passively senseless. Schuller, *The Biopolitics of Feeling: Race, Sex, and Science in the Nineteenth Century* (Durham, NC: Duke University Press, 2018), 6–8. This is an astute and productive distinction for the purpose of understanding how certain scientific discourses default to temporalizing frameworks in order to mobilize power, or in Schuller's project, of making life productive in a biopolitical mode. I am not entirely convinced, however, that this distinction applies to racializing discourses of impressionability in Romantic-era cultural or scientific discourses. But, more significant, there are features of impression and impressionability that get lost in its absorption into entirely progressive and temporal understandings of history, in particular, important aspects of the material conditions of capital that are left to the side by this distinction.

23. Priestley, *A Course of Lectures*, 288.

24. Ibid., 288. In *Speech and Phenomena*, Derrida provides a footnote that brings this matter into contemporary phenomenology, saying that for Husserl, what must be "excluded from pure expression as such is indication, and thus the association in the sense of empirical psychology. It is the empirical mental experiences which must be bracketed in order to recognize the ideality of meaning at work." Derrida, *Speech and Phenomena and Other Essays on Husserl's Theory of Signs*, trans. David B. Allison (Evanston, IL: Northwestern University Press, 1973), 30.

25. Joseph Priestley, *Hartley's Theory of the Human Mind, on the Principle of the Association of Ideas*, 2nd ed. (London: Printed for J. Johnson, 1790), 126, 115.

26. Ibid., 226.

27. Ibid.

28. *Oxford English Dictionary*, s.v., "Superfluous," https://www.oed.com/view/Entry/194328?redirectedFrom=superfluous#eid.

29. Ibid., s.v. "Subsistence," https://www-oed-com.proxy.library.nyu.edu/view/Entry/193020?redirectedFrom=subsistence#eid.

30. Newton Garver points to examples such as "the colorless green ball" and "the alert response of the dead man" (x). On the contestation between logic and rhetoric in the philosophy of language, see Garver, Preface to *Speech and Phenomena and Other Essays on Husserl's Theory of Signs*, trans. David B. Allison (Evanston, IL: Northwestern University Press, 1973), ix–xvii.

31. J. L. Austin, "Lecture VIII," in *How to Do Things with Words* [1977], Oxford Scholarship Online.

32. The phonetic and speculative connections between "vagrant," "vague," and "way" would move from the Latin *vagārī*, to wander; to *vagus*, wandering, inconstant, uncertain; and to the Old Saxon *weg* and the Old Swedish *vägher*. *Oxford English Dictionary*, s.v., "Way," https://www-oed-com.proxy.library.nyu.edu/view/Entry/226469?rskey=YtJ1yW&result=1&isAdvanced=false#eid. Thanks to David Lloyd and Fred Moten for pushing me toward these connections.

33. For an excellent account of Wordsworth's power of remediation, see Maureen N. McLane, "Dating Orality, Thinking Balladry: Of Milkmaids and Minstrels in 1771," *Eighteenth Century* 47, no. 2/3 (2006): 131–149.

34. Priestley, *A Course of Lectures*, 50.

35. William Wordsworth, "Note to 'The Thorn,'" in *The Major Works*, 593.

36. Coleridge, *Biographia Literaria*, 171.

37. Ibid., 313.

38. This phrasing of rebellion is taken from E. P. Thompson's parody of the riot in "The Moral Economy of the English Crowd in the Eighteenth Century," in *The Essential E. P. Thompson*, ed. Dorothy Thompson (New York: New Press, 2001).

39. Coleridge, *Biographia Literaria*, 171.

40. Wordsworth, "Note to 'The Thorn,'" 593.

41. Coleridge, *Biographia Literaria*, 157.

42. Marx, *Capital*, 1:139.

43. Alfred Sohn-Rethel, *Intellectual and Manual Labor: A Critique of Epistemology* (Atlantic Highlands, NJ: Humanities Press, 1978), 26.

44. Karl Marx, "The Value-Form."

45. Ibid., 157–178.

46. Marx, *Capital*, 1:915.

47. Denise Ferreira da Silva, "*Transversing* the Circuit of Dispossession," *Eighteenth Century* 55, nos. 2–3 (2014): 285.

48. Simpson, *Wordsworth, Commodification and Social Concern*, 4.

49. Marx, *Capital*, 1:163, emphasis added.

50. Alice Becker-Ho, *The Essence of Jargon*, trans. John McHale (New York: Autonomedia, 2015).

51. In the most famous passage of "The Task of the Translator," Walter Benjamin discusses the "way of meaning" (*Brot* and *pain* in German and French), words that "signify the very same thing" but are also "not interchangeable" and "strive to exclude each other" (257). For Benjamin, we must understand this referential sameness through a historical and transient way of meaning that is only ever a provisional condensation of the essential supplementariness of language, in which a universal *way* of meaning will never be achieved but in which the emergence of any mother tongue through heterogeneous languages bears the potential of a universal relation. Benjamin, "The Task of the Translator," in *Selected Writings*, vol. 1: *1913–1926*, trans. Edmund Jephcott et al., ed. Marcus Bullock and Michael W. Jennings (Cambridge, MA: Harvard University Press, 2004).

52. Marx, *Capital*, 1:874.

53. Ibid.

54. Rosa Luxemburg, *The Complete Works of Rosa Luxemburg*, vol. 2: *Economic Writings 2*, ed. Peter Hudis and Paul Le Blanc (New York: Verso, 2015), 302–303.

55. *Oxford English Dictionary*, s.v., "Schema," https://www-oed-com.proxy.library.nyu.edu/view/Entry/172307?redirectedFrom=schema#eid.

56. For more on this point, see Alyssa Adamson, "Against a Single History, for a Revaluation of Power," in *Creolizing Rosa Luxemburg*, ed. Drucilla Cornell and Jane Anna Gordon (New York: Rowman & Littlefield, 2021).

57. Kanyal Sanyal, *Rethinking Capitalist Development: Primitive Accumulation, Governmentality, and Post-colonial Capitalism* (London: Routledge, 2007), 39.

58. Michael T. Taussig, *The Devil and Commodity Fetishism in South America: Thirtieth Anniversary Edition with a New Chapter by the Author*, 2nd ed. (Chapel Hill: University of North Carolina Press, 2010), 17.

59. Ibid.

60. Edmund Burke, "Thoughts and Details on Scarcity," in *Miscellaneous Writings*, ed. Francis Canavan (Indianapolis: Liberty Fund, 1999), 71–72.

61. Thompson, "Moral Economy."

62. Rosa Luxemburg, *The Mass Strike, the Political Party, and the Trade Unions* [1906], trans. Patrick Lavin, Marxists.org, 1999.

63. This use of apostrophe doubles down on its sensational derivations from Latin as tumultuousness, disturbance, agitation, excitement; and the French *émeute*, to agitate, from *émouvir*, to touch, to move, to be touched by.

64. Hilary Beckles, "Sex and Gender in the Historiography of Caribbean Slavery," in *Engendering History*, ed. Verene Shepherd, Bridget Brereton, and Barbara Bailey (New York: Palgrave Macmillan, 1995), 132.

65. Cedric Robinson, *Black Marxism: The Making of the Black Radical Tradition*, 2nd ed. (Chapel Hill: University of North Carolina Press, 2005), 42.

66. In keeping with the actual historical variation of terms provided by written texts, and in order to maintain the critical uncertainty of its referent, I have chosen to use *Obeah* and *Obi* as both nouns and adjectives throughout the book.

67. Saree Makdisi, *Making England Western: Occidentalism, Race, and Imperial Culture* (Chicago: University of Chicago Press, 2014), 1–38.

68. "Quite simply, the problems we faced in making *Handsworth* were very practical ones—to do with melodrama—orchestrating means of identification, rather than distancing people and dazzling them with techniques. The editing might be considered unconventional, but the techniques are very straightforward." John Akomfrah in Coco Fusco, "An Interview with Black Audio Film Collective: John Akomfrah, Lina Gopaul, Avril Johnson, and Reece Auguiste," in *Young, British & Black: A Monograph on the Work of Sankofa Film/Video Collective and Black Audio Film Collective* (Buffalo, NY: Hallwalls / Contemporary Arts Center, 1988), 49–50.

69. Daniel Stout, "Associationist Aesthetics: Priestley's Materialism and the Radical Picturesque," *European Romantic Review* 3, no. 31 (2020): 267–283. See also Devin Griffiths, *The Age of Analogy: Science and Literature between the Darwins* (Baltimore: Johns Hopkins University Press, 2016).

70. Denise Ferreira da Silva, *Toward a Global Idea of Race* (Minneapolis: University of Minnesota Press), xvii–17.

71. Jacques Derrida, *Of Grammatology* (Baltimore: Johns Hopkins University Press, 1998), 101–102.

72. Percy Shelley, "Triumph of Life," in *Shelley's Poetry and Prose*, 2nd ed., ed. Donald H. Reiman and Neil Freistat (London: W. W. Norton, 2002), 141.

Chapter 1: Apostrophe and Riot

1. This aspect of primitive accumulation, Federici argues, is "a true vivisection of the body whereby it was decided which of its properties could live and which, instead, had to die." According to Federici, it is the subsumption of the body to the demands of capitalist production that truly marks the onset of the capitalist mode of production. Federici, *Caliban and the Witch*, 138.

2. William Wordsworth, "An Evening Walk," in *The Major Works: Including "The Prelude,"* 2nd ed., ed. Stephen Gill (Oxford: Oxford University Press, 2008).

3. Johnson, "Apostrophe, Animation, and Abortion," 30; Guyer, *Romanticism after Auschwitz*, 146; Culler, "Apostrophe," 59.

4. Thompson, "Moral Economy," 333. Along with Thompson, the following

works provide accounts of the combined effects of the end of feudalism, the oscillations between active and suspended foreign wars, intense state oppression of internal critics, massive food shortages, and the significant transitions toward the formal subsumption of capital in the 1790s: David Collings, *Monstrous Society: Reciprocity, Discipline, and the Political Uncanny, c. 1780–1848* (Lewisburg, PA: Bucknell University Press, 2001); Mary Fairclough, *The Romantic Crowd: Sympathy, Controversy and Print Culture* (Cambridge: Cambridge University Press, 2013); Ian Haywood, *Bloody Romanticism: Spectacular Violence and the Politics of Representation 1777–1832* (Basingstoke, UK: Palgrave Macmillan, 2004); Georgina Green, *The Majesty of the People: Popular Sovereignty and the Role of the Writer in the 1790s* (Oxford: Oxford University Press, 2014); Perry Anderson, *Lineages of the Absolutist State* (New York: Verso, 2013); and Peter Linebaugh, *The London Hanged: Crime and Civil Society in the Eighteenth Century*, 2nd ed. (New York: Verso, 2003).

5. Linebaugh, *Red Round Globe Burning Hot*, 2019.

6. S. T. Coleridge, "Introductory Address," in *Collected Works: Lectures 1795 on Politics and Religion*, vol. 1, ed. Lewis Patton and Peter Mann (Princeton, NJ: Princeton University Press, 1971), 45, emphasis added. Earlier, Coleridge writes, "For can we wonder that men should want humanity, who want all the circumstances of life that humanize? Can we wonder that with the ignorance of Brutes they should unite their ferocity? . . . But let us shudder to hear from Men of dissimilar opportunities sentiments of similar revengefulness. The purifying alchemy of Education may transmute the fierceness of an ignorant man into virtuous energy—but what remedy shall we apply to him, whom Plenty has not softened, whom Knowledge has not taught Benevolence" (39).

7. Ibid., 43.

8. Ibid., 40, 39. We find a similar sentiment in the preface to Burke's *Thoughts and Details on Scarcity* by French Laurence and Walker King. There Laurence and King describe the food riots as the result of "gross minds [that] distorted (convictions) into authorities to prove that there was plenty in the land, and that the arts of greedy and unfeeling men alone intercepted the bounty of Providence. Meetings were called; non-consumption agreements were signed, to fix a compulsory price, and associations were formed, chiefly in cities and great towns, to prosecute those, without whom cities and great towns can never be regularly fed. There is no weak, no wild, no violent project, which did not find countenance in some quarter or the other . . . and the multitude began to pursue their usual course of providing in the shortest way for their instant wants, or of terrifying, or punishing those, whom they had been taught to consider as their oppressors." French Laurence and Walker King, preface to *Miscellaneous Writings: Thoughts and Details on Scarcity*, by Edmund Burke, ed. Francis Canavan (Indianapolis: Liberty Fund, 1999).

9. Ian Balfour, *The Rhetoric of Romantic Prophecy* (Stanford, CA: Stanford University Press, 2002), 282–283, 254.

10. Here Coleridge follows the mechanistic doctrine espoused by Julian Offray de La Mettrie, who wrote in *Man as Machine* that: "1) the more *ferocious* animals are, the less brain they have; 2) this organ seems to grow, as it were, in relation to their docility; 3) [and] that what is gained on the side of intelligence is lost on the side of instinct." See La Mettrie, *Machine Man and Other Writings*, ed. Ann Thompson (Cambridge: Cambridge University Press, 1996), 10. Later, Condillac would worry about the power of reason in the face of the supposed extremity of need. See Lorraine Daston, *Classical Probability in the Enlightenment* (Princeton, NJ: Princeton University Press, 1988), 210.

11. See Priestley, *Hartley's Theory*, 32.

12. Ibid.

13. Ibid., 32–33, emphasis added.

14. Kevis Goodman, "'Uncertain Disease': Nostalgia, Pathologies of Motion, Practices of Reading," *Studies in Romanticism* 49, no. 2 (Summer 2010): 212.

15. Coleridge's appeal for indirect speech to the poor is based on this distinction between "the avowal of *political* Truth among those only whose minds are susceptible of reasoning" and "the multitude, who *ignorant and needy* must necessarily act from the *impulse of inflamed Passions*." Coleridge, *Conciones ad Populum*, in *Collected Works: Lectures 1795 on Politics and Religion*, vol. 1, ed. Lewis Patton and Peter Mann (Princeton, NJ: Princeton University Press, 1971), 51, emphasis added.

16. Maureen N. McLane has argued that we should pay more attention to Malthus as a theorist of desire and not just of restraint. I would only add that the excesses of desire attendant upon this aspect of his work are still bound up with the just as necessary elimination of the excesses of poor in numerical terms. See McLane, "Malthus Our Contemporary? Toward a Political Economy of Sex," *Studies in Romanticism* 52 (Fall 2013): 337–362.

17. For Marx's critique of Malthus on the production of surplus populations as an effect of technological "advances" rather than of an iron law of scarcity, see Marx, *Capital*, 1:781–793.

18. Marx writes that "within the capitalist system all methods for raising the social productivity of labour are put into effect at the cost of the individual worker; that all means for the development of undergo a dialectical inversion so that they become means of domination and exploitation of the producers; they distort the worker into a fragment of a man, they degrade him to the level of an appendage of a machine, they destroy the actual content of his labour by turning it into a torment; they alienate from him the intellectual potentialities of the labour process. . . . It makes an accumulation of misery a necessary condition, corresponding to the ac-

cumulation of wealth. Accumulation of wealth at one pole is, therefore, at the same time, accumulation of misery, the torment of labour, slavery, ignorance, brutalization and moral degradation at the opposite pole, i.e. on the side of the class that produces its own product as capital." Ibid., 1:799.

19. Elsewhere Marx emphasizes this point further, writing that "the worker is often compelled to make his individual consumption into a merely *incidental* part of the production process; he provides himself with means of subsistence in order to keep his labour-power in motion, just as coal and water are supplied to the steam-engine, and oil to the wheel." Ibid., 1:717.

20. Ibid., 1:799.

21. "The demand for labor is not identical with increase of capital, nor is supply of labour identical with increase of the working class. It is not a case of two independent forces working on each other. *Les dés sont pipés*. Capital acts on both sides at once." Ibid., 1:793.

22. Burke, "Thoughts and Details," 72. Here Burke refers to the Speenhamland system, which inspired Burke to write this memorandum to William Pitt. In 1782, Parliament had enacted Gilbert's Act, which authorized local governments to grant allowances in aid of wages. Subsidizing the wages of the poor was not even then a new departure in English law. On this basis, in 1795 the magistrates of Berkshire, a county adjacent to Burke's Buckinghamshire, met in the Pelican Inn in Speenhamland and adopted a scheme to ensure laborers a living wage. A minimum wage was fixed, which varied with the price of corn; if wages actually fell below that, they would be supplemented from the poor rates." Laurence and King, "Preface," 64.

23. For instance, Burke's Malthusian position was pitted against the decision made by many parishes to subsidize the devastated wages of agricultural workers, thus enabling them to purchase goods during what was approaching a true famine situation. In contrast, Coleridge's "Letter to Famine" appeals to "viceregents" to unseal their ears and do exactly what Burke recommends against.

24. *Oxford English Dictionary*, s.v., "Indirect," https://www-oed-com.proxy.library.nyu.edu/view/Entry/94531?redirectedFrom=indirect#eid.

25. See Thompson, "Moral Economy"; and Joshua Clover, *Riot. Strike. Riot* (New York: Verso, 2016), 1–35.

26. For a discussion of the term *phenomenophilia*, see Rei Terada, *Looking Away: Phenomenality and Dissatisfaction, Kant to Adorno* (Cambridge, MA: Harvard University Press, 2009), 3–4. Terada describes this as "particularly ephemeral perceptual experiences" such as "looking away at the colored shadow on the wall, or keeping the head turned to the angle at which the sunspot stays in view" (3–4).

27. It included an epigraph from Aristophanes that reads, "So here I'm waiting, thoroughly prepared / To riot, wrangle, interrupt the speakers / Whene'er they

speak of anything but Peace" (trans. Benjamin Bickley Rogers) and a preface invoking Ecclesiastes. Coleridge, *Conciones ad Populum*, 26.

28. Coleridge, "Letter to Famine," in *Collected Works: Lectures 1795 on Politics and Religion*, vol. 1, ed. Lewis Patton and Peter Mann (Princeton, NJ: Princeton University Press, 1971), 31.

29. I take this phrasing from Thompson, "Moral Economy."

30. Burke, "Thoughts and Details," 71.

31. Ibid.

32. Of this conundrum for capitalism, Jordy Rosenberg humorously proposes that "you can speed up the production process through massive innovations in technology, but you still can't exploit a robot arm. You can only invest money in it, and if it breaks, you can't expect the robot arm's wife to take care of it for a couple of unpaid weeks; you have to fix it yourself. Surplus comes from exploitation—the difference between what someone is paid, and what they produce for the capitalist. You can only exploit living people, because only living people expend energy on their own survival." See Rosenberg, "Becoming Hole (The Hiddener Abode)," *World Picture Journal* 11 (Summer 2016).

33. Antonella Picchio, *Social Reproduction: The Political Economy of the Labour Market* (Cambridge: Cambridge University Press, 1992), 9, emphasis added. Picchio writes in useful ways about the *organizational* nature of the division of labor, which "occurred merely at the level of organization, as [processes of production and the processes of social reproduction] were interconnected, and both were necessary for the reproduction of the system as a whole. . . . The separation was not spontaneous and it was not accomplished by impersonal market forces: laws, orders, courts, evictions and workhouses forced the changes into social practice" (ibid.).

34. See Hannah More's poems "The Riot; or, Half a Loaf Is Better Than No Bread" (Perth: R. Morison, 1800) and "A Hymn of Praise for the Abundant Harvest of 1796" (London: J. Marshall, 1796) for examples of the active remaking of the Thompsonian "moral economy" into one based on a capitalist system of commodity exchange. More's moral economy follows what Picchio describes as the meeting of needs set by the parameters of profit. In that shifting of economies, the "laboring population no longer reproduces itself with self-produced goods or with market goods acquired by direct exchange of its own products; its reproduction depends on the sale of its labour." Picchio, *Social Reproduction*, 9.

35. Ross's history of the Paris Commune begins with an apostrophe uttered two years in advance at a workers' gathering and with journeyman Louis Alfred Briosne's "direct second-person address" to his audience as "Citoyennes et citoyens" rather than "Mesdames et messieurs." Ross writes that such apostrophe "[cre-

ates] that gap or division in the now, in the contemporary moment constituted by the speech act" and "interpellates listeners to be part of that present." Kristen Ross, *Communal Luxury: The Political Imaginary of the Paris Commune* (New York: Verso, 2015), 16–17. See also Michael Hardt and Antonio Negri's short text on the global uprisings of 2011, *Declaration* (New York: Argo Navis, 2012), itself a form of apostrophe that remains less certain of the future than does the manifesto.

36. Saidiya Hartman, "The Anarchy of Colored Girls Assembled in a Riotous Manner," *South Atlantic Quarterly* 117, no. 3 (2018): 465–490.

37. Karl Marx, *Grundrisse: Foundations of the Critique of Political Economy*, trans. Martin Nicolaus (London: Penguin Books, 1973), 101.

38. Jackie Wang, *Carceral Capitalism* (Cambridge, MA: MIT Press, 2018).

39. Desmond King-Hele, *Erasmus Darwin: A Life of Unequalled Achievement* (London: DLM, 2000), 47. The *Aris Gazette* was also the paper in which a well-known illustration of the burning of Albion Mills was published.

40. For his own part, Burke advocated for "protecting" the bodies of those hanged in response to the Gordon Riots in the following manner: "Afterwards, great care should be taken, that their bodies may not be delivered to their friends, or to others, who may make them objects of compassion, or even veneration; some instances of the kind have happened, with regard to the bodies of those killed in riots." See Burke, "Some Thoughts on the Approaching Executions," in *On Empire, Liberty, and Reform: Speeches and Letters*, ed. David Bromwich (New Haven, CT: Yale University Press, 2000), 199–210.

41. See Linebaugh, *The London Hanged*; and Jordy Rosenberg, "Trans/War Boy/Gender: The Primitive Accumulation of T," *Salvage*, December 21, 2015.

42. On the other hand, as Rosenberg notes, Daniel Defoe argued that the living labor that could be put to work in the colonies was far more productive of securing an empire. Ibid.

43. See Linebaugh, *The London Hanged*, "Part Three."

44. Along with such bloody criminalization, the mid- to late eighteenth century and the early Romantic period were, as Londa Schiebinger's work has shown in the global and colonial contexts, an incredibly messy, contingent, and open-ended accumulation and study of subsistence-style means of life that would only later come to be classified and erased in their commodification. See Schiebinger, *Plants and Empire: Colonial Bioprospecting in the Atlantic World* (Cambridge, MA: Harvard University Press, 2004), 194–219.

45. Erasmus Darwin, *Zoonomia; or, The Laws of Organic Life*, vol. 1 (London: Printed for J. Johnson, [1794]), 112. In his most famous scientific treatise, *Zoonomia*, Darwin was deeply concerned with those same materialist theories of habituated and equilibrating physiologies that Hartley had termed secondary

automation. Translating Hartley's more mechanistic terms into the language of sensible, animated matter, Darwin theorized that all material motions resulted from the giving or receiving of motion by one body to or from another. All bodies came to be regulated through the development of in-tandem and reciprocal relations of the kind Hartley also laid out. Animal movements functioned either by association, causation, catenation, or habit, "that is, by frequent repetition." Habit, as contemporaries of Darwin would also explain, was the result of internalized causation rather than external stimulation and was generated through the involuntary memory of motion. Unlike responses to stimuli, which created motion at the extremities of the body, habit resulted from internally generated motion catalyzed by the repeated association of sensation and trains of thought.

46. Ibid., 6.

47. Georg Simmel develops the term "societalization" to designate such relations. This refers to a series of reciprocal interactions through which human activity, over time, develops into objective and natural forms that determine human activity beyond our intention or control. For an explanation of Simmel's concept of societalization, see Matthias Gross, "Unexpected Interactions: Georg Simmel and the Observation of Nature," *Journal of Classical Sociology* 1, no. 3 (2001): 395–414. In a formulation that would be significant for Benjamin, Simmel writes that "as soon as the human-made work is completed, it not only has an objective being and an individual existence independent of humans, but it also holds in its being . . . strengths and weaknesses, components and significances, that we are completely innocent of and which often take us by surprise." Simmel qtd. in ibid., 399. As Gross writes, Simmel understood the aim of sociology to be to track this movement of "sociation" or "societalization" (397).

48. Maureen McNeil, *Under the Banner of Science: Erasmus Darwin and His Age* (Manchester, UK: Manchester University Press, 1987), 153.

49. Under "senses relating to speech or expression," articulation refers to the utterance of the distinct elements of speech; (*Phonetics*) the formation of speech sounds by the control of the air flow in the vocal tract by vocal organs." *Oxford English Dictionary*, s.v. "Articulation," https://www-oed-com.proxy.library.nyu.edu/view/Entry/11196?redirectedFrom=articulation#eid.

50. Brenna Bhandar, *Colonial Lives of Property: Law, Land, and Racial Regimes of Ownership* (Durham, NC: Duke University Press, 2018), 9.

51. Walter Benjamin qtd. in Susan Buck-Morss, *The Dialectics of Seeing: Walter Benjamin and the Arcades Project* (Cambridge, MA: MIT Press, 1991), 59.

52. For instance, Theresa M. Kelley writes that when "botanical particulars resist or exceed conceptual location, either because they are hybrid, morphologically resistant, or because their names invite imagining them beyond the cate-

gories they putatively occupy and instantiate," they "speak to the possibility of a material and aesthetic pleasure that cannot be economized." Kelley, *Clandestine Marriage: Botany and Romantic Culture* (Baltimore: Johns Hopkins University Press, 2015), 13–14.

53. McNeil, *Under the Banner of Science*, 159.

54. See Goodman, "'Uncertain Disease,'" 214.

55. Bhandar, following Hall, describes conjunctures as "a formation whose genesis cannot be reduced to any one singular system or structure [in which] political ideologies, economic rationalities, and cultural and juridical practices operate in conjunction to produce structures of domination." Bhandar, *Colonial Lives of Property*, 9.

56. Erasmus Darwin, *Phytologia; or the Philosophy of Agriculture and Gardening* (London: Printed for J. Johnson, St. Paul's Church-Yard; by T. Bensley, Bolt Court, Fleet Street, 1800). Coleridge expresses a similar sentiment about the development of coralline in an essay unpublished in his lifetime, in which he describes the ossifying decay of its reproduction, as an entity that "grows ... even as gristle becomes bone,—and thus we may truly say, lives by dying." "Hints towards the Formation of a More Comprehensive Theory of Life," in *The Collected Works of Samuel Taylor Coleridge*, vol. 11, ed. H. J. Jackson and J. R. de J. Jackson (Princeton, NJ: Princeton University Press, 1995), 1030.

57. Amanda Jo Goldstein, *Sweet Science: Romantic Materialism and the New Logics of Life* (Chicago: University of Chicago Press, 2017), 148.

58. Picchio, *Social Reproduction*, 21. According to David Ricardo, "The power of the labourer to support himself, and the family which may be necessary to keep up the number of labourers, does not depend on the quantity of money which he may receive for wages, but on the quantity of food, necessaries and conveniences that become essential to him from habit." Ricardo qtd. in ibid., 17.

59. Such an assessment of the historical, which is to say, at this point, rhetorical nature of capital nuances Thompson's landmark account of the eighteenth-century riot, which was already structured by the mechanics of supply and demand that Picchio articulates as only dominant in the later nineteenth century.

60. Ibid., 2.

61. See Georgiana Green's work for a description of the formation of popular sovereignty in the nineteenth century through its "exclusive preoccupation with satisfying the need for bare necessities." According to her, the ambivalence of the structure of constituent power has to do with this incorporation of the state of nature within the structure of sovereignty not as "the power of command" but as "the power to form governments." Green, *Majesty of the People*, 10, 7. Green's formulation points to the problem of bare necessities that Lorraine Daston has argued

was the end point of early modern empiricism and its presumption of a stable and uniform nature underlying the social formation of habits. According to Daston, the French Revolution sealed the fate of an epistemology already troubled by the constitutive trembling between subjective perception and an objective, uniform world. Daston, *Classical Probability*, 188–224.

62. Jason W. Moore, *Capitalism in the Web of Life: Ecology and the Accumulation of Capital* (New York: Verso, 2015), 61–79.

63. Rosenberg, "Becoming Hole."

64. Denise Ferreira da Silva, "On Difference without Separability," catalogue for the 32nd Sao Paulo Art Biennial (November 2016).

65. Balfour, *Rhetoric of Romantic Prophecy*, 44.

66. Ibid., 316.

67. For an example of a more conventional Romanticism, see the London Corresponding Society pamphlet *Reformers no Rioters* ([London]: Printed by order of the London Corresponding Society, [1794]), which declares that "one of the fundamental principles of this society . . . is that riot, tumult, and violence are not the fit means of obtaining a redress of grievances" (2). They conclude the tract in quite Wordsworthian fashion, writing that "this great end (we answer) is attainable solely by the *whole nation*, deeply impressed with a sense of its wrongs, *uniting*, as it were with one voice . . . and an equal representation of the whole body of the people" (5).

68. Anonymous qtd. in Thompson, "Moral Economy," 359.

69. Thelwall qtd. in Coleridge, *Collected Works*, 1:xxix. It is perhaps in this sense that we can understand the uncanny continuity between Hartley, Coleridge, and Walter Benjamin, who writes in *The Arcades Project* that "the idea of revolution [is] an innervation of the technical organs of the collective." His example of such innervation is "the (analogy with the child who learns to grasp by trying to get hold of the moon)" (W7,4).

Chapter 2: Anachronism, Dreams, and Enclosure

1. John Hunter, *Lectures on the Principles of Surgery* [1775] (Philadelphia: Haswell, Barrington, and Haswell, 1839), 121.

2. Bhandar cites Hall's concept as one in which "the different levels of articulation do not by any means simply correspond [to] or 'mirror' one another." She explains that articulation "produce[s] uneven, nonlinear, and sometimes contradictory effects" and "stresses the contingency present in the development of social formations" while still "defin[ing] the social formation as a 'structure in dominance,' in order to emphasize its determinate and systemic qualities." Bhandar, *Colonial Lives of Property*, 11.

3. Mary Robinson, *Memoirs of Mary Robinson*, ed. J. Fitzgerald Molloy (Philadelphia: J. B. Lippincott, 1895), 219.

4. Ibid.

5. Jonathan Sheehan and Dror Wahrman, *Invisible Hands: Self-Organization and the Eighteenth Century* (Chicago: University of Chicago Press, 2015), xii.

6. Ibid., 203. While I mainly address Sheehan and Wahrman's assessment of analogy in the eighteenth-century life sciences, cognitive sciences, and social systems, other recent works also locate analogy as central to a more dynamic and contingent epistemology of science up to the mid-nineteenth century. For Devin Griffiths, "harmonic" analogies were a crucial resource of knowledge production in nineteenth-century science and literature because they "work from the bottom up, exploring a pattern between two different sets of relationships" that "disclose new commonalities and distinctions." See Griffiths, *The Age of Analogy: Science and Literature between the Darwins* (Baltimore: Johns Hopkins University Press, 2016), 19, 20. Richard Sha's argument about the role of imagination in Romantic science is analogical in everything but name, as imagination for Sha generates an "ability to see relationality among differences" and allows for the constitution of a whole whose meaning is given by its parts and "for the contingent to have shaped any current view of the universal." See Sha, *Imagination and Science in Romanticism* (Baltimore: Johns Hopkins University Press, 2018), 3. One might also read analogy implicitly at the center of Caroline Levine's recent revisions of formal hierarchy, which for her is a field of plural and dynamic relations that constitute wholes without fixed order. See Levine, *Forms: Whole, Rhythm, Hierarchy, and Network* (Princeton, NJ: Princeton University Press, 2017). In contrast to these more stable binaries assigned to analogy, see Taylor Schey on its constitutively limited nature, which resists any ontological definition of analogy in favor of its "obstinate rhetoricity and its inability to establish clear-cut distinctions between sameness and difference." As Schey has argued, a "skeptical" strain of analogy persisted in Romantic poetry and philosophy, "precisely because of its failure to establish clear-cut identities and differences—precisely, that is, because of its epistemic instability and 'merely' rhetorical nature." See Schey, "Limited Analogies: Reading Relations in Wordsworth's *The Borderers*," *Studies in Romanticism*, no. 56 (Summer 2017): 197, 180.

7. Sheehan and Wahrman, *Invisible Hands*, xii.

8. On metaphor, see M. H. Abrams, *The Mirror and the Lamp: Romantic Theory and the Critical Tradition* (Oxford: Oxford University Press, 1953); Paul de Man, "Semiology and Rhetoric," in *Allegories of Reading: Figural Language in Rousseau, Nietzsche, Rilke, and Proust* (New Haven, CT: Yale University Press, 1979); and W. K. Wimsatt Jr. and M. C. Beardsley, "The Intentional Fallacy," *Sewanee Review* 57, no. 3 (Winter 1946): 468–488. On apostrophe, see Jonathan Culler, "Apostrophe"; and Barbara Johnson, "Apostrophe, Animation, and Abortion."

9. Romantic poetics, with its ever-ambivalent slippage between spontaneity and association, automation and autonomy, has long been a particularly overdetermined site of (ongoing) experimentation with such limit cases, in both poetry and criticism alike. Indeed, the significance, and signification, of apparently self-generating and self-organizing processes has motivated much Romantic literary criticism of one kind or another, including the ideology critique of fetishistic relations as well as more recent turns to the affective and emergent causality of autopoiesis. On the one hand, critics have read the concerns over mechanism and organicism in Romantic poetry as an extended engagement with dancing tables and ghostly animation. On the other hand, much recent criticism eschews such concerns as suspicious, even quasi-metaphysical, in favor of figurations of atomic swerves and feedback loops. But both sides of this critical divide share in the presupposition that increasing standardization and homogeneity characterized the more oppressive and exploitative dynamics of late eighteenth-century and Romantic forms of life. Rather than autopoiesis, the phenomenon at the center of much recent work on eighteenth-century and Romantic-era life sciences and poetry actually seems more aptly captured by the term "sympoeisis" that Donna Haraway borrows from M. Beth Dempster, as "collectively-producing systems that do not have self-defined or temporal boundaries" and in which "information and control are distributed among components." Donna Haraway, "Staying with the Trouble," in *Anthropocene or Capitalocene: Nature, History, and the Crisis of Capitalism*, ed. Jason W. Moore (Oakland, CA: PM Press, 2016), 37.

10. David Hartley, *Observations on Man, His Frame, His Duty, and His Expectations*, vol. 1 (London: Printed by S. Richardson; for James Leake and Wm. Frederick, Booksellers in Bath: and sold by Charles Hitch and Stephen Austen, Booksellers in London, M.DCC.XLIX. [1749]), 385–386.

11. Hunter, *Lectures*, 122.

12. *Oxford English Dictionary*, s.v. "Simultaneity," https://www-oed-com.proxy.library.nyu.edu/view/Entry/180022?redirectedFrom=simultaneity#eid.

13. Hartley, *Observations on Man*, 386.

14. Ibid., 389.

15. For Orrin Wang, this limit point of epistemology is "the space of figure," in which the "indeterminacies of deep history, uneven development, long centuries, and ambivalent prophecy play themselves out." See Wang, *Romantic Sobriety: Sensation, Revolution, Commodification, History* (Baltimore: Johns Hopkins University Press, 2011), 2.

16. Celeste Langan, *Romantic Vagrancy: Wordsworth and the Simulation of Freedom* (Cambridge: Cambridge University Press, 1995), 2.

17. Ibid., 2.

18. Gavin Walker, *The Sublime Perversion of Capital: Marxist Theory and the Politics of History in Modern Japan* (Durham, NC: Duke University Press, 2018), 83.

19. Langan, *Romantic Vagrancy*, 1. *Oxford English Dictionary*, s.v. "Contiguous," https://www-oed-com.proxy.library.nyu.edu/view/Entry/40227?redirectedFrom =contiguous.

20. Federici, *Caliban and the Witch*, 61–133.

21. According to Debra Hawhee, *accumulatio* was a rhetorical tool emphasized by Desiderius Erasmus for "developing an abundant style" and was meant to cultivate a rhetoric of "resourcefulness" through a "dazzling spectacle of a seeming infinite variety of things." For Hawhee, *accumulatio* "shape[d] the prevailing early modern habit of accumulation" (135) and entwined rhetoric, culture, and natural history in the early modern period. See Hawhee, *Rhetoric in Tooth and Claw: Animals, Language, Sensation* (Chicago: University of Chicago Press, 2017). But we could argue that, by the eighteenth-century, analogy—better suited to the suturing of natural history and political economy—had come to figure accumulation. As Jordy Rosenberg has argued, eighteenth-century commentators such as Locke and Shaftesbury explicitly distinguished modernity through its economic, moral, and aesthetic moderation, which for Rosenberg accompanied the "vanishing" of capital into colonial endeavors and investments in the slave trade. Analogy is a trope that preserves dissimilarity, thus accommodating an "infinite variety of things," but establishes equilibrium and harmony among its parts. In this sense, analogy might be said to be the figure of capital accumulation, along with its rhetorical and cultural traces, in the transition from an early modern to an Enlightenment-era mode. See Jordy Rosenberg, *Critical Enthusiasm: Capital Accumulation and the Transformation of Religious Passion* (Oxford: Oxford University Press, 2011).

22. Many Marxian-influenced readings of Romanticism have helped us sort through the dialectical complexities of commodity fetishism, along with equally uncanny effects and brutal enforcements of the equivalences and standardizations that attend it. Such analyses are immensely useful in showing that Romantic poetry was not strictly an ideology of such fetishism but rather works in a deeply prescient way to demonstrate the spectral complexities of, as David Simpson has put it, "industrial time, machine-driven labor and commodity form." Simpson, *Wordsworth, Commodification and Social Concern*, 4.

23. Schey, "Limited Analogies," 180.

24. Sheehan and Wahrman, *Invisible Hands*, xxi.

25. Bhattacharya, "Introduction," 19. Of course, much of Marx's own writing can be located as the genesis of this division, confirming as it does a historically progressive tendency in standardization and universal equivalence.

26. I take this formulation of accumulation by dispossession from David Harvey, which he details at length in *The New Imperialism*, 2nd ed. (Oxford: Oxford University Press, 2005), 137–182. As Harvey makes clear, one of the most significant

aspects of this mode of accumulation is its reliance on the state and its monopoly of violence, which "goes back a long way, keeping the territorial and capitalistic logics of power always intertwined though not necessarily concordant" (145).

27. Robinson, *Memoirs*, 218.

28. Mary Robinson, "The Maniac," in *Mary Robinson: Selected Poems*, ed. Judith Pascoe (Peterborough, ON: Broadview Press, 2000), 41, 78, 29–30.

29. Ibid., 1–2.

30. I take this phrasing from Orrin Wang's *Romantic Sobriety*. More generally, Wordsworth's position within the science and poetry of regulation, physiological and political, has been frequently debated. His poetry serves as something of a crucible for the ambivalent intersection of disciplinary knowledge and palliative poetics in the Romantic period, extending out to a larger debate over the proto-biopolitical nature of Romantic poetics more generally. Such debates have sometimes tended to inscribe an unhelpful and distinctly non-Foucauldian sense of regulation and governance as totalizing and uniform rather than as that more genealogical entanglement of gray zones, petty malices, jolts, feverish agitations, unpalatable defeats, and palimpsestic rewriting. See Michel Foucault, "Nietzsche, Genealogy, History," in *Language, Counter-Memory, Practice: Selected Essays and Interviews*, ed. D. F. Bouchard (Ithaca, NY: Cornell University Press, 1977).

31. Coleridge provides a similar description of the simultaneously excessive and restrained nature of Robinson's form: "There was a poem of [Robinson's] in this Morning's paper which both in metre and matter pleased me much—She overloads everything; but I never knew a human Being with so *full* a mind—bad, good, & indifferent, I grant, but full, & overflowing" S. T. Coleridge, "Letter to Southey: Saturday, January 27, 1800," in *Collected Letters of S. T. Coleridge*, vol. 1, ed. Earl Leslie Griggs (Oxford: Clarendon Press, 1956), 562.

32. Elizabeth Fay discusses the relevance of this refusal at length in "Mary Robinson," in *The Encyclopedia of Romantic Literature*, vol. 3, ed. Frederick Burwick, Nancy Moore Goslee, and Diane Long Hoeveler (Chichester, UK: Wiley-Blackwell, 2012).

33. Robinson, "The Maniac," 1–2.

34. Ibid., 7, 13, 19, 25.

35. Ibid., 52–53.

36. Griffiths, *Age of Analogy*, 28.

37. Schey, "Limited Analogies," 180.

38. Robinson, "The Maniac," 35–36.

39. William Wordsworth, "Preface to Lyrical Ballads (1802)," in *The Major Works*, 595.

40. Langan, *Romantic Vagrancy*, 11.

41. In a headnote to Wordsworth's "The Solitude of Binnorie," Coleridge acknowledges, on Wordsworth's behalf, the influence of Robinson's meter upon the poem: "This acknowledgment will not appear superfluous to those who have felt the bewitching effect of that absolutely original stanza in the original Poem, and who called to mind that the invention of a metre has so widely diffused the name of Sappho and almost constitutes the present celebrity of Alcaeus." Sappho here refers to Robinson and Alcaeus to Wordsworth. S. T. Coleridge, "To the Editor of the Morning Post," *Morning Post*, October 14, 1800.

42. Robinson, "The Maniac," 103–114.

43. This line of inquiry could be usefully applied to the vestiges of the history of primitive accumulation in Wordsworth's "Goody Blake and Harry Gill," a poem that weaves together gender, the supernatural, and the criminalization of wood theft, which, according to Engels, prompted Marx's turn away from law and toward political economy: "I always heard Marx say that it was through study of the law on theft of wood and the situation of the Moselland peasants that he was led to go over from pure politics to the study of economic questions and thereby even to socialism." Michael Löwy, *The Theory of Revolution in Young Marx* (Leiden: Brill, 2003), 25.

44. Schey, "Limited Analogies," 184.

45. Goldstein, *Sweet Science*, 188.

46. Johnson, "Apostrophe, Animation, and Abortion," 33.

47. Hartley, *Observations*, 13.

48. Sheehan and Wahrman, *Invisible Hands*, 198. Kyla Schuller has done remarkable work on the racialized origins and uneven classifications of such sensation histories. See Schuller, *Biopolitics of Race*.

49. Coleridge, *Biographia Literaria*, 313.

50. Wimsatt and Beardsley write in "The Intentional Fallacy" that "there is a gross body of life, of sensory and mental experience, which lies behind and in some sense causes every poem, but can never be and need not be known in the verbal and hence intellectual composition which is the poem. For all the objects of our manifold experience, especially for the intellectual objects, for every unity, there is an action of the mind which cuts off roots, melts away context" (479). Compare to the *Biographia*, where Coleridge writes that "the Imagination, then, I consider either as primary or secondary. The primary Imagination I hold up to be the living Power and prime Agent of all human Perception, and as a repetition in the finite mind of the eternal act of creation in the infinite I Am. The secondary I consider as an echo of the former. . . . It dissolves, diffuses, dissipates in order to re-create. . . . Fancy, on the contrary, has no other counters to play with, but fixities and definites. The Fancy is, indeed, no other than a mode of Memory emancipated from the order of

time and space, and blended with, and modified by, that empirical phenomenon of the will which we express by the word Choice. But, equally with the ordinary memory, it must receive all its materials ready made from the law of association" (173).

51. Ibid., 313.

52. Davis's precise description of the function of gender within a capitalist system of production is that "women filter through the prevailing ideology as anachronisms" alongside "awesome but increasingly irrational technological achievements." Angela Davis, "Women and Capitalism: Dialectics of Oppression and Liberation," in *The Black Feminist Reader*, ed. Joy James and Tracy Sharpley-Whiting (Malden, MA: Blackwell, 2000), 148.

53. As Amy De'Ath writes, the "unwaged reproductive work [that] cannot be rationalized towards the production of relative surplus value and thus resists productivity increases" is the condition of possibility for the production of equivalent commodities and standardized labor that underlies commodity fetishism. De'Ath, "Reproduction," in *The Bloomsbury Companion to Marx*, ed. Andrew Pendakis, Jeff Diamanti, and Imre Szeman (New York: Bloomsbury Academic, 2019), 400.

54. Daniel Hartley, "The Person, Historical Time and the Universalization of Capital," *Salvage*, no. 6 (2018): 206.

55. William J. Chambliss, "A Sociological Analysis of the Law of Vagrancy," *Social Problems* 12, no. 1 (Summer 1964): 70.

56. Ibid., 71. According to Chambliss, these shifts were "tied to the securitization of commodity circulation across borders.... This shift also meant that new categories within the category of vagrancy came to be made" (ibid.).

57. See Hartley, "The Person," 206.

58. This category also included "all fencers, bearwards, common players in interludes, and minstrels ... all jugglers, pedlars, tinkers, chapmen ... and all counterfeiters of licenses, passports and users of the same." Chambliss, "Sociological Analysis," 73.

59. C. S. L. Davis, "Slavery and Protector Somerset: The Vagrancy Act of 1547," *Economic History Review* 19, no. 3 (1966): 534–535.

60. William Hawkins and John Curwood, *A Treatise of the Pleas of the Crown; A System of the Principal Matters Relating to That Subject*, 8th ed., vol. 1 (London: S. Sweet, 1824), 690.

61. Federici, *Caliban and the Witch*, 184.

62. Marx, *Capital*, 1:916.

63. Saidiya V. Hartman, "The Anarchy of Colored Girls Assembled in a Riotous Manner," *South Atlantic Quarterly* 117, no. 3 (July 2018): 475. On the other side of accumulation-by-pleasure, see Hartman's use of "fungibility" as a rhetorical and

affective conjuncture of the spectacularized violence of slavery and the exchange form of the commodity in *Scenes of Subjection: Terror, Slavery, and Self-Making in Nineteenth-Century America* (Oxford: Oxford University Press, 1997), 21, 26.

64. Hartman, "Anarchy of Colored Girls," 475.

65. Ibid. Hartman writes elsewhere in the essay that "vagrancy was a status, not a crime. . . . Status offenses were critical to the remaking of a racist order in the aftermath of slavery and accelerated the growing disparity between black and white rates of incarceration in northern cities at the beginning of the twentieth century. . . . Involuntary servitude wasn't one condition—chattel slavery—nor was it fixed in time and place; rather it was an ever-changing mode of exploitation, domination, accumulation (the severing of will, the theft of capacity, the appropriation of life), and confinement" (ibid., 474).

66. Davis, "Women and Capitalism."

67. Joel Faflak, introduction to *Confessions of an Opium-Eater* by Thomas De Quincey, ed. Faflak (Peterborough, ON: Broadview, 2009), 39.

68. As many have pointed out, the history of enclosure is also emancipated from the order of time and space that Hartley, as well as Sheehan and Wahrman, have in mind. Marx gives us the basis for this emancipated reading when he tells us the (his)story of so-called primitive accumulation as a theological idyll that "plays approximately the same role in political economy as original sin does in theology. Adam bit the apple, and thereupon sin fell on the human race. Its origin is supposed to be explained when it is told as an anecdote about the past. Long, long ago there were two sorts of people; one, the diligent, intelligent and above all frugal élite; the other, lazy rascals, spending their substance, and more, in riotous living," Marx, *Capital*, 1:873. Rather than an examination of "the actual historical contours of feudalism," as Jordy Rosenberg notes, Marx's attention to enclosure was a full-blown philosophy of history in which capitalist modes of production and development occurred through the continuity of radically different forms of dispossession. See Rosenberg, "'The Original Sin Is at Work Everywhere': Marx's Concept of Primitive Accumulation," in *The Bloomsbury Companion to Marx*, ed. Andrew Pendakis, Jeff Diamanti, and Imre Szeman (New York: Bloomsbury Academic, 2019), 368.

69. Goldstein, *Sweet Science*, 118.

70. In this sense, Robinson's poem might be considered as the dream, or the Fancy, of sensation histories of a self-organizing mind. In this sense, it offers a prototype of Walter Benjamin's principle of collective history embedded in dreams in *The Arcades Project*, a principle itself drawn from eighteenth-century sensibility theory. Particularly relevant for me are the ways that Benjamin analogizes dreams to physiological processes in describing them as a collective unconscious, making both living bodies and the arcades into reservoirs of accumulated histories and

memories. In *The Arcades Project*, he writes that in the nineteenth century "the collective consciousness sinks into an ever deeper sleep. But just as the sleeper—in this respect like the madman—sets out on the macrocosmic journey through his own body, and the noises and feelings of his insides, such as blood pressure, intestinal churn, heartbeat, and muscle sensation . . . generate, in the extravagantly inner awareness of the sleeper, illusion or dream imagery which translates and accounts for them, so likewise for the dreaming collective, which, through the arcades, communes with its own insides" (K1,4).

71. Walker, *Sublime Perversion of Capital*, 83.

72. Wang, *Carceral Capitalism*, 99–112.

73. In this sense, commentators are absolutely right to point to the fact that eighteenth-century epistemologies were not nearly as fixed and totalizing as they have sometimes been depicted. Nonetheless, resituating such epistemologies as more heterogeneous and contingent in their empirical orientations does not save them from histories of capital accumulation and colonialism if the latter processes do not always look the way we think they do. Rather, as Ann Laura Stoler has recently argued, we might best understand the endurance and duress of colonial histories by attending to sentiments and sensibilities, simultaneous temporalities, degrees of sovereignty, the productive nature of messy borders, uncertain epistemologies, and zones of ambiguity rather than to the supremacy of reason, clearly defined categories, and fixed orders of things. See Stoler, *Duress: Imperial Durabilities in Our Times* (Durham, NC: Duke University Press, 2016), 3–37.

74. Fred Moten, *Stolen Life*, vol. 2 of *consent not to be a single being* (Durham, NC: Duke University Press, 2018), 87.

75. Ibid., x.

76. De Man, "Epistemology of Metaphor," 6.

77. De'Ath and Bhattacharya qtd. in De'Ath, "Reproduction," 401.

78. George Caffentzis, in *Letters of Blood and Fire: Work, Machines, and the Crisis of Capitalism* (Oakland, CA: PM Press, 2012), 40, 260.

79. Antonella Picchio describes this paradox as one in which "the capitalist economy uses the reproduction of the laboring population for the accumulation of capital. Hence capital must be understood not only physically, as tools or goods, but as a specific historical relationship between the laboring population and its means of reproduction." Picchio, *Social Reproduction*, 9.

Chapter 3: Tautology, Witchcraft, and a Thingly Commons

1. The case of the Norwood gypsies is documented by Owen Davies in *Witchcraft, Magic and Culture 1736–1951* (Manchester, UK: Manchester University Press, 1999), 55–56.

2. As Paton notes, a variety of terms including "obi, obey, oby, obia, and obeah" were used to refer to such practices. Diana Paton, *The Cultural Politics of Obeah: Religion, Colonialism and Modernity in the Caribbean World* (Cambridge: Cambridge University Press, 2015), 31.

3. The full title of the act was "An Act to Remedy the Evils arising from Irregular Assemblies of Slaves and to prevent their possessing arms and ammunition and going from place to place without tickets, and for preventing the practice of obeah, and to restrain overseers from leaving the estates under their care on certain days, and to oblige all free negroes, mulattoes or Indians, to register their names in the vestry books of the respective parishes of this Island, and to carry about them the certificate, and wear the badge of their freedom; and to prevent any captain, master or supercargo of any vessel bringing back slaves transported off this Island."

4. Paton, *Cultural Politics of Obeah*, 21; Srinivas Aravamudan, introduction to *Obi; or, the History of Three-Fingered Jack* (Peterborough, ON: Broadview, 2005), 32. As Paton writes, "Where colonists in most parts of the Americas assimilated African practices to European witchcraft, Jamaican authorities distanced the two. The new crime of obeah drew on the legal definition of witchcraft, but named it as something else" (Paton, *Cultural Politics of Obeah*, 21). Other formative readings of Obeah in this same vein include Vincent Brown, *The Reaper's Garden: Death and Power in the World of Atlantic Slavery* (Cambridge, MA: Harvard University Press, 2008); and Jenny Davidson, *Ghosts of Slavery* (Minneapolis: University of Minnesota Press, 2002). On Obeah and the British Romantic context, see also Alan Richardson, "Romantic Voodoo: Obeah and British Culture, 1797–1807," *Studies in Romanticism* 32 (Spring 1993): 3–28; Elizabeth S. Kim, "Maria Edgeworth's *The Grateful Negro*: A Site for Rewriting Rebellion," *Eighteenth-Century Fiction* 16, no. 1 (October 2003): 103–126; Charles J. Rzepka, "Thomas De Quincey's "Three-Fingered Jack": The West Indian Origins of the "Dark Interpreter," *European Romantic Review* 8, no. 2 (1997): 117–138; and Alan Bewell, "A 'Word Scarce Said': Hysteria and Witchcraft in Wordsworth's 'Experimental' Poetry of 1797–1798," *ELH* 53, no. 2 (Summer 1986): 357–390.

5. Alan Bewell has most explicitly presented the emergence of a medicalized approach to hysteria as a break with witchcraft, in the "transformation of the witch and her victim into melancholy or hysterical women." Bewell, "A 'Word Scarce Said,'" *ELH* 53, no. 2 (Summer 1986): 364.

6. Federici, *Caliban and the Witch*, 62.

7. M. H. Abrams, *Natural Supernaturalism: Tradition and Revolution in Romantic Literature* (New York: W. W. Norton, 1973).

8. Claude Lévi-Strauss, *The Savage Mind* (London: Weidenfeld & Nicolson, 1966), 14.

9. Ibid., 20–21.

10. Diana Paton notes that practitioners of what was consolidated under the name of Obeah in the nineteenth century "often make use of designations that invoke the modernity rather than the primitivism of their knowledge, such as 'science-man,' 'scientist,' 'doctor-man,' or 'professor'" (Paton, *Cultural Politics of Obeah*, 2).

11. Here Moseley provides the following footnote: "See *Isaiah*, c. lxvi. v. 17. also, PIERIUS on the Egyptian hieroglyphs." Benjamin Moseley, *A Treatise on Sugar*, 2nd ed. (London: Printed by J. Nichols, 1800), 191.

12. Darwin, *Zoonomia*, 482.

13. "*Mania mutabilis.* Mutable madness. Where the patients are liable to mistaken ideas of sensation for those from irritation, that is, imaginations for realities, if cured of one source of insanity, they are liable in a few months to find another source in some new mistaken or imaginary idea." Erasmus Darwin, *Zoonomia; or, the Laws of Organic Life*, vol. 2 (London: Printed for J. Johnson, in St. Paul's Church-Yard, [1796]), 270.

14. Marcel Mauss, *A General Theory of Magic*, trans. Robert Brain (London: Routledge, 2001), 15.

15. Darwin, *Zoonomia*, 1:135.

16. Ibid., 1:128–129.

17. David Lloyd, "The Racial Thing," *Texte zur Kunst* 29, no. 117 (March 2020): 86.

18. G. W. F. Hegel, *Hegel's Phenomenology of Spirit*, trans. A. V. Miller (Oxford: Oxford University Press, 1977), 68, 73.

19. Given both Hegel's and Darwin's interest in the movement forward from such associated things to complex and reflexive subjects, there is an immediate social implication to these taste tests that David Lloyd identifies in Hegel specifically. For Lloyd, the subsistence relations of things here show us a sensing subject that is composed of manifold perceptions that allows for the possibility of relations between things and others organized in coexistence but not identification. Or, as he puts it, there is a "social life of things" that aspires not to autonomy but to an organizing principle that is dispossessed, with only the "property to defy appropriation" but "the sealed and bounded unity of the individual. Lloyd, "The Racial Thing," 86.

20. Mauss, *General Theory of Magic*, 15.

21. Federici, *Caliban and the Witch*, 174.

22. In this context of Romantic empiricism and phenomenology, the following superstition offered by Michelle Cliff in her novel *Abeng* is quite striking: "Before the slaves came to Jamaica, the old women and men believed, before they had to eat

salt during their sweated labor in the canefields, Africans could fly. They were the only people on this earth to whom God had given this power. Those who refused to become slaves and did not eat salt flew back to Africa, those who did these things, who were slaves and ate salt to replenish their sweat, had lost the power because the salt made them heavy, weighed down." Michelle Cliff, *Abeng* (New York: Plume Press, 1995), 63.

23. The full title of Moseley's treatise is *A Treatise on Sugar, Medical Tracts. I. On Sugar. II. On the Cow Pox. III. On the Yaws. IV. On Obi, or African Witchcraft. V. On the Plague; and Yellow Fever of America VI. On Hospitals. VII. On Bronchocele. VIII. On Prisons*. As we read Moseley's interest in the diseases of slaves and the role of doctors more generally in the plantation economy, it is helpful to keep Robert Wedderburn's description of his slave-owning, rapist father in mind: "[James Wedderburn] adopted the medical profession; and in Jamaica he was Doctor and Man-Midwife, and turned an honest penny by drugging and physicing the poor blacks, where those that were cured, he had the credit for, and for those he killed, the fault was laid to their obstinancy." Wedderburn, *Horrors of Slavery*, 46.

24. Moseley, *Treatise on Sugar*, 5.

25. Ibid., 23.

26. Ibid., 63. On this point, Sidney Mintz writes, "Only in recent years have the civilizational accomplishments of the Arab world begun to receive fair attention in the West. . . . Though we never quite bring ourselves to say so baldly, the western view is one of amazement that the aesthetic capacities of other peoples are not confined by their technical limitations." Mintz, *Sweetness and Power: The Place of Sugar in Modern History* (New York: Penguin Books, 1985), 24.

27. Moseley, *Treatise on Sugar*, 56.

28. Ibid., 55.

29. Charles Mackey's narrativization of the pandemonium of superstition is useful here: "Every calamity that befell [man] he attributed to a witch. If a storm arose and blew down his barn, it was witchcraft; if his cattle died of a murrain . . . they were not visitations of Providence, but the works of some neighbouring hag, whose wretchedness or insanity caused the ignorant to raise their finger and point at her as a witch." Mackey, *Extraordinary Popular Delusions and the Madness of Crowds* (New York: Noonday Press, 1932), 463.

30. Wordsworth, "The Thorn," in *The Major Works*, 232–235.

31. Ibid., 196–198.

32. Oxford English Dictionary, s.v. "Hearsay," https://www-oed-com.proxy.library.nyu.edu/view/Entry/85059?rskey=5f1lf4&result=2&isAdvanced=false.

33. Federici, *Caliban and the Witch*, 186.

34. James I, "News from Scotland," in *William Shakespeare: Macbeth Texts and Contexts*, ed. William C. Carroll (Boston: Bedford / St. Martin's, 1999), 318.

35. Federici, *Caliban and the Witch*, 165, 171. The juridical acceptance of women's testimony in these cases even initiated the first instances of women's recognition as subjects qualified to testify in court in Europe.

36. Wordsworth, "Note to 'The Thorn,'" 594.

37. Ibid.

38. Ibid., 593.

39. Wordsworth, "Preface to *Lyrical Ballads* (1802)," 609.

40. One thing that seems useful about Wordsworth's articulation of tautology is that it is not primarily bound up with the classical philosophical problem of the ironically self-positing subject and its ungrounded repetitions. The problem with tautology tends to be routed through the "auto" and its sense of the selfsame, leading us to stay with the construction of the individual and self-possessed subject of Romantic ideology. Such a subject is the tautological conundrum of the selfsame repetition of "I am," the same kind of subject that Paul de Man once described as necessarily violent in its groundless positing. See his "Epistemology of Metaphor," 34–51.

41. In this way, tautology and repetition are not opposed to one another. They remain entangled in the body, even generating certain instances in which the difference is not clear at all. After all, there is no absolute difference between a word that is "weighed in the balance of feeling" and one that is "measured by the space they occupy on the page." Ostensibly, according to Wordsworth's own theory of meter, the balance of feeling has everything to do with the space and duration of words on the page. In this supposed distinction, there is actually a set of relations that is established in the progression from superstition to feeling, from sensation to self-regulation. Instead, they are arranged as a movement from external things to internal reflection and from the animal manifold of sensorial experience to the complex variety of human feeling.

42. *Brill Indo-European Etymological Dictionaries Online*. s.v. "autos" and "logos."

43. On this point in German, Greg Bird writes that "'same' . . . stems from *same/sama* (Old Norse). Like '*zusammen*,' it is rooted in the Proto-Germanic term *samon*, which connotes a process that gathers things together. The gathered-together appear as if they are the same. . . . In German, *Sammlung zusammen* is an obvious tautology, gathering toward the gathering—and it is less commonly used than its English equivalent gathering together.' But unlike its English counterpart, it clearly emphasizes how sameness is synthetically produced." Bird, *Containing Community: From Political Economy to Ontology in Agamben, Esposito, and Nancy* (Albany, NY: SUNY Press, 2016), 213n9.

44. Wordsworth, "Note to 'The Thorn,'" 593.

45. Rosalind Shaw, *Memories of the Slave Trade: Ritual and the Historical Imagination in Sierra Leone* (Chicago: University of Chicago Press, 2002): 16.

46. Ibid., 27.

47. Ibid., 17, 42.

48. Olaudah Equiano, *The Interesting Narrative of the Life of Olaudah Equiano or Gustauvus Vassa, the African. Written by Himself*, 2nd ed. [1789] (New York: Penguin Books, 2003), 57.

49. Alexander X. Byrd, *Captives & Voyagers: Black Migrants across the Eighteenth-Century British Atlantic World* (Baton Rouge: Louisiana State University Press, 2008), 30.

50. Brown, *Reaper's Garden*, 151.

51. Shaw, *Memories of the Slave Trade*, 3.

52. Wordsworth, "The Thorn," 1, 7–16.

53. Oxford English Dictionary, s.v., "Wretched, adj.," https://www-oed-com.proxy.library.nyu.edu/view/Entry/230658?rskey=EOpODw&result=2&isAdvanced=false.

54. William Shakespeare, *Macbeth: The Arden Shakespeare Third Series*, ed. Sandra Clark and Pamela Mason (London: Bloomsbury Arden Shakespeare, 2015), 227n122.

55. Wordsworth, "Note to 'The Thorn,'" 593.

56. Fred Moten, *The Universal Machine*, vol. 3 of *consent not to be a single being* (Durham, NC: Duke University Press, 2018), 9.

57. Moseley, *Treatise on Sugar*, 119–120.

58. This refrain comes from some of the best-known lines from "The Thorn." In *Sweetness and Power*, Sidney Mintz offers a similar perspective on the wide availability of the saccharine principle: "[R.J. Forbes accepts Dioscorides, who wrote: 'There is a kind of concreted honey, called *saccharon*, found in reeds in India and Arabia Felix, like in consistence to salt, and brittle to be broken between the teeth, as salt is. . . .' He reminds us, however, that terms like *saccharon* and even 'manna' were used for a variety of sweet substances, including plant secretions, the excreta of plant life, the mannite exudation of *Fraxinus ornus* (the so-called manna ash tree), etc." (20). Unlike Moseley's desire to establish sugar as a commodity, however, Mintz writes that sugar was "no single homogeneous substance" (27).

59. Moseley, *Treatise on Sugar*, 64.

60. Ibid., 164.

61. Ibid.

62. John Stuart Mill, "Of the Competition of Different Countries in the Same Market," in *Principles of Political Economy with Some of Their Applications to Social Philosophy* [1848], ed. J. M. Robson (Toronto: University of Toronto Press, 1965), 693. For more on the relevance of this internalization to the global form of capitalism particular to the British Empire, see Giovanni Arrighi, *The Long Twentieth Century: Money, Power and the Origins of Our Times* (New York: Verso, 2010).

63. See Mintz, *Sweetness and Power*: "Plantations were highly speculative enterprises. While they eventuated in enormous profits for fortunate investors, bankruptcies were common; some of the most daring plantation entrepreneurs ended their days in debtors' prison. Sugar was never a sure thing, despite the unfailingly optimistic predictions of its protagonists" (44–45).

64. Perhaps the most extensive, exoticizing, and dehumanizing account of maroons' ways of living is provided in the work of Bryan Edwards, *The Proceedings of the Governor and Assembly of Jamaica, in Regard to the Maroon Negroes* (London: Printed for John Stockdale, 1796); and Edward Long, *The History of Jamaica*, vol. 2: *Reflections on Its Situation, Settlements, Inhabitants, Climate, Products, Commerce, Laws, and Government* [1774] (Montreal McGill-Queen's University Press, 2005), 176–182.

65. "The planters who remained [post-emancipation] did not manage to organize law and penalty in such a way as to create a large-scale captive labor force or to proletarianize the population so as to force them into full-time wage work. Freedpeople, given the options by their ability to resist proletarianization, did not willingly submit to the plantation wage labor that was offered them. Instead, they tried to construct a peasant way of life. They thus removed themselves as far as possible from the subordination inherent in wage labor in plantation societies, a form of subordination that in fact echoed, rather than stood apart from, slavery." Diana Paton, *No Bond but the Law: Punishment, Race, and Gender in Jamaican State Formations, 1780–1870* (Durham, NC: Duke University Press, 2004), 9.

66. Wedderburn, *Horrors of Slavery*, 48–49.

67. Paton, *No Bond but the Law*, 15. See also Vincent Brown, *Reaper's Garden*.

68. Coleridge performs a similar distancing effect in his preface to "The Three Graves," where he writes that "the following humble fragment . . . is therefore presented as the fragment, not of a Poem, but of a common Ballad-tale. Whether this is sufficient to justify the adoption of such a style, in any metrical composition not professedly ludicrous, the Author is himself in some doubt." Coleridge, "The Three Graves," in *Sibylline Leaves* (Garden City, NY: Dolphin Books, n.d.), 171.

69. Federici, *Caliban and the Witch*, 204.

70. Coleridge, "Three Graves," 170. Moseley also recalls the superstition of witchcraft as more of a recent than a long-ago belief: "There was a time, and that not very long ago, when poverty, ugliness, and wrinkles, with palsied head and trembling limbs, constituted suspicions of Obi in England; and for which many old women have been tried, condemned, and hanged, as perpetrators of every untoward accident in their neighborhood." Moseley, *Treatise on Sugar*, 194.

71. Coleridge, "Three Graves," 172–173.

72. Edmund Burke, *A Philosophical Enquiry into the Origin of Our Ideas of the Sublime and Beautiful*, ed. J. T. Boulton (New York: Columbia University Press, 1958), 13.

73. Immanuel Kant, "Dreams of a spirit-seer elucidated by dreams of metaphysics," *Theoretical Philosophy*, ed. David Wolford (Cambridge: Cambridge University Press, 1992), 307–360.

74. Coleridge uses the phrase "fast-linked" to describe Edward's affections for both Mary and Ellen: Now Ellen was a darling love/ In all his joys and cares: / And Ellen's name and Mary's name / *Fast-linked they both together came*. / Whene'er he said his prayers / And in the moment of his prayers / *He lov'd them both alike*." Coleridge, "Three Graves," 178.

75. Ibid., 180.

76. Ibid.

77. Ibid., 172.

78. Beckles, "Sex and Gender," 132; emphasis added.

79. Hortense Spillers's account of ungendering and undifferentiation is very complex, and I cannot pretend to do justice to it here. Most relevant to my argument, though, is Spillers's claim that dispossession is a "loss of gender" that constitutes the abjection through which female slaves are simultaneously erased from histories of slavery and remain outside gender as defined by the domestic. Spillers tracks a genealogy of the absence of the father that produces a pathology of the mother, but her aim is not to save the mother as a substitution for the father and claims of rights and of property, but rather to suggest that there is a long tradition of illegitimacy to be read and invented in the history of female slaves. Thus, dispossession is the vestibulary space for the imagination and creation of "illegitimate" female relations and kinship relations that have already been constituted within the history of slavery. Spillers, "Mama's Baby, Papa's Maybe: An American Grammar Book," *Diacritics* 17, no. 2 (Summer 1987): 64–81.

80. Beckles, "Sex and Gender," 135.

81. Spillers, "Mama's Baby, Papa's Maybe," 77.

82. Alexander G. Weheliye, *Habeas Viscus: Racializing Assemblages, Biopolitics, and Black Feminist Theories of the Human* (Durham, NC: Duke University Press, 2014), 125.

83. Moseley, *Treatise on Sugar*, 166.

84. As Joseph Priestley describes it, the "science of language" can be plotted along the arc from archaic hieroglyphs to the progress of the written alphabet. Priestley, *A Course of Lectures*.

85. Moseley, *Treatise on Sugar*, 188. For a powerful reworking of this trope of affectability, see Opal Palmer-Adisa's short story "The Living Roots," in which enslaved women escape by growing into the environment: "I cannot tell you how we did it, except that once the ship docked and we were relieved from our chains, we each ran, and to keep from being detected, our bodies transformed and

we found ourselves being pulled more deeply into the earth.... From there we learned what we had always been taught, that we could become whatever the occasion demanded.... We grew roots and dug more securely into the ground and gave birth." Palmer-Adisa, *So Long Been Dreaming: Postcolonial Science Fiction & Fantasy*, ed. Nalo Hopkinson and Uppinder Mehan (Vancouver, BC: Arsenal Pulp Press, 2004), 230–242.

86. Moseley, *Treatise on Sugar*, 189.
87. Ibid., 188.
88. Spillers, "Mama's Baby, Papa's Maybe," 66.
89. Ferreira da Silva, *Toward a Global Idea*, 24.
90. Mauss, *General Theory of Magic*, 15.

91. Robinson writes that "the negations resultant from capitalist modes of production, relations of production, and ideology did not manifest themselves as an eradication of opposites among the working classes. Instead, the dialectic of proletarianization disciplined the working classes to the importance of distinctions: between ethnics and nationalities; between skilled and unskilled workers; and ... between races. The persistence and creation of such oppositions within the working classes were a critical part of the triumph of capitalism in the nineteenth century." Robinson, *Black Marxism*, 42.

92. In this sense, what Maureen McLane describes as Wordsworth's remediation of the oral in ballad poetry might extend far beyond poetic or anthropological concerns. For McLane, central to Wordsworth's remediating writing is that he "resists consigning [poetry] to a 'closed past'" in favor of "an utterly contemporary chronotype, featuring speech 'in the now,'" in which the past is both marked off and rewritten. From my perspective, Wordsworth's own entanglement with tautology is not a purely poetic project but one of those images of the material reconstructions of subsistence ongoing, inverted, and recalcitrant throughout Romanticism, processes that cannot be relegated to the residual. McLane, "Minstrelsy, or, Romantic Poetry," in *Balladeering, Minstrelsy, and the Making of British Romantic Poetry* (Cambridge: Cambridge University Press, 2008), 158.

93. Lloyd, "The Racial Thing," 90.

Chapter 4: Figure, Space, and Race between 1769 and 1985

1. The 1981 uprising in Brixton, South London, was a response to continuing police violence against the Black community, which had most recently been expressed via the formation of "'Swamp 81,' a special operation to combat 'muggings' and street crime" ("Notes and Documents," *Race and Class* 23, no. 2/3 [1981]: 224). The 1985 uprisings were a response to the police shooting of Dorothy "Cherry" Groce, a Black woman, as the police searched her home for her son, and shortly

thereafter the death of Cynthia Jarrett, another Black mother who died of a heart attack as a result of a violent search of her home in Tottenham. The Black Audio Film Collective was formed in this historical context and "was launched with three principal aims. Firstly, to attempt to look critically at how racist ideas and images of black people are structured and presented as self-evident truths in cinema. What we are interested in here is how these 'self-evident truths' become the conventional pattern through which the black presence in cinema is secured." John Akomfrah, "Black Independent Film-Making: A Statement by the Black Audio Film Collective," in Eshun and Sagar, *Ghosts of Songs*, 144.

2. Fusco, "Interview," 19.

3. "What we decided to do . . . was to appropriate classical or neoclassical images. But we appropriated them using methods of avant-garde photography which effectively began with Alexander Rodchenko—extremely angular kinds of framing, etc. That was the key difference. If you look at the formalist work on the other hand, the methods of composition were extremely straightforward. Henri Cartier Bresson could have done it. What people found unnerving about what we were doing was the play of postmodernism wasn't there." Akomfrah in ibid., 48.

4. Seymour Chatman ctd. In Wendy Xin, "The Secret Lives of Plot" (unpublished manuscript), 25. As Xin argues, montage reveals the materiality of the film strip that the form of the plot of cinema always works to suture. In her reading, montage becomes a way to theorize the relationship between what is inside and what is outside aesthetic form as a continual negotiation of mastery over its arrangement not through the successfulness of order but through the awareness of materiality's constructedness. Marjorie Perloff cites the Group Mu manifesto on this point, who write that in collage, "each cited element breaks the continuity or linearity of the discourse and leads necessarily to a double reading: that of the fragment perceived in relation to its text of origin; that of the same fragment as incorporated into a new whole, a different totality. The trick of collage consists also of never entirely suppressing the alterity of these elements reunited in a temporary composition." Perloff, "Collage and Poetry," in *Encyclopedia of Aesthetics*, vol. 1, ed. Michael Kelly (Oxford: Oxford University Press, 1998), 385.

5. Neill McKindrick, "Progress and the Lunaticks," *New York Times*, January 1, 1964. See also Robert Schofield, *Mechanism and Materialism: British Natural Philosophy in the Age of Reason* (Princeton, NJ: Princeton University Press, 1970); and Maureen McNeil, *Under the Banner of Science*, for a comprehensive overview of the role of the Lunar Society within the Industrial Revolution and their broader interests in capital investment, labor disciplining, and infrastructural schemes. Of particular interest to the Romantic period is James Watt and his partner, Michael Boulton's, opening of a giant flour mill in London that was to be powered by

Watt's rotating engine. The Albion Mills ran from 1786 until its destruction by fire in March 1791. As E. P. Thompson notes in "The Moral Economy of the Working Class," "the Albion Mills at Blackfriar's Bridge (London's first steam mills) were governed by a quasi-philanthropic syndicate; yet when they burned down in 1791 Londoners danced and sang ballads rejoicing in the streets." According to Thompson, such mills "were the visible, tangible targets of some of the most serious urban riots of the century." For a poetic depiction of such mills, one need look no further than William Blake's famous depiction of the "dark Satanic mills" of England.

6. "Look at that bird on the branch: it always seems ready to take flight. The imagination is the same, always carried away by the vortex of blood and the spirits; one wave leaves a trace which is erased by the following one. The soul runs after them, often in vain. It must expect to regret those it was not quick enough to seize and keep. Thus the imagination, in the true likeness of time, is perpetually renewed and destroyed." La Mettrie, *Machine Man*, 49.

7. Reece Auguiste, "Black Cinema, Poetics, and New World Aesthetics," in Eshun and Sagar, *Ghosts of Songs*, 159.

8. Kodwo Eshun and John Akomfrah, "An Absence of Ruins: John Akomfrah in Conversation with Kodwo Eshun," in Eshun and Sagar, *Ghosts of Songs*, 131.

9. Guyer, *Romanticism*, 146–147.

10. Auguiste, "Black Cinema," 154.

11. Chatman ctd. in Xin, "Secret Lives of Plot," 25.

12. Eshun and Akomfrah, "Absence of Ruins," 134.

13. As they remark in the interview with Fusco in "Interview with Black Audio Film Collective," the BAFC were interested in "representation because it seemed to be partly a way of prying open a negative/positive dichotomy. It seemed to be a way of being able to bypass certain boundaries" (43).

14. Daniel Rosenberg, "Joseph Priestley and the Graphic Invention of Modern Time," *Studies in Eighteenth-Century Culture* 36 (2007): 57.

15. Joseph Priestley, *A Description of a New Chart of History*, 7th ed. (London: Printed for J. Johnson, No. 72, St. Paul's Church Yard, 1789).

16. Rosenberg, "Joseph Priestley and the Graphic Invention of Modern Time," 55. Rosenberg does not describe the tradition of historiography in which he is working as Western, choosing instead to describe it as a historiographic tradition that ranges from "the most ancient of times to the most modern" (ibid.).

17. Priestley, *Description*, 5.

18. Ibid., 15.

19. Jonathan Sachs, *The Poetics of Decline in British Romanticism* (Cambridge: Cambridge University Press, 2018), 52.

20. Ibid., 62.

21. Rosenberg, "Joseph Priestley," 75.
22. Ibid., 81.
23. Sachs, *Poetics of Decline*, 44.
24. Ibid., 43.
25. Ibid., 52. For Sachs, it is such linearity and uniformity that enables the depiction of new scales of time, and it is this aspect of Priestley's chart that William Playfair later adopts in order to "underscore his argument that decline is a relative category . . . but also [to examine] the movement of empires over a nearly four-thousand-year period" (ibid.). A long scholarly history positions the late Enlightenment and the eighteenth century as the age in which epistemologies and technologies of standardization were most fully realized. Among others, see Stephen Gaukorger, "The Mathematical Principles of Natural Philosophy" and "The Fortunes of a Mechanical Model for Natural Philosophy" in *The Collapse of Mechanism and the Rise of Sensibility: Science and the Shaping of Modernity, 1680–1760* (Oxford: Oxford University Press, 2010), 55–83, 293–317; Schiebinger, *Plants and Empire*; John Gascoigne, *Science in the Service of Empire: Joseph Banks, the British State and the Uses of Science in the Age of Revolution* (Cambridge: Cambridge University Press, 1998); Tim Fulford, Debbie Lee, and Peter Kitson, *Literature, Science, and Exploration in the Romantic Era: Bodies of Knowledge* (Cambridge: Cambridge University Press, 2004); and McNeil, *Under the Banner of Science*. Critical works concerned with the relationship between science and commodification tend to emphasize the significance of standardizing epistemologies as well. The exemplary account here is Theodor Adorno and Max Horkheimer, *The Dialectic of Enlightenment: Philosophical Fragments*, trans. Edmund Jephcott (Stanford, CA: Stanford University Press, 2002). There is perhaps even more scholarship that sets itself up against a presupposed hegemony of standardization and commodification and in defense of more aesthetic or poetic modes of conceiving and perceiving the natural world. See, for instance, Theresa M. Kelley's recent *Clandestine Marriage: Botany and Romantic Culture* (Baltimore: Johns Hopkins University Press, 2015), which argues for a counterdiscourse to the standardization and classification of eighteenth-century sciences through the material resistance of plant life to such categorization; Goldstein, *Sweet Science*; Griffiths, *Age of Analogy*; Tim Fulford, "Science and Poetry in 1790s Somerset: The Self-Experiment Narrative, the Aeriform Effusion, and the Greater Romantic Lyric," *ELH* 85, no. 1 (2018): 85–118; Kate Singer, "Limpid Waves and Good Vibrations: Charlotte Smith's New Materialist Affect," in *Essays in Romanticism* 23, no. 2 (2016): 175–192; and Marjorie Levinson, "Of Being Numerous," *Studies in Romanticism* 49 (Winter 2010): 633–657. Mary Louise Pratt's *Imperial Eyes: Travel Writing and Transculturation*, 2nd ed. (London: Routledge, 2008) probably still stands as the best complicating account of the in-

terchangeability of classificatory and standardizing epistemologies with more sensational and sentimental ones.

26. Benjamin, *Arcades Project*, 391.
27. Ferreira da Silva, *Toward a Global Idea*, 2.
28. Priestley, *Description*, 5.
29. Fulford, "Science and Poetry," 92.
30. Sachs, *Poetics of Decline*, 62.
31. Rosenberg, "Joseph Priestley," 64.
32. Ibid., 77, emphasis added.
33. Priestley, *Description*, 8.
34. Darwin, *Zoonomia*, 1:113.
35. Ibid., 1:117. A similar sentiment is reflected in Priestley's edited republication of David Hartley's *Observations on Man*, where the linguistic notion of figure is shown to be the materialist product of associated differences: "The principle relation, which gives rise to figures, is that of likeness; and this may be either a likeness in *shape*, and *visible appearance*, or one *in application, use*, &c. Now it is very evident from the nature of association, that objects which are like to a given one in visible appearance, *will draw to themselves* the word by which this is expressed." Priestley, *Hartley's Theory*, 125.
36. Ferreira da Silva, *Toward a Global Idea*, xxxviii.
37. Darwin, *Zoonomia*, 1:42–43.
38. Priestley, *Description*, 10.
39. Ibid., 14. This relation between coexistence and progress lays a sensational groundwork for what Rei Terada has located as the racial logic of Kantian categories of space and time. See Terada, "The Racial Grammar of Kantian Time," *European Romantic Review* 28, no. 3 (2017): 267–278.
40. Gaukroger, *Collapse of Mechanism*, 418. This concern over excitation is characteristic of the broader conception of life and health in materialist and sensationalist perspectives. Indeed, one of the earliest physiological articulations of regulation as a defining feature of animate matter comes in James Parsons's 1752 *Philosophical Observations on the Analogy between the Propagation of Animals and Vegetables*: "The animating principle has the regulating power which renders the action of organization compatible with social Harmony . . . prevents Interruption, corrects Movements of all its springs, makes the distinction between use and abuse, and propagates virtue and truth, instead of vice and confusion by its guidance of the organization," 195. See also Goodman, "'Uncertain Disease'"; Noel Jackson, *Science and Sensation in Romantic Poetry* (Cambridge: Cambridge University Press, 2008); Paul Youngquist, "Lyrical Bodies: Wordsworth's Physiological Aesthetics," *European Romantic Review* 10 (1999): 152–162. On excitation

as a politico-physiological concern in the Romantic period, see Mary Fairclough, *Romantic Crowd*.

41. According to Rosenberg, "Priestley carried forward the linear concept from his *Chart of Biography* to his *Chart of History*, but there it functioned in a somewhat different way . . . Priestley sought to establish the relationship between ideas of place and time. This created a productive tension" due to the fact that the "principle divisions are geographic." "Joseph Priestley and the Graphic Invention of Modern Time," (81).

42. In Priestley's edition of Hartley's *Observations on Man*, a singularly influential text for Priestley, we can glimpse his own sense of history as the sedimented effect of figure. There, Hartley writes that "many, or most common figures, pass so far into literal expressions by use, i.e. association, that we do not attend at all to their figurative nature. And thus by degrees figurative senses become a foundation for successive figures, in the same manner, as originally literal senses." Priestley, *Hartley's Theory*, 126. Over time, figures are forgotten and being forgotten, they become succession and origin alike. While an impression on the eye is the foundation for our idea of history, this foundation is itself not temporally uniform.

43. Rosenberg, "Joseph Priestley," 77, emphasis added.

44. In this creative presentation of history, Priestley's distribution of space follows what Alan Bewell has recently argued was the constructivist approach that was exemplary of the eighteenth- century social and intellectual milieu in which Priestley circulated. Writing primarily about reconstructions of nature in imperial botanic gardens, Bewell notes that "What is distinctive about the botanic gardens of the second half of the eighteenth century is that they were more prospective than retrospective in character, less about the recovery of a lost order of nature than about making something new." "Erasmus Darwin's Cosmopolitan Nature," *ELH*, 76.1 (Spring 2009): 33.

45. Sachs, *Poetics of Decline*, 52.

46. Priestley, *Description*, 10.

47. Frank Palmieri, *States of Nature, Stages of Society: Enlightenment Conjectural History and Modern Social Discourse* (New York: Columbia University Press, 2016), 34.

48. Ibid. Rosenberg notes this as well, writing that the Chart "rel[ies] as much on the effects of simultaneity as of sequence . . . in the field of history [Priestley] always expressed frustration at the constraints of narrative." Rosenberg, "Joseph Priestley," 88–89.

49. Palmieri, *States of Nature*, 35.

50. Maureen N. McLane, *Romanticism and the Human Sciences* (Cambridge: Cambridge University Press, 2000), 133.

51. Walter Benjamin, "On the Concept of History," in *Selected Writings*, vol. 4:

1938–40, trans. Edmund Jephcott et al., ed. Howard Eiland and Michael W. Jennings (Cambridge, MA: Harvard University Press, 2003), 390.

52. Previous criticism of eighteenth-century materialist empiricism depicts the tradition of associationism as a predominantly mechanistic one, in which matter was characterized through passivity, necessity, and uniformity. Lorraine Daston depicts associationism as a theory of sensorially derived knowledge that is stabilized by a presupposed continuity between natural and psychological operations. See Daston, *Classical Probability*, 191–210. For a more specific account of materialism as it was theorized by David Hartley, see Jess Kaiser, "Plastic Matters," in *The New Politics of Materialism*, ed. Sarah Ellenzweig and John H. Zammito (London: Routledge, 2017), 66–86. More recent readings of empiricism attend more closely to its heterogeneity and complicate the tendency within new materialism and object-oriented ontology to treat "mechanistic materialism" as either a transcendental or binaristic affair.

53. Benjamin, *Arcades Project*, 475.

54. Ferreira da Silva, *Toward a Global Idea*, 39.

55. Eshun and Akomfrah, "Absence of Ruins," 133.

56. Edward George, "Introductions to Reflections of the Black Experience," in Eshun and Sagar, *Ghosts of Songs*, 151.

57. Benjamin, *Arcades Project*: "The compelling—the drastic experience, which refutes everything 'gradual' about becoming and shows all seeming 'development' to be dialectical reversal, eminently and thoroughly composed, is the awakening from a dream" (838).

58. Sachs, *Poetics of Decline*, 57.

59. Writing in his preface to *A Sermon on the Subject of the Slave Trade* (Birmingham, UK: Printed for the author, by Pearson and Rollason and sold by J. Johnson, 1788), Priestley relies explicitly on a stagism that defends the commonality of the human species. He declares that the "distinction" of the slave is "unnatural and improper . . . among those who are partakers of the same common nature" (22) and that those persons who "have long been in the habit of being served by slaves" are debased and "unfit for the society of his equals" (21). He writes elsewhere that "Christianity teaches us to consider all mankind as *brethren*, equally the subjects of God's moral government here, and alike heirs of immortality hereafter. Now, whether it can be proved that these principles necessarily lead to the emancipation of slaves or not (any more than they lead to take away all inequalities among men, those of rich and poor, masters and servants, &c) yet they certainly lead us to give every individual of the human race, at least sufficient, advantages for improving his nature, and preparing for a future state." (15).

60. Roxanne Wheeler, *The Complexion of Race: Categories of Race in Eighteenth-Century British Culture* (Philadelphia: University of Pennsylvania Press), 35, emphasis added.

61. Jairus Banaji, "State and Capital in the Era of Primitive Accumulation," Academic.edu, 3.

62. Marlon B. Ross, "The Race of/in Romanticism: Notes toward a Critical Race Theory," *Race, Romanticism and the Atlantic*, ed. Paul Youngquist (Farnham, UK: Ashgate, 2013), 26, 37. As Ross persuasively argues, it is at that messy and incoherent intersection of the surface of bodies and the level of the gut-instinctual and affective that race gets naturalized, experienced both as familiar and known as well as inarticulable and unstable. For Ross, it seems that British Romantic remakings of race came about in part through the increasing status of Black workers in domestic positions throughout the eighteenth century, which, coupled with discourses about Africa, made Blackness familiar and unfamiliar at the same time. As I argue, such a familiar/unfamiliar logic also extends to the continual discursive production and distribution of the affectability and pleasures of subsistence that remain a part of contemporary life.

63. Such relationality mirrors what Foucault presented as the logic of accumulation constructed through a new episteme of living organisms in the eighteenth century. Focusing not on representations of history but on the ordering of organisms in historical time, he sketched a spatiotemporal heuristic of living bodies and historical ordering in which hierarchies of structure existed alongside the relational and common functions of organisms. In the shattering of earlier orders of representation, an order of things that could accommodate both the relational and the discontinuous nature of living things was composed. Presented as "a series of oppositions, of which the two terms are never on the same level," Foucault's schematization of historical organisms highlights a more general asymmetry in which relationality could be organized along differential lines. Michel Foucault, *The Order of Things: An Archaeology of the Human Sciences* (New York: Random House, 1970), 268–269. Romantic and nineteenth-century scholars have had much to say about the flaws in Foucault's epistemic models in *The Order of Things*. Nonetheless, the noncontradiction between relationality and hierarchy he captured there is quite useful. By describing the onset of accumulation logics as an asymmetrical totality and distributed relationality, Foucault located the basic structure of what more recent scholars have described as that of global capital accumulation through racialization.

64. Ferreira da Silva, *Toward a Global Idea of Race*, xxxviii.

65. For the most thorough account of the racialization of the English working class through the framework of Orientalism, see Makdisi, *Making England Western*.

66. Priestley, *An Account*, 4–5.

67. Sandro Mezzadra describes how the extension of the working day has typically been understood by Marxist theorists, as the "'formal subsumption' of labor

under capital . . . (achieved by means of a constant increase of the length of the working day)" was for Marx a way of understanding the emergence of capitalism under different modes of production in which, and here he quotes Marx, "the capitalist mode of production did not display a specifically capitalist character." Mezzadra complicates the potential primitivization of formal subsumption in a later section of the text, where, again quoting Marx, he notes that under "'this primary or first period of capital' . . . a set of fundamental conditions of the capitalist mode of production ('a certain level of skill, instrument as means of labor, etc.') are 'already available.' . . . On the other hand, this peculiar temporal structure (where the time of capital is dependent on other historical times that are not its own) characterizes 'formal subsumption.'" Sandro Mezzadra, "The Topicality of Prehistory: A New Reading of Marx's Analysis of 'So-Called Primitive Accumulation.'" *Rethinking Marxism* 23, no. 3 (2011): 313–314.

68. Priestley here presupposes the natural division between the costs of production and reproduction that we discussed in Chapter 1. For instance, the fund he proposes assumes that capitalists are only responsible for covering the present costs of workers' reproduction rather than the cost of their health risks and late life as well. It also assumes that unwaged labor can only secure what is needed for short-term subsistence, which, as Antonella Picchio's and David Lloyd's work has shown, is simply not the case.

69. Priestley, *An Account*, 7.

70. Robert Schofield, *The Lunar Society of Birmingham: A Social History of Provincial Science and Industry in Eighteenth-Century England* (Oxford: Clarendon Press, 1963), 151.

71. Cedric Robinson, "Atlantic Slave Trade and African Labor," in *Black Marxism*, 101–116.

72. Ruth Wilson Gilmore, "Fatal Couplings of Power and Difference: Notes on Racism and Geography," *Professional Geographer* 54, no. 1 (2002): 16.

73. For more on this point, see Wang, *Carceral Capitalism*.

74. Fred Moten, *In the Break: The Aesthetics of the Black Radical Tradition* (Minneapolis: University of Minnesota Press, 2003), 6.

75. Auguiste, "Black Cinema," 154.

76. In contrast, Ferreira da Silva suggests more rather than less "critique of the context and conditions of production of the tools that set up and sustain this rather efficient biopolitical arsenal" of death-dealing. Denise Ferreira da Silva, "Notes for a Critique of the 'Metaphysics of Race,'" *Theory, Culture & Society* 28, no. 1 (2011): 147.

77. See McNeil, *Under the Banner of Science*, 161–163.

78. Priestley, *An Account*, 7.

79. Monique Allewaert, *Ariel's Ecology: Plantations, Personhood, and Colonialism in the American Tropics* (Minneapolis: University of Minnesota Press, 2013), 61. For a similar reading of Priestley, see Stout, "Associationist Aesthetics."

80. Daniel Nemser, *Infrastructures of Race: Concentration and Biopolitics in Colonial Mexico* (Austin: University of Texas Press, 2017), 157.

81. Alexander von Humboldt, *Political Essay on the Kingdom of New Spain* (London: Printed for Longman, Hurst, Rees, Orme, and Brown, 1822), 235.

82. Ibid., 261, emphasis added.

83. David Lloyd, *Irish Culture and Colonial Modernity, 1800–2000: The Transformation of Oral Space* (Oxford: Oxford University Press, 2011), 33, emphasis added. Elsewhere, Lloyd argues that such trajectories of modernization made available by developmentalist discourses depict responses to what he has called "the historical processes of colonization, survival and transformation" as traditional and backward. Quite to the contrary, however, he argues that what appear as backward or primitive practices are "alternative forms that persist at [the] violent interfaces" of colonial and capitalist development. That is, what gets presented as most archaic in developmentalist narratives is entirely contemporary, activated by historical processes that sever people from tradition and have "the contradictory effect of preserving the social formation through antagonism to colonialism. David Lloyd, "Rethinking National Marxism: James Connolly and 'Celtic Communism,'" *Interventions: International Journal of Postcolonial Studies* 5, no. 3 (2003): 345–370.

84. Fusco, "Interview," 52.

85. Okwui Enwezor, "Coalition Building, Black Audio Film Collective and Transnational Post-colonialism," in Eshun and Sagar, *Ghosts of Songs*, 120.

86. Fusco, "Interview," 43.

87. Ibid., 52. Similarly, postcolonial scholar David Lloyd describes race as "constitutive of and marginal to the history of global capitalism." Lloyd, "Rethinking National Marxism," 345. Lloyd's analysis resonates with Sandro Mezzadra's, for whom a fundamental "disconnection defines the relationship between the history and 'prehistory' of capital." Such disconnection, which "is always open in capitalist development" ("Topicality of Prehistory," 314) is no general abstraction. It is, as Priestley's chart and supplementary text helps to show, a more concrete abstraction, in which representations of history are inseparable from the production of race.

88. Stoler, *Duress*, 239. On this point, see also Ruth Wilson Gilmore, who writes that "if race has not essence, racism does. Racism is singular because, whatever its place-based particularities, its practitioners exploit and renew *fatal* power-difference couplings" (Wilson Gilmore, "Fatal Couplings of Power and Difference," 16).

Coda

1. Benjamin, *Arcades Project*, K1,4.
2. Sabina Spielrein, "Destruction as the Cause of Coming into Being" [1912], *Journal of Analytic Psychology* 39 (1994): 157.
3. Ibid., 156–157.
4. My use of the term women throughout refers not only to those designated by medical professionals and the state as biological women but also to those who become women later in life.
5. Ibid., 157.
6. Arien Austen, "Journals of Originary Accumulation: Introduction to Silvia Federici's Nigerian Writings," *differences: A Journal of Feminist Cultural Studies* 51, no. 5 (2021): 123.
7. Mezzadra, "Topicality of Prehistory," 305.
8. Daston, *Classical Probability*, 209–210.
9. Forest Pyle and Jacques Khalip, "Introduction: The Present Darkness of Romanticism," in *Constellations of a Contemporary Romanticism*, ed. Pyle and Khalip (New York: Fordham University Press, 2016), 5.
10. Benjamin, "On the Concept of History," 391.
11. Foucault, "Nietzsche, Genealogy, History," 154.
12. Robinson qtd. in Harriet Guest, *Unbounded Attachment: Sentiment and Politics in the Age of the French Revolution* (Oxford: Oxford University Press, 2013), 34.
13. "Mr Robinson had much business to transact in London, and I was almost perpetually alone at Finchley. Of our domestic establishment there was only one who did not desert us, and he was a negro!—one of that despised, degraded race, who wear the colour on their features which too often characterizes the hearts of their fair and unfeeling oppressors. I have found, during my journey through life, that the two male domestics who were most attached to my interest and most faithful to my fortunes were both *negroes!*" Robinson, *Memoirs*, 89.
14. Ibid., 18.
15. Ibid., 13.
16. Ibid., 14.
17. Ibid., 46.
18. Ibid., 22.
19. Ibid., 27.
20. Ibid., 14, 46, 26–27.
21. Foucault qtd. In Mezzadra, "Topicality of Prehistory," 305.
22. Darwin, *Zoonomia*, 356–357.
23. Judith Butler describes the production of the relation between the subject and its (gendered) essence through the figure of scene and stage, including "the ar-

chitectonics of its theatre, its framing in space-time, its geometric organization, its props, its actors, their respective positions, their dialogues, indeed their tragic relations, without over-looking the mirror, most often hidden, that allows the logos, the subject, to reduplicate itself, to reflect itself by itself. All these are interventions on the scene; they ensure its coherence so long as they remain uninterpreted." Judith Butler, *Bodies That Matter* (Abingdon, UK: Routledge, 1993), 3.

24. Ruba Salih and Sophie Richter-Devroe, "Palestine beyond National Frames: Emerging Politics, Cultures, and Claims," *South Atlantic Quarterly* 117, no. 1 (January 2018): 4.

25. Spielrein, "Destruction," 157.

26. Brian Whitener, "Countering Counterinsurgency: Social Reproduction and Emancipatory Thought" (unpublished manuscript), 3. See also Nathan K. Hensley, *Forms of Empire: The Poetics of Victorian Sovereignty* (Oxford: Oxford University Press, 2016), 1–32.

27. Foucault, "Nietzsche, Genealogy, History," 145.

28. Nazan Üstündağ, "Mother, Politician, and Guerilla: The Emergence of a New Political Imagination in Kurdistan through Women's Bodies and Speech," *differences: A Journal of Feminist Cultural Studies* 50, no. 2 (2019): 122.

29. The fuller context provided by Bülent Kücük and Ceren Özselçuk is as follows: "As the world's largest stateless people, dispersed across four nation-states, Kurds emerge as an empowered actor in the midst of the dramatic social and political upheavals that reconfigure the Middle East and transform the region into a political battlefield of local, regional, and global forces. . . . After the heroic defense of Kobane (a city in the larger region of Rojava) in the autumn of 2014, carried out by the People's Protection Units and Women's Protection Units against the invasive and cruel attacks of the Islamic State, this small town located on the Syrian-Turkish border has expanded into a metaphor for liberation (especially women's liberation." Bülent Kücük and Ceren Özselçuk, "The Rojava Experience: Possibilities and Challenges of Building a Democratic Life," *South Atlantic Quarterly* 115, no. 1 (January 2016): 184.

30. Üstündağ, "Mother, Politician, and Guerilla," 134.

31. Benjamin, "On the Concept of History," 394.

32. Silvia Federici, "Nigerian Writings," *differences: A Journal of Feminist Cultural Studies* 51, no. 5 (2021): 141, 143.

33. Foucault, "Nietzsche, Genealogy, History," 151.

34. De Man, "Epistemology of Metaphor," 44.

35. "What I would like to show is this: that statelessness is not relative nothingness; that insofar as blackness is and comes, rather, from absolutely nothing it is, indeed, something after all, namely, the commonness of the improper," Moten, *Stolen Life*, 26.

36. Clifford ctd. in Salih and Richter-Devroe, "Palestine beyond National Frames," 5.

37. On the history of this incorporation of diversity, see Roderick Ferguson, *The ReOrder of Things: The University and Its Pedagogies of Minority Difference* (Minneapolis: University of Minnesota Press, 2012).

38. Modern Language Association, "Resolutions from the 2017 Delegate Assembly," mla.org.

39. On the history and strategy of the academic and cultural boycott, see Uri Yacobi Keller, "The Economy of the Occupation," *Socioeconomic Bulletin*, nos. 23–24 (2009): 1–64. Keller writes, "All main Israeli academic institutions are involved in the occupation. Indeed, all major Israeli academic institutions, certainly the ones with the strongest international connections, were found to provide unquestionable support to Israel's occupation" (5). Keller also discusses the difference between the tactics of economic and cultural boycotts and the significant distinctions between these campaigns in the context of Israeli and South African apartheid regimes.

40. Jeffrey Sacks, "The Resistance to Boycott: Palestine, BDS, and the Modern Language Association," *Radical History Review* 134 (May 2019): 241–242.

41. Benjamin, "On the Concept of History," 391. For an extensive review of the relationship between BDS, language, and international higher education, see Rebecca Comay, Margaret Ferguson, Lenora Hanson, David Lloyd, Julie Rak, and David Simpson, "A Report on MLA Members' Visit to Palestine," MLA Members for Justice in Palestine, December 6, 2016.

42. The "question of Palestine" tends to be deferred, when taken up at all, to the Victorian period and the British Mandate. See Stephan Wade, *Spies in the Empire: Victorian Military Intelligence* (London: Anthem Press, 2007); Mark Crinson, *Empire Building: Orientalism and Victorian Architecture* (London: Routledge, 1996); and John James Moscrop, *Measuring Jerusalem: The Palestine Exploration Fund and British Interests in the Holy Land* (London: Leicester University Press, 2000).

43. Hamid Dibashi, "Afterword: Palestine without Borders," *South Atlantic Quarterly* 117, no. 1 (January 2018): 180–181.

44. Ilan Pappe, "Indigeneity as Cultural Resistance: Notes on the Palestinian Struggle within Twenty-First-Century Israel," *South Atlantic Quarterly* 117, no. 1 (January 2018): 168, 170. As Pappe writes, the use of the term "indigeneity" in a Palestinian context has been fraught, owing both to the pseudo-national framework established by the Oslo Accords as well as to Palestinian concerns that claims to indigeneity would "tally with the Israeli politics of dividing the Palestinians into religious and cultural minorities and question their national cohesive identity." In contrast, he invokes James Clifford's notion of indigeneity "not as a fixed identity but rather as a dynamic identity that one can grow into" (158).

45. Ruba Salih and Sophie Richter-Devroe, "Palestine beyond National Frames: Emerging Politics, Cultures, and Claims," *South Atlantic Quarterly* 117, no. 1 (January 2018), 2.

46. Ibid., 2–3.

47. Stoler, *Duress*, 37–67.

48. Moten, *Stolen Life*, 3.

49. See Moten on this point as well: "The poetics of nonsense arises within the horizon of this discursive system, in the border area between late Enlightenment and early romanticism." Moten, *Stolen Life*, 4.

50. Linebaugh, *Red Round Globe Burning Hot*. In Linebaugh's most recent work, Romanticism is found across Great Britain, Ireland, the West Indies, and Nicaragua.

51. Even Pier Paolo Pasolini reads Palestinian faces in this manner, saying that "they have pre-Christian faces, pagan, indifferent, happy, savage," and comparing them to the European lumpenproletariat. Pasolini, *Seeking Locations in Palestine for the Film "The Gospel According to Matthew"* (1965).

Bibliography

Abrams, M. H. *The Mirror and the Lamp: Romantic Theory and the Critical Tradition*. Oxford: Oxford University Press, 1953.
Adamson, Alyssa. "Against a Single History, for a Revaluation of Power: Luxemburg, James, and a Decolonial Critique of Political Economy." In *Creolizing Rosa Luxemburg*, edited by Drucilla Cornell and Jane Anna Gordon. New York: Rowman & Littlefield, 2021.
Adorno, Theodor and Max Horkheimer. *The Dialectic of Enlightenment: Philosophical Fragments*. Translated by Edmund Jephcott. Stanford, CA: Stanford University Press, 2002.
Akomfrah, John. "Black Independent Film-Making: A Statement by the Black Audio Film Collective." In Eshun and Sagar, *The Ghosts of Songs*.
Allewaert, Monique. *Ariel's Ecology: Plantations, Personhood, and Colonialism in the American Tropics*. Minneapolis: University of Minnesota Press, 2013.
Anderson, Perry. *Lineages of the Absolutist State*. New York: Verso, 2013.
Aravamudan, Srinivas. Introduction to *Obi; or, the History of Three-Fingered Jack*. Edited by Srinivas Aravamudan. Peterborough, ON: Broadview, 2005.
Arrighi, Giovanni. *The Long Twentieth Century: Money, Power and the Origins of Our Times*. New York: Verso, 2010.
Auguiste, Reece. "Black Cinema, Poetics, and New World Aesthetics." In Eshun and Sagar, *The Ghosts of Songs*.

Austen, Arien. "Journals of Originary Accumulation: Introduction to Silvia Federici's 'Nigerian Writings.'" *differences: A Journal of Feminist Cultural Studies* 51, no. 5 (2021): 117–155.

Austin, J. L. "Lecture VIII." In *How to Do Things with Words*. 1977. Oxford Scholarship Online. October 2011. doi:10.1093/acprof:oso/9780198245537.001.0001.

Balfour, Ian. *The Rhetoric of Romantic Prophecy*. Stanford, CA: Stanford University Press, 2002.

Banaji, Jairus. "State and Capital in the Era of Primitive Accumulation." https://www.historicalmaterialism.org/book-review/state-and-capital-era-primitive-accumulation.

Becker-Ho, Alice. *The Essence of Jargon*. Translated by John McHale. New York: Autonomedia, 2015.

Beckles, Hilary. "Sex and Gender in the Historiography of Caribbean Slavery." In *Engendering History: Caribbean Women in Historical Perspective*, edited by Verene Shepherd, Bridget Brereton, and Barbara Bailey. New York: Palgrave Macmillan, 1995.

Benjamin, Walter. *The Arcades Project*. Translated by Howard Eiland and Kevin Mclaughlin. Cambridge, MA: Harvard University Press, 1999.

———. "On the Concept of History." In *Selected Writings*, vol. 4: *1938–1940*, translated by Edmund Jephcott et al., edited by Howard Eiland and Michael Jennings. Cambridge, MA: Harvard University Press, 2006.

———. "The Task of the Translator." In *Selected Writings*, vol. 1: *1913–1926*, translated by Harry Zohn, edited by Marcus Bullock and Michael W. Jennings. Cambridge, MA: Harvard University Press, 2004.

Bewell, Alan. "Erasmus Darwin's Cosmopolitan Nature." *ELH* 76, no. 1 (Spring 2009): 19–48.

———. "A 'Word Scarce Said': Hysteria and Witchcraft in Wordsworth's 'Experimental' Poetry of 1797–1798." *ELH* 53, no. 2 (Summer 1986): 357–390.

Bhandar, Brenna. *Colonial Lives of Property: Law, Land, and Racial Regimes of Ownership*. Durham, NC: Duke University Press, 2018.

Bhattacharya, Tithi. "Introduction: Mapping Social Reproduction Theory." In *Social Reproduction Theory: Remapping Class, Recentering Oppression*, edited by Tithi Bhattacharya. London: Pluto Press, 2017.

Bird, Greg. *Containing Community: From Political Economy to Ontology in Agamben, Esposito, and Nancy*. Albany, NY: SUNY Press, 2016.

Brown, Vincent. *The Reaper's Garden: Death and Power in the World of Atlantic Slavery*. Cambridge, MA: Harvard University Press, 2008.

Buck-Morss, Susan. *The Dialectics of Seeing: Walter Benjamin and the Arcades Project*. Cambridge, MA: MIT Press, 1991.

Burke, Edmund. *A Philosophical Enquiry into the Origin of Our Ideas of the Sublime and Beautiful*. Edited by J. T. Boulton. New York: Columbia University Press, 1958.

———. "Some Thoughts on the Approaching Executions." In *On Empire, Liberty, and Reform: Speeches and Letters*, edited by David Bromwich. New Haven, CT: Yale University Press, 2000.

———. "Thoughts and Details on Scarcity." In *Miscellaneous Writings*, edited by Francis Canavan. Indianapolis: Liberty Fund, 1999.

Butler, Judith. *Bodies That Matter*. Abingdon, UK: Routledge, 1993.

Byrd, Alexander X. *Captives & Voyagers: Black Migrants across the Eighteenth-Century British Atlantic World*. Baton Rouge: Louisiana State University Press, 2008.

Caffentzis, George. In *Letters of Blood and Fire: Work, Machines, and the Crisis of Capitalism*. Oakland, CA: PM Press, 2012.

Chambliss, William. "A Sociological Analysis of the Law of Vagrancy." *Social Problems* 12, no. 1 (Summer 1964): 67–77.

Clare, John. "The Eternity of Nature." In *I Am: The Selected Poetry of John Clare*, edited by Jonathan Bate. New York: Farrar, Straus & Giroux, 2003.

Cliff, Michelle. *Abeng*. New York: Plume Press, 1995.

Clover, Joshua. *Riot. Strike. Riot*. New York: Verso, 2016.

Coleridge, S. T. *Biographia Literaria*. In *Samuel Taylor Coleridge: The Major Works*, edited by H. J. Jackson. Oxford: Oxford University Press, 2008.

———. *Collected Letters of S. T. Coleridge*. Vol. 1. Edited by Earl Leslie Griggs. Oxford: Clarendon Press, 1956.

———. *The Collected Works of Samuel Taylor Coleridge*. Vol. 11. Edited by H. J. Jackson and J. R. de J. Jackson. Princeton, NJ: Princeton University Press, 1995.

———. *Conciones ad Populum*. In *Collected Works: Lectures 1795 on Politics and Religion*, vol. 1, edited by Lewis Patton and Peter Mann. Princeton, NJ: Princeton University Press, 1971.

———. "Introductory Address." In *Collected Works: Lectures 1795 on Politics and Religion*, vol. 1, edited by Lewis Patton and Peter Mann. Princeton, NJ: Princeton University Press, 1971.

———. "The Three Graves." In *Sibylline Leaves*. Garden City, NY: Dolphin Books, n.d. http://www.jackdeland.com/content/resources/pdfs/h-autography/sibylline_leaves.pdf.

———. "To the Editor of the Morning Post." *Morning Post*, October 14, 1800. Seventeenth and Eighteenth Century Burney Newspapers Collection.

Collings, David. *Monstrous Society: Reciprocity, Discipline, and the Political Uncanny, c. 1780–1848*. Lewisburg, PA: Bucknell University Press, 2001.

Comay, Rebecca, Margaret Ferguson, Lenora Hanson, David Lloyd, Julie Rak, and David Simpson. "A Report on MLA Members' Visit to Palestine." MLA Members for Justice in Palestine, December 6, 2016, https://mlaboycott.wordpress.com/2016/12/06/report-on-mla-members-trip-to-the-west-bank-and-israel/.

Crinson, Mark. *Empire Building: Orientalism and Victorian Architecture*. London: Routledge, 1996.

Culler, Jonathan. "Apostrophe." *Diacritics* 7, no. 4 (Winter 1977): 59–69.

Darwin, Erasmus. *Phytologia; or the Philosophy of Agriculture and Gardening*. London: Printed for J. Johnson, St. Paul's Church-Yard; by T. Bensley, Bolt Court, Fleet Street, 1800. Eighteenth Century Collections Online. https://link.gale.com/apps/doc/CW0109294142/ECCO?u=new64731&sid=bookmark-ECCO&xid=3ca36dc8&pg=1.

———. *Zoonomia; or, the Laws of Organic Life*. Vol. 1. London: Printed for J. Johnson, [1794]. Eighteenth Century Collections Online. https://link.gale.com/apps/doc/CW0109312786/ECCO?u=new64731&sid=bookmark-ECCO&xid=4a9a94fc&pg=1.

———. *Zoonomia; or, the Laws of Organic Life*. Vol. 2. London: Printed for J. Johnson, in St. Paul's Church-Yard, [1796]. Eighteenth Century Collections Online. https://link.gale.com/apps/doc/CW0109564210/ECCO?u=new64731&sid=bookmark-ECCO&xid=d01c33cf&pg=1.

Daston, Lorraine. *Classical Probability in the Enlightenment*. Princeton, NJ: Princeton University Press, 1988.

Davidson, Jenny. *Ghosts of Slavery*. Minneapolis: University of Minnesota Press, 2002.

Davies, Owen. *Witchcraft, Magic and Culture 1736–1951*. Manchester, UK: Manchester University Press, 1999.

Davis, Angela. "Women and Capitalism: Dialectics of Oppression and Liberation." In *The Black Feminist Reader*, edited by Joy James and Tracy Sharpley-Whiting. Malden, MA: Blackwell, 2000.

Davis, C. S. L. "Slavery and Protector Somerset: The Vagrancy Act of 1547." *Economic History Review* 19, no. 3 (1966): 533–549.

De'Ath, Amy. "Reproduction." In *The Bloomsbury Companion to Marx*, edited by Jeff Diamanti, Andrew Pendakis, and Imre Szeman. New York: Bloomsbury Academic, 2019.

de Man, Paul. "The Epistemology of Metaphor." In *Aesthetic Ideology*, edited by Andrejz Warminksi. Minneapolis: University of Minnesota Press, 1996.

———. "Semiology and Rhetoric." In *Allegories of Reading: Figural Language in Rousseau, Nietzsche, Rilke, and Proust*. New Haven, CT: Yale University Press, 1979.

Derrida, Jacques. *Of Grammatology*. Baltimore: Johns Hopkins University Press, 1998.

———. *Speech and Phenomena and Other Essays on Husserl's Theory of Signs*. Translated by David B. Allison. Evanston, IL: Northwestern University Press, 1973.

de Sousa Santos, Boaventura. "Public Sphere and Epistemologies of the South." *Africa Development* 37, no. 1 (2012): 43–67.

Dibashi, Hamid. "Afterword: Palestine without Borders." *South Atlantic Quarterly* 117, no. 1 (January 2018): 179–187.

Edwards, Bryan. *The Proceedings of the Governor and Assembly of Jamaica, in Regard to the Maroon Negroes*. London: Printed for John Stockdale, 1796. Caribbean History and Culture, 1535–1920. https://infoweb-newsbank-com.proxy.library.nyu.edu/iw-search/we/Evans?p_theme=eai&p_product=EAIX&d_collections=CRBHCC&d_collectionName=CRBHCC&p_action=search&d_searchform=customized&p_text_custbase-0=3420&p_field_custbase-0=docnum&p_sort=YMD_date%3AA&s_startsearch=&s_pagesearch=&p_perpage=10&d_subcat=&p_nbid=C5DU50DKMTY1Mjg4MjgzNy4oNTk2NDg6MT0xNDoxMjguMTIyLjE0OS45Mg.

Enwezor, Okwui. "Coalition Building: Black Audio Film Collective and Transnational Post-colonialism." In Eshun and Sagar, *The Ghosts of Songs*.

Equiano, Olaudah. *The Interesting Narrative of the Life of Olaudah Equiano or Gustauvus Vassa, the African: Written by Himself*. 1789. 2nd ed. New York: Penguin Books, 2003.

Eshun, Kodwo, and John Akomfrah. "An Absence of Ruins: John Akomfrah in Conversation with Kodwo Eshun." In Eshun and Sagar, *The Ghosts of Songs*.

Eshun, Kodwo, and Anjalika Sagar. *The Ghosts of Songs: The Film Art of the Black Audio Film Collective*. Edited by Kodwo Eshun and Anjalika Sagar. Liverpool, UK: Liverpool University Press, 2007.

Faflak, Joel. Introduction to *Confessions of an Opium-Eater* by Thomas De Quincey. Edited by Joel Faflak. Peterborough, ON: Broadview, 2009.

Fairclough, Mary. *The Romantic Crowd: Sympathy, Controversy and Print Culture*. Cambridge: Cambridge University Press, 2013.

Fay, Elizabeth. "Mary Robinson." In *The Encyclopedia of Romantic Literature*, edited by Frederick Burwick, Nancy Moore Goslee, and Diane Long Hoeveler. Vol. 3. Chichester, UK: Wiley-Blackwell, 2012.

Federici, Silvia. *Caliban and the Witch*. New York: Autonomedia, 2004.

———. "Nigerian Writings." *differences: A Journal of Feminist Cultural Studies* 51, no. 5 (2021): 117–155.

Ferguson, Roderick. *The ReOrder of Things: The University and Its Pedagogies of Minority Difference*. Minneapolis: University of Minnesota Press, 2012.

Ferreira da Silva, Denise. "Notes for a Critique of the 'Metaphysics of Race.'" *Theory, Culture & Society* 28, no. 1 (2011): 138–148.

———. "On Difference without Separability." Catalogue for the 32nd Sao Paulo Art Biennial, November 2016. https://issuu.com/amilcarpacker/docs/denise_ferreira_da_silva.

———. *Toward a Global Idea of Race*. Minneapolis: University of Minnesota Press, 2007.

———. "*Transversing* the Circuit of Dispossession." *Eighteenth Century* 55, nos. 2–3 (2014): 283–288.

Foucault, Michel. "Nietzsche, Genealogy, History." In *Language, Counter-Memory, Practice: Selected Essays and Interviews*, edited by D. F. Bouchard. Ithaca, NY: Cornell University Press, 1977.

———. *The Order of Things: An Archaeology of the Human Sciences*. New York: Random House, 1970.

Fulford, Tim. "Science and Poetry in 1790s Somerset: The Self-Experiment Narrative, the Aeriform Effusion, and the Greater Romantic Lyric." *ELH* 85, no. 1 (2018): 85–118.

Fulford, Tim, Debbie Lee, and Peter Kitson. *Literature, Science, and Exploration in the Romantic Era: Bodies of Knowledge*. Cambridge: Cambridge University Press, 2004.

Fusco, Coco. "An Interview with Black Audio Film Collective: John Akomfrah, Lina Gopaul, Avril Johnson, and Reece Auguiste." In *Young, British & Black: A Monograph on the Work of Sankofa Film/Video Collective and Black Audio Film Collective*. Buffalo, NY: Hallwalls / Contemporary Arts Center, 1988.

Garver, Newton. Preface to *Speech and Phenomena and Other Essays on Husserl's Theory of Signs*. Translated by David B. Allison. Evanston, IL: Northwestern University Press, 1973.

Gascoigne, John. *Science in the Service of Empire: Joseph Banks, the British State and the Uses of Science in the Age of Revolution*. Cambridge: Cambridge University Press, 1998.

Gaukorger, Stephen. *The Collapse of Mechanism and the Rise of Sensibility: Science and the Shaping of Modernity, 1680–1760*. Oxford: Oxford University Press, 2010.

George, Edward. "Introductions to Reflections of the Black Experience." In Eshun and Sagar, *The Ghosts of Songs: The Film Art of the Black Audio Film Collective*. Liverpool, UK: Liverpool University Press, 2007.

Goldstein, Amanda Jo. *Sweet Science: Romantic Materialism and the New Logics of Life*. Chicago: University of Chicago Press, 2017.

Goodman, Kevis. "'Uncertain Disease': Nostalgia, Pathologies of Motion, Practices of Reading." *Studies in Romanticism* 49, no. 2 (Summer 2010): 197–227.

Green, Georgiana. *The Majesty of the People: Popular Sovereignty and the Role of the Writer in the 1790s*. Oxford: Oxford University Press, 2014.

Griffiths, Devin. *The Age of Analogy: Science and Literature between the Darwins*. Baltimore: Johns Hopkins University Press, 2016.

Gross, Matthias. "Unexpected Interactions: Georg Simmel and the Observation of Nature." *Journal of Classical Sociology* 1, no. 3 (2001): 395–414.

Guest, Harriet. *Unbounded Attachment: Sentiment and Politics in the Age of the French Revolution*. Oxford: Oxford University Press, 2013.

Guyer, Sara. *Reading with John Clare: Biopoetics, Sovereignty, Romanticism*. New York: Fordham University Press, 2015.

———. *Romanticism after Auschwitz*. Stanford, CA: Stanford University Press, 2007.

Haraway, Donna. "Staying with the Trouble." In *Anthropocene or Capitalocene: Nature, History, and the Crisis of Capitalism*, edited by Jason W. Moore. Oakland, CA: PM Press, 2016.

Hardt, Michael and Antonio Negri. *Declaration*. New York: Argo Navis, 2012.

Hartley, Daniel. "The Person, Historical Time and the Universalization of Capital." *Salvage*, no. 6 (2018): 193–212.

Hartley, David. *Observations on Man, His Frame, His Duty, and His Expectations*. Vol. 1. London: Printed by S. Richardson; for James Leake and Wm. Frederick, Booksellers in Bath: and sold by Charles Hitch and Stephen Austen, Booksellers in London, M.DCC.XLIX. [1749]. Eighteenth Century Collections Online. https://link.gale.com/apps/doc/CW0121618548/ECCO?u=new64731&sid=bookmark-ECCO&xid=04ad81aa&pg=407.

Hartman, Saidiya V. "The Anarchy of Colored Girls Assembled in a Riotous Manner." *South Atlantic Quarterly* 117, no. 3 (July 2018): 465–490.

———. *Scenes of Subjection: Terror, Slavery, and Self-Making in Nineteenth-Century America*. Oxford: Oxford University Press, 1997.

Harvey, David. *The New Imperialism*. 2nd ed. Oxford: Oxford University Press, 2005.

Hawhee, Debra. *Rhetoric in Tooth and Claw: Animals, Language, Sensation*. Chicago: University of Chicago Press, 2017.

Hawkins, William, and John Curwood. *A Treatise of the Pleas of the Crown, or, A System of the Principal Matters Relating to That Subject*. 8th ed. Vol. 1. London: S. Sweet, 1824. https://link.gale.com/apps/doc/F0105420786/MOML?u=new64731&sid=bookmark-MOML&xid=e3a4a6a3&pg=1.

Haywood, Ian. *Bloody Romanticism: Spectacular Violence and the Politics of Representation 1777–1832*. Basingstoke, UK: Palgrave Macmillan, 2004.

Hegel, G. W. F. *Hegel's Phenomenology of Spirit*. Translated by A. V. Miller. Oxford: Oxford University Press, 1977.

Hensley, Nathan K. *Forms of Empire: The Poetics of Victorian Sovereignty*. Oxford: Oxford University Press, 2016.

Humboldt, Alexander von. *Political Essay on the Kingdom of New Spain*. London: Printed for Longman, Hurst, Rees, Orme, and Brown, 1822.

Hunter, John. *Lectures on the Principles of Surgery*. 1775. Philadelphia: Haswell, Barrington, and Haswell, 1839. https://archive.org/details/56830620R.nlm.nih.gov.

Jackson, Noel. *Science and Sensation in Romantic Poetry*. Cambridge: Cambridge University Press, 2008.

James I. "News from Scotland." In *William Shakespeare: Macbeth Texts and Contexts*, edited by William C. Carroll. Boston: Bedford / St. Martin's, 1999.

Johnson, Barbara. "Apostrophe, Animation, and Abortion." *Diacritics* 16, no. 1 (Spring 1986): 28–47.

———. *Persons and Things*. Cambridge, MA: Harvard University Press, 2008.

Kant, Immanuel. "Dreams of a Spirit-seer Elucidated by Dreams of Metaphysics." In *Theoretical Philosophy*, edited by David Wolford. Cambridge: Cambridge University Press, 1992.

Kaiser, Jess. "Plastic Matters." In *The New Politics of Materialism*, edited by Sarah Ellenzweig and John H. Zammito. London: Routledge, 2017.

Keller, Uri Yacobi. "The Economy of the Occupation." *Socioeconomic Bulletin*, nos. 23–24 (2009): 1–64.

Kelley, Theresa M. *Clandestine Marriage: Botany and Romantic Culture*. Baltimore: Johns Hopkins University Press, 2015.

Khalip, Jacques. *Anonymous Life: Romanticism and Dispossession*. Stanford, CA: Stanford University Press, 2008.

Kim, Elizabeth S. "Maria Edgeworth's *The Grateful Negro*: A Site for Rewriting Rebellion." *Eighteenth-Century Fiction* 16, no. 1 (October 2003): 103–126.

King-Hele, Desmond. *Erasmus Darwin: A Life of Unequalled Achievement*. London: DLM, 2000.

Kornbluh, Anna. *Realizing Capital: Financial and Psychic Economies in Victorian Form*. New York: Fordham University Press, 2013.

Küçük, Bülent, and Ceren Özselçuk. "The Rojava Experience: Possibilities and Challenges of Building a Democratic Life." *South Atlantic Quarterly* 115, no. 1 (January 2016): 184–196.

La Mettrie, Julian Offray de. *Machine Man and Other Writings*. Edited by Ann Thompson. Cambridge: Cambridge University Press, 1996.

Langan, Celeste. *Romantic Vagrancy: Wordsworth and the Simulation of Freedom*. Cambridge: Cambridge University Press, 1995.

Laurence, French, and Walker King. Preface to *Miscellaneous Writings: Thoughts and Details on Scarcity,* by Edmund Burke. Edited by Francis Canavan. Indianapolis: Liberty Fund, 1999.

Levinson, Marjorie. "Of Being Numerous." *Studies in Romanticism* 49 (Winter 2010): 633–657.

Lévi-Strauss, Claude. *The Savage Mind.* London: Weidenfeld & Nicolson, 1966.

Linebaugh, Peter. *The London Hanged: Crime and Civil Society in the Eighteenth Century.* 2nd ed. New York: Verso, 2003.

———. *Red Round Globe Burning Hot: A Tale at the Crossroads of Commons and Closure, of Love and Terror, of Race and Class, and of Kate and Ned Despard.* Oakland, CA: University of California Press, 2019.

Lloyd, David. *Irish Culture and Colonial Modernity, 1800–2000: The Transformation of Oral Space.* Oxford: Oxford University Press, 2011.

———. "The Racial Thing: On Appropriation, Black Studies, and Thingliness." *Texte zur Kunst* 29, no. 117 (March 2020): 74–95.

———. "Rethinking National Marxism: James Connolly and 'Celtic Communism.'" *Interventions: International Journal of Postcolonial Studies* 5, no. 3 (2003): 345–370. doi:10.1080/1369801032000135611.

London Corresponding Society. *Reformers No Rioters.* [London]: Printed by order of the London Corresponding Society, [1794]. Eighteenth Century Collections Online. https://link.gale.com/apps/doc/CW0105551163/ECCO?u=new64731&sid=bookmark-ECCO&xid=e609ce8d&pg=1.

Long, Edward. *The History of Jamaica*, vol. 2: *Reflections on Its Situation, Settlements, Inhabitants, Climate, Products, Commerce, Laws, and Government.* 1774. Montreal: McGill-Queen's University Press, 2005. https://ebookcentral.proquest.com/lib/nyulibrary-ebooks/detail.action?docID=3331793.

Löwy, Michael. *The Theory of Revolution in Young Marx.* Leiden: Brill, 2003.

Luxemburg, Rosa. *The Complete Works of Rosa Luxemburg*, vol. 2: *Economic Writings 2.* Edited by Peter Hudis and Paul Le Blanc. New York: Verso, 2015.

———. *The Mass Strike, the Political Party, and the Trade Unions.* 1906. Translated by Patrick Lavin. Marxists.org, 1999. https://www.marxists.org/archive/luxemburg/1906/mass-strike/.

Mackey, Charles. *Extraordinary Popular Delusions and the Madness of Crowds.* New York: Noonday Press, 1932.

Makdisi, Saree. *Making England Western: Occidentalism, Race, and Imperial Culture.* Chicago: University of Chicago Press, 2014.

Marx, Karl. *Capital: A Critique of Political Economy.* Vol. 1. Translated by Ben Fowkes. London: Penguin Books, 1976.

———. *Grundrisse: Foundations of the Critique of Political Economy.* Translated by Martin Nicolaus. London: Penguin Books, 1973.

———. "The Value-Form: Appendix to the 1st German Edition of *Capital*, Vol. 1, 1867." Marxists.org. https://www.marxists.org/archive/marx/works/1867-c1/appendix.htm.

Mauss, Marcel. *A General Theory of Magic*. Translated by Robert Brain. London: Routledge, 2001.

McKindrick, Neill. "Progress and the Lunaticks." *New York Times*, January 1, 1964.

McLane, Maureen N. "Dating Orality, Thinking Balladry: Of Milkmaids and Minstrels in 1771." *Eighteenth Century* 47, no. 2/3 (2006): 131–149.

———. "Malthus Our Contemporary? Toward a Political Economy of Sex." *Studies in Romanticism* 52 (Fall 2013): 337–362.

———. "Minstrelsy, or, Romantic Poetry." In *Balladeering, Minstrelsy, and the Making of British Romantic Poetry*. Cambridge: Cambridge University Press, 2008.

———. *Romanticism and the Human Sciences: Poetry, Population, and the Discourse of Species*. Cambridge: Cambridge University Press, 2000.

McNeil, Maureen. *Under the Banner of Science: Erasmus Darwin and His Age*. Manchester, UK: Manchester University Press, 1987.

Mezzadra, Sandro. "The Topicality of Prehistory: A New Reading of Marx's Analysis of 'So-Called Primitive Accumulation.'" *Rethinking Marxism* 23, no. 3 (2011): 302–321.

Mill, John Stuart. "Of the Competition of Different Countries in the Same Market." In *Principles of Political Economy with Some of Their Applications to Social Philosophy*. 1848. Edited by J. M. Robson. Toronto: University of Toronto Press, 1965.

Mintz, Sidney. *Sweetness and Power: The Place of Sugar in Modern History*. New York: Penguin Books, 1985.

Modern Language Association. "Resolutions from the 2017 Delegate Assembly." mla.org. https://www.mla.org/About-Us/Governance/Delegate-Assembly/Motions-and-Resolutions/Resolutions-Ratified-by-the-Membership/Resolutions-from-the-2017-Delegate-Assembly.

Moore, Jason W. *Capitalism in the Web of Life: Ecology and the Accumulation of Capital*. New York: Verso, 2015.

More, Hannah. "A Hymn of Praise for the Abundant Harvest of 1796." London: J. Marshall, 1796. Eighteenth Century Collections Online.

———. "The Riot; or, Half a Loaf Is Better Than No Bread." Perth: R. Morison, 1800. Eighteenth Century Collections Online.

Moscrop, John James. *Measuring Jerusalem: The Palestine Exploration Fund and British Interests in the Holy Land*. London: Leicester University Press, 2000.

Moseley, Benjamin. *A Treatise on Sugar: Medical Tracts. I. On Sugar. II. On the Cow Pox. III. On the Yaws. IV. On Obi, or African Witchcraft. V. On the Plague; and*

Yellow Fever of America VI. On Hospitals. VII. On Bronchocele. VIII. On Prisons. 2nd ed. London: Printed by J. Nichols, 1800. The Making of the Modern World, Part 1. https://www.gale.com/c/making-of-the-modern-world-part-i

Moten, Fred. *Black and Blur.* Vol. 1 of *consent not to be a single being.* Durham, NC: Duke University Press, 2017.

———. *In the Break: The Aesthetics of the Black Radical Tradition.* Minneapolis: University of Minnesota Press, 2003.

———. *Stolen Life.* Vol. 2 of *consent not to be a single being.* Durham, NC: Duke University Press, 2018.

———. *The Universal Machine.* Vol. 3 of *consent not to be a single being.* Durham, NC: Duke University Press, 2018.

Nemser, Daniel. *Infrastructures of Race: Concentration and Biopolitics in Colonial Mexico.* Austin: University of Texas Press, 2017.

"Notes and Documents." *Race and Class* 23, no. 2/3 (1981).

Palmer-Adisa, Opal. "The Living Roots." In *So Long Been Dreaming: Postcolonial Science Fiction & Fantasy,* edited by Nalo Hopkinson and Uppinder Mehan. Vancouver, BC: Arsenal Pulp Press, 2004.

Palmeri, Frank. *States of Nature, Stages of Society: Enlightenment Conjectural History and Modern Social Discourse.* New York: Columbia University Press, 2016.

Pappe, Ilan. "Indigeneity as Cultural Resistance: Notes on the Palestinian Struggle within Twenty-First-Century Israel." *South Atlantic Quarterly* 117, no. 1 (2018): 157–178.

Parsons, James. *Philosophical Observations on the Analogy between the Propagation of Animals and That of Vegetables.* London: Printed for C. Davis, 1752. Eighteenth Century Collections Online. https://link.gale.com/apps/doc/CW0110541635/ECCO?u=new64731&sid=bookmarkECCO&xid=49b917df&pg=1.

Pasolini, Pier Paolo. *Seeking Locations in Palestine for the Film "The Gospel According to Matthew."* 1965. UbuWeb. https://ubu.com/film/pasolini_palestine.html.

Paton, Diana. *The Cultural Politics of Obeah: Religion, Colonialism and Modernity in the Caribbean World.* Cambridge: Cambridge University Press, 2015.

———. *No Bond but the Law: Punishment, Race, and Gender in Jamaican State Formations, 1780–1870.* Durham, NC: Duke University Press, 2004.

Perloff, Marjorie, "Collage and Poetry." In *Encyclopedia of Aesthetics.* Vol. 1. Edited by Michael Kelly. Oxford: Oxford University Press, 1998.

Picchio, Antonella. *Social Reproduction: The Political Economy of the Labour Market.* Cambridge: Cambridge University Press, 1992.

Pierrot, Gregory, with Gabriella I. Johnson. "A Collaborative Review of Francis Botkin's *Thieving Three-Fingered Jack* and Cedric Robinson's *Black Marxism.*" Romantic Circles Reviews and Receptions. https://romantic-circles.org/re

views-blog/collaborative-review-frances-botkin%E2%80%99s-thieving-three-fingered-jack-and-cedric-robinson.

Pratt, Mary Louise. *Imperial Eyes: Travel Writing and Transculturation*. 2nd ed. London: Routledge, 2008.

Priestley, Joseph. *An Account of a Society, for Encouraging the Industrious Poor*. Birmingham, UK: Printed by Pearson and Rollason, 1787. Eighteenth Century Collections Online. link.gale.com/apps/doc/CB0126685958/ECCO?u=new64731&sid=bookmark-ECCO&xid=bd507765&pg=1.

———. *A Course of Lectures on the Theory of Language, and Universal Grammar*. Warrington, UK: Printed by W. Eyres, 1762. Eighteenth Century Collections Online. https://link.gale.com/apps/doc/CW0111634446/ECCO?u=new64731&sid=bookmark-ECCO&xid=c1457453&pg=1

———. *A Description of a New Chart of History*. 7th ed. London: Printed for J. Johnson, No. 72, St. Paul's Church Yard, 1789. Eighteenth Century Collections Online. https://link.gale.com/apps/doc/CW0101172118/ECCO?u=new64731&sid=bookmark-ECCO&xid=8db8d2a6&pg=1.

———. *Hartley's Theory of the Human Mind, on the Principle of the Association of Ideas*. 2nd ed. London: Printed for J. Johnson, 1790. Eighteenth Century Collections Online. https://link.gale.com/apps/doc/CW0107910017/ECCO?u=new64731&sid=bookmark-ECCO&xid=be0ceee2&pg=1.

———. *A Sermon on the Subject of the Slave Trade*. Birmingham, UK: Printed for the author, by Pearson and Rollason and sold by J. Johnson, 1788. Slavery and Anti-slavery: A Transnational Archive. https://link.gale.com/apps/doc/DS0103720619/SAS?u=new64731&sid=bookmark-SAS&xid=2f6e8fb0&pg=1.

Pyle, Forest, and Jacques Khalip. "Introduction: The Present Darkness of Romanticism." In *Constellations of a Contemporary Romanticism*, edited by Pyle and Khalip. New York: Fordham University Press, 2016.

Richardson, Alan. "Romantic Voodoo: Obeah and British Culture, 1797–1807." *Studies in Romanticism* 32 (Spring 1993): 3–28.

Robinson, Cedric. *Black Marxism: The Making of the Black Radical Tradition*. 2nd ed. Chapel Hill: University of North Carolina Press, 2005.

Robinson, Mary. "The Maniac." In *Mary Robinson: Selected Poems*, edited by Judith Pascoe. Peterborough, ON: Broadview Press, 2000.

———. *Memoirs of Mary Robinson, "Perdita," from the Edition by Her Daughter*. Edited by J. Fitzgerald Molloy. Philadelphia: J. B. Lippincott, 1895. https://digital.library.upenn.edu/women/robinson/memoirs/memoirs.html.

Rosenberg, Daniel. "Joseph Priestley and the Graphic Invention of Modern Time." *Studies in Eighteenth-Century Culture* 36 (2007): 55–103. doi:10.1353/sec.2007.0013.

Rosenberg, Jordy. "Becoming Hole (The Hiddener Abode)." *World Picture Journal* 11 (Summer 2016). http://www.worldpicturejournal.com/WP_11/Rosenberg_11.html.

———. *Critical Enthusiasm: Capital Accumulation and the Transformation of Religious Passion*. Oxford: Oxford University Press, 2011.

———. "'The Original Sin Is at Work Everywhere': Marx's Concept of Primitive Accumulation." In *The Bloomsbury Companion to Marx*, edited by Andrew Pendakis, Jeff Diamanti, and Imre Szeman. New York: Bloomsbury Academic, 2018.

———. "Trans/War Boy/Gender: The Primitive Accumulation of T." *Salvage*. https://salvage.zone/in-print/trans-war-boy-gender/.

Ross, Kristen. *Communal Luxury: The Political Imaginary of the Paris Commune*. New York: Verso, 2015.

Ross, Marlon B. "The Race of/in Romanticism: Notes toward a Critical Race Theory." In *Race, Romanticism and the Atlantic*, edited by Paul Youngquist. Farnham, UK: Ashgate, 2013.

Rzepka, Charles J. "Thomas De Quincey's 'Three-Fingered Jack': The West Indian Origins of the 'Dark Interpreter.'" *European Romantic Review* 8, no. 2 (1997): 117–138.

Sachs, Jonathan. *The Poetics of Decline in British Romanticism*. Cambridge: Cambridge University Press, 2018.

Sacks, Jeffrey. "The Resistance to Boycott: Palestine, BDS, and the Modern Language Association." *Radical History Review* 134 (May 2019): 233–244.

Salih, Ruba, and Sophie Richter-Devroe. "Palestine beyond National Frames: Emerging Politics, Cultures, and Claims." *South Atlantic Quarterly* 117, no. 1 (January 2018): 1–20.

Sanyal, Kanyal. *Rethinking Capitalist Development: Primitive Accumulation, Governmentality, and Post-colonial Capitalism*. London: Routledge, 2007.

Schey, Taylor. "Limited Analogies: Reading Relations in Wordsworth's *The Borderers*." *Studies in Romanticism*, no. 56 (Summer 2017): 177–201.

Schiebinger, Londa. *Plants and Empire: Colonial Bioprospecting in the Atlantic World*. Cambridge, MA: Harvard University Press, 2004.

Schofield, Robert E. *The Lunar Society of Birmingham: A Social History of Provincial Science and Industry in Eighteenth-Century England*. Oxford: Clarendon Press, 1963.

———. *Mechanism and Materialism: British Natural Philosophy in the Age of Reason*. Princeton, NJ: Princeton University Press, 1970.

Schuller, Kyla. *The Biopolitics of Feeling: Race, Sex, and Science in the Nineteenth Century*. Durham, NC: Duke University Press, 2018.

Sha, Richard. *Imagination and Science in Romanticism.* Baltimore: Johns Hopkins University Press, 2018.
Shakespeare, William. *Macbeth: The Arden Shakespeare Third Series.* Edited by Sandra Clark and Pamela Mason. London: Bloomsbury Arden Shakespeare, 2015.
Shaw, Rosalind. *Memories of the Slave Trade: Ritual and the Historical Imagination in Sierra Leone.* Chicago: University of Chicago Press, 2002.
Sheehan, Jonathan, and Dror Wahrman. *Invisible Hands: Self-Organization and the Eighteenth Century.* Chicago: University of Chicago Press, 2015.
Shelley, Percy. "Triumph of Life." In *Shelley's Poetry and Prose,* 2nd ed., edited by Donald H. Reiman and Neil Freistat. London: W. W. Norton, 2002.
Singer, Kate. "Limpid Waves and Good Vibrations: Charlotte Smith's New Materialist Affect." *Essays in Romanticism* 23, no. 2 (2016): 175–192.
Sohn-Rethel, Alfred. *Intellectual and Manual Labor: A Critique of Epistemology.* Atlantic Highlands, NJ: Humanities Press, 1978.
Spielrein, Sabina. "Destruction as the Cause of Coming into Being." 1912. *Journal of Analytic Psychology* 39 (1994): 155–186.
Spillers, Hortense. "Mama's Baby, Papa's Maybe: An American Grammar Book." *Diacritics* 17, no. 2 (Summer 1987): 64–81.
Stoler, Ann Laura. *Duress: Imperial Durabilities in Our Times.* Durham, NC: Duke University Press, 2016.
Stout, Daniel. "Associationist Aesthetics: Priestley's Materialism and the Radical Picturesque." *European Romantic Review* 3, no. 31 (2020): 267–283.
Taussig, Michael T. *The Devil and Commodity Fetishism in South America: Thirtieth Anniversary Edition with a New Chapter by the Author.* 2nd ed. Chapel Hill: University of North Carolina Press, 2010.
Terada, Rei. *Looking Away: Phenomenality and Dissatisfaction, Kant to Adorno.* Cambridge, MA: Harvard University Press, 2009.
———. "The Racial Grammar of Kantian Time." *European Romantic Review* 28, no. 3 (2017): 267–278.
Thompson, E. P. "The Moral Economy of the English Crowd in the Eighteenth Century." In *The Essential E. P. Thompson,* edited by Dorothy Thompson. New York: New Press, 2001.
Üstündağ, Nazan. "Mother, Politician, and Guerilla: The Emergence of a New Political Imagination in Kurdistan through Women's Bodies and Speech." *differences: A Journal of Feminist Cultural Studies* 50, no. 2 (2019): 115–145.
Wade, Stephan. *Spies in the Empire: Victorian Military Intelligence.* London: Anthem Press, 2007.
Walker, Gavin. *The Sublime Perversion of Capital: Marxist Theory and the Politics of History in Modern Japan.* Durham, NC: Duke University Press, 2018.

Wang, Jackie. *Carceral Capitalism*. Cambridge, MA: MIT Press, 2018.
Wang, Orrin. *Romantic Sobriety: Sensation, Revolution, Commodification, History*. Baltimore: Johns Hopkins University Press, 2011.
Wedderburn, Robert. *The Horrors of Slavery and Other Writings*. Edited by Iain McCalman. Princeton, NJ: Markus Wiener, 1991.
Weheliye, Alexander G. *Habeas Viscus: Racializing Assemblages, Biopolitics, and Black Feminist Theories of the Human*. Durham, NC: Duke University Press, 2014.
Wheeler, Roxann. *The Complexion of Race: Categories of Race in Eighteenth-Century British Culture*. Philadelphia: University of Pennsylvania Press, 2000.
Whitener, Brian. "Countering Counterinsurgency: Social Reproduction and Emancipatory Thought." Unpublished manuscript.
Wilson Gilmore, Ruth. "Fatal Couplings of Power and Difference: Notes on Racism and Geography." *Professional Geographer* 54, no. 1 (2002): 15–24.
Wimsatt, W. K., Jr., and M. C. Beardsley. "The Intentional Fallacy." *Sewanee Review* 53, no. 3 (Winter 1946): 468–488.
Wordsworth, William. *The Major Works: Including "The Prelude."* 2nd ed. Edited by Stephen Gill. Oxford: Oxford University Press, 2008.
Youngquist, Paul. "Lyrical Bodies: Wordsworth's Physiological Aesthetics." *European Romantic Review* 10 (1999): 152–162.
Xin, Wendy. "The Secret Lives of Plot." Unpublished manuscript.

Index

Abrams, M. H., 9n
accumulation, 139–40, 165, 173, 198; *accumulatio* and, 228n21; capitalist violence and, 195; cycles of, 170; of data, 152; debt as mechanism of, 202; of differences, 3, 77, 85, 89, 147, 174, 212n7; by dispossession, 58, 72, 78, 125, 186, 187, 203, 228–29n26, 228n26; enclosure as, 90; of equivalence, 136; of experiences, 202; figural mode operation of, 61; forms of, 170; gender difference as mechanism of, 202; of gendered reproduction, 203; global cycles of, 174; of history, 185; history of, 187; involuntary servitude and, 232n65; logic of, 248n63; of misery, 219–20n18; of motley ways of use, 21; of noncapitalist ways of living, 202; of nonlinear time, 183; progress and, 156; repetitions of dispossession, 202; in Romantic period, 222n44; separability and, 114; social reproduction and, 184; of spaces and "simple elements," 178; thorny mode of, 125; through social reproduction, 132; of time, 116, 117
accumulation, capital, 1, 161, 169; analogy and, 228n21; apostrophe's necessity to, 45, 66, 67; basic structure of, 248n63; of bourgeois, 23; catachrestic historical realities and, 172; concrete forms of life destroyed by, 33; constitutive exclusion and, 198; construction of surplus populations and, 44; coralline nature of, 61; Darwin's theory of nature and, 58, 59, 63; by dispossession, 71–72; enclosure origins of, 93, 180; the everyday and, 26; excess and

271

272 INDEX

accumulation, capital (cont.)
unmeasurable needs and, 28; feminist and colonialist accounts of, 64; fertile soil of, 29; figuration and, 64, 65, 66, 67, 72, 160, 188; gender and enclosure relationship to, 87; global process of, 18–19; global system of, 25; globality of, 200; history of, 8, 24, 75, 87, 92, 93, 98, 233n73; infinite circulation and, 76, 77; Marx as theorist of, 16; means of subsistence necessary for, 65; modernity and, 160–61; originary violence of, 71; primitive nature of, 202; processes of, 24, 99, 100, 104; racial origins of, 164; racializing and gendering origins of, 77; relations of, 67; remaking of subsistence in, 202; repetition characterizes, 138; reproduction and, 65, 91, 196; reproduction of laboring population for, 233n79; resistance to, 124; rhetoric of, 22, 26; riot as immanent domain of, 53; Romantic critical depictions of, 78; romanticism and, 208; soil of, 130, 132; subsistence and, 191; superstitions and, 112; "The Thorn" archives, 123; thorny mode of, 125; violences of, 197; witch hunts' importance to, 112
accumulation, collective, 184
accumulation, discontinuous, 31
accumulation, historical, 146
accumulation, material, 189
accumulation, originary, 23, 195
accumulation, primitive, 8, 17, 18; abjection attendant on, 136; the body and, 217n1; bourgeois myth of, 202; bricolage and, 100; capitalism and, 31, 186; capitalism's simultaneity, 164, 168, 170, 171; constitutive exclusion and, 198; continuous discontinuity of, 113–14, 208–9; death-dealing abstractions of, 180; of differences, 147; differences of race and gender and, 89; dispossession and, 180; enclosure and, 89; exploitation and expropriation and, 93; gender and vagrancy and, 29; in "Goody Blake and Harry Gill," 230n43; heterogeneous processes attendant on, 89; hierarchies in, 95; hierarchies produced by, 175, 212n7; history of capitalism originating in, 163; likeness and unsameness and, 129; Marx's critique of, 78; mythic origins of, 22; necessity of, 24; ongoing nature of, 25; racializing work of, 174; recursive process of, 124; repetitions of, 130, 203, 207; Robinson and, 193; subsistence and, 32, 188, 194, 197; superstitions and, 118; as theological idyll, 232n68; theorists of, 23; "The Thorn" and, 125; of witch hunts, 137
accumulation, racialized, 171
accumulation, sensorial, 163
accumulation, speculative, 196
accumulation, temporally successive, 26
affectability, 140, 151, 162, 163, 165, 167, 196; associated with ways of living, 30; of material bodies, 26; in primitive accumulation, 25; racial analytics of, 147; spatialized, 142; of subsistence, 248n62; of unformed bodies, 134
affectable bodies, 8, 25, 31, 164, 174, 180

INDEX 273

affectable things, 126–38, 161
Africa, 130, 137, 165, 236n22; discourses about, 248n62; enslaved captured from, 18, 170; origin of Obeah, 98, 114, 134, 135; witchcraft and, 31, 106, 138, 234n4
Afro-Caribbeans, 140
age of analogy, 73
Albion Mills, 51–52, 243n5
allegory, 27, 48, 67, 84–85; Hartley's, 41, 42, 56; of historical processes, 195
Allewaert, Monique, 175
alterity, 2, 6, 84, 147, 242n4
America, 18, 130, 156, 159, 192, 234n4. See also North America, South America; Indigenous peoples of, 126; Spanish, 175
anachronism, ludicrous, 28, 29, 74, 92
Antoinette, Marie, 190
Arabs, 104–5, 121, 134, 236n26
Aravamudan, Srinivas, 98
Aristophanes, 220n27
articulation, 11, 58, 59, 65, 72, 76, 154, 225n2
associationism, 42, 44, 103, 187–88; of Hartley, 152; hopes for a better future, 38; mechanistic, 53, 247n52; origins of language and knowledge, 12; proto-psychoanalytic language of, 210; theories of mind and body, 9
Auguiste, Reece, 171
Austin, J. L., 12, 13
Australia, 206
automation, 42, 43, 47, 222–23n45, 227n9

Bacon, Francis, 161
BAFC (Black Audio Film Collective), 143, 147, 161, 162, 177, 179; on belonging and displacement, 140; on Blackness, 139; formation of, 242n1; interested in representation, 243n13; nondichotomous approach to history, 146; provide images of capitalism, 31
Balfour, Ian, 39, 68
Banaji, Jairus, 164
Beardsley, M. C., 86, 230n50
Becker-Ho, Alice, 20
Beckles, Hilary, 29, 130, 131, 132, 133
Benjamin, Walter, 33, 146, 160, 199, 205, 216n51, 223n47; approach to translation, 21–22; *The Arcades Project*, 139, 183; constellation, 188; on dreams, 75; on history, 163, 181, 189, 190, 207; narcotic historicism, 151; principle of collective history, 232n70; on revolution, 225n69
Bewell, Alan, 59, 234n5, 246n44
Bhandar, Brenna, 58, 224n55, 225n2
binaries, 2, 5, 8, 11, 25, 61, 121, 181; essential, 24; sedimented, 78; stable, 226n6; suspended, 56
binarism, 7, 140, 198, 247n52
binarization, 36, 59, 73, 99, 122, 147, 175
biopoetics, 95
Black Audio Film Collective. See BAFC (Black Audio Film Collective)
Blackness, 8, 139, 248n62, 252n35
Blackstone, William, 90
Blake, William, 35, 209, 243n5
Bloody Laws, 55, 90. See also vagrancy laws
bodies, affectable, 8, 25, 31, 164, 174, 180
bodies, material, 114; colonized affectability of, 26; features of racialized, 180; kept in motion, 37; relational

bodies, material (*cont.*)
    resources of, 95; rhetorical relations of, 43; stuck in space of apostrophe, 40; subject to economy of lack, 39; subsist in noncapitalist ways, 30; tautological thingliness of, 30
body of life, gross, 36, 86, 230n50
body of the Malefactor, 53, 54, 63
body-without-equivalence, 61
Boulton, Michael, 148, 169, 242n5
bourgeoisie, 4, 23, 189, 190, 202
bricolage, 99–101, 104, 112, 133
Briosne, Louis Alfred, 221n35
British Empire, 120, 140, 179. *See also* England
Brown, John, 59, 60
Brown, Vincent, 113, 114
Burke, Edmund, 67, 220n22, 220n23, 222n40; discourse on common sense, 127; division of unmeasured labor, 63; on habits, 64, 66; indirect reproduction in, 45–53; on riots, 27
Butler, Judith, 251–52n23
Byrd, Alexander X., 113

Caffentzis, George, 95
Camarda, Julie, 110
Canada, 191, 201, 206. *See also* North America
capital accumulation. *See* accumulation, capital
capitalism, 2–3, 6, 14, 19, 31, 35, 137, 148, 167; carceral, 27, 53, 56, 67; history of, 90, 99, 112, 163, 164; industrial, 26, 32, 36, 59, 140, 168, 170; modern, 5, 89, 99, 151, 168, 169; primitive accumulation and, 31, 163, 164, 168, 170, 171, 186; racial, 32, 147, 168, 169, 171, 177

Caribbean, 130, 133, 140, 206. *See also* West Indies
cartographization, 150, 151, 155, 162
causality, 4, 42, 102, 111, 130, 136, 188, 227n9
central Africa, 113. *See also* Africa
Chambliss, William, 87, 88, 231n56
chatter, 8, 12, 107, 108; superstitious, 105, 111, 123, 124, 129; of women, 51, 122
Clare, John, 1, 2, 3
classic form, 24. *See also* form
Clover, Joseph, 46
coherence, 73, 80
Coleridge, Samuel Taylor, 32, 82, 130, 133, 240n74. *See also* "Three Graves, The"; address to Famine, 28; appeal for indirect speech, 219n15; associates rhetoric and subsistence, 38; convention of deviations, 62–69; on coralline, 224n56; follows mechanistic doctrine, 219n10; global commons of susceptibility, 136; on humanity, 218n6; on Imagination, 230n50; indirect reproduction in, 45–53; language and, 9, 14, 15; notion of degraded Fancy, 86; on the Oppressed, 39, 41; on revolution, 225n69; rhetorical paths and, 16; on riots, 27, 40, 42; on Robinson, 229n31, 230n41; on subsistence, 7; on the supernatural, 99; "The Three Graves," 30, 97, 126–28, 239n68; witchcraft in poetry of, 132
colonialism, 64, 76, 122, 191, 233n73, 250n83; human suffering caused by, 213n14; in Palestine, 204, 207–8; slavery and, 170
commensurability, 76–77, 79, 87, 93

commodification, 59, 61, 65, 66, 222n44, 244n25
commodity form. *See* form, commodity
commodity production, 1, 3, 29, 30, 64, 138, 170
common differentiation, 8, 28
commonality, 30, 85, 116, 226n6, 247n59
common-in-variety, 117
commons, 31, 33, 71, 108, 138; global, 8, 30, 133, 135, 136; sufficient, 14, 30, 115–26, 132
conjunctures, 5, 52, 56, 76, 224n55, 232n63
constellations, 26, 146, 175, 179, 181, 189, 207; accumulated, 186; Benjamin's versions of, 188; dreamlike form of, 185; of figures, 81, 200; generated by dispossession, 197; of global interrelation, 194; of instants, 160; of mother, daughter, witch, teacher, and addict, 196; of sensation, figure, use, and need, 16; of spatialized sensations, 143; Spielrein's, 193; of times, 184
contingency, 77, 78, 92, 112, 125, 225n2; analogy and, 73; in context of accumulation by dispossession, 72; of a material system, 64; relation with death, 69; subsistence and, 63
contradictions, 12, 24; capitalism and, 2–3; dispossession and, 23; internal to money form, 121; Marx on, 18; noncontradiction, 214n18, 248n63; of simultaneity, 8
coralline, 55, 56, 58–59, 61, 62, 66, 224n56
creoles, creolization, 98, 99, 131, 170
criminalization, 13, 27, 36, 54, 91, 194, 222n44; of gleaning, 114; means of subsistence, 37; meeting needs outside exchange economy, 55; of mobility, 88; of nonwork, 58, 90, 95; of socially rejected practices, 89; of vagrancy, 28, 29, 87; of witchcraft, 31, 89, 98; of women, 201; of wood theft, 230n43
Culler, Jonathan, 36

da Silva, Denise Ferreira, 135, 167, 171, 179, 213n14; on death-dealing, 249n76; on exteriority, 140, 146; on history of perception, 161; post-Enlightenment transparency thesis of, 151; on the racial, 147, 162, 168, 174, 175; on racism, 32; stage of exteriority of, 163
Dabashi, Hamid, 206
Darwin, Erasmus, 31, 101–2, 171, 179, 194, 235n19; articulation of reproduction, 53–62; convention of deviations, 62–69; figural epistemology of, 153, 154, 155, 162, 164, 178; on industrialization, 147; on material motions, 222–23n45; on progress and improvement, 148; on salt and sugar, 103, 105, 107, 112, 115, 116, 135; on the supernatural, 136; on witches, 193
Daston, Condillac, 187, 224–25n61, 247n52
Davies, C. S. L., 88
Davis, Angela, 29, 87, 89, 90, 91, 231n52
de Man, Paul, 4, 6, 68, 69, 95, 212–13n10, 237n40
de Sousa Santos, Boaventura, 213n14
De'Ath, Amy, 231n53
Defoe, Daniel, 131, 222n42
Dempster, M. Beth, 227n9

276 INDEX

Derrida, Jacques, 162, 214n24
Description of a Curious Sea Plant, A, 57
Description of the Habits of the Many Countries of the World, A, 166
deviations, 41, 59, 188; material, 199; of rhetorical language, 6
deviations from convention, 9, 43, 45, 47, 48, 50; apostrophic, 36–38; Coleridge's and Darwin's, 62–69
Dibashi, Hamid, 208
Dickens, Charles, 49
dispossession, 6, 8, 19, 22, 24, 200; accumulation by, 58, 72, 78, 125, 186, 203, 228n26; conjuncture of, 5, 56; differential, 94, 193, 197; enclosure and, 2, 205, 207; enslavement and, 113, 114, 191; history of, 3, 78, 94, 146; of identity, 206, 210
divisions, 65, 228n25; accumulation of, 212n7; in apostrophic economy, 53; class, 125; compulsive vs. free, 68; between costs of production and reproduction, 249n68; in divergent back-stories, 85; figural vs. mechanical form of life, 66; gendered, 14; intraclass, 189; of living bodies, 56; mechanist vs. materialist, 175; in the now, 222n35; principle, 246n41; progressive, 50; social, 201; of spaces and the bodies, 93; of subsistence, 3; workers and slaves, 137
divisions of labor, 71, 75, 88, 89, 92, 99, 109, 112, 202; organizational nature of, 221n33; productive of surplus vs. not capable of equalization, 27; productivity and capital and, 151; unmeasured, 63; value form of equivalence, 17; within capitalism, 14
dream economies, 79–85

dream frame, 28, 77
Duncan, Gilles, 108

economies, 7, 28, 39, 41, 61, 63, 75; capitalist, 58, 233n79; dream, 79–85; exchange, 51, 55, 212n10; moral, 26, 27, 40, 221n34; plantation, 120–21, 123, 131, 132, 236n23; of subsistence, 40, 46, 50, 55, 56, 64
economy, political, 8, 38, 59, 66, 78, 91, 228n21, 230n43, 232n68
Edwards, Bryan, 100, 127
empiricism, 55, 73, 112, 225n61, 235n22, 247n52
enclosure, history of, 75, 76, 117, 122, 232n68
enclosure poetics, 71–78
England, 201, 206. *See also* British Empire; 1795 riots, 26; becomes Western, 30, 171; Bloody Laws, 90; colonial and capitalist endeavors, 196; dark Satanic mills, 243n5; dispossession in, 192; enclosures in, 17, 18; industrialization of, 19, 136; Moseley compares to Jamaica, 134; Newgate prison, 49, 52; Obi in, 239n70; rural villagers in, 114; slavery in, 95, 121; subsidizing poor wages in, 220n22; subsistence ways of living in, 37, 163; supernatural beliefs in, 99; superstition in, 126; thorn trees, 108, 116; threat of superstition in, 112; tropical commodities sold in, 120; wage laborers in, 170; witch hunts in, 138; Witchcraft Act, 98; witchcraft criminalized in, 31; workers of, 4, 24
Enlightenment, 16, 39, 98, 100, 123, 151, 228n21; late, 7, 9, 244n25, 254n49

enslaved, 4, 121, 136, 196, 199; binarizing history of, 122; captured from Africa, 18, 170; in Caribbean, 133; in history of capitalism, 90; in Jamaica, 207; labor of, 125; Moseley on, 120; reproduction of, 137; terrorized, 113; women, 130, 131, 132, 240n85
enslavement, 18, 22, 23, 113, 114, 191. *See also* slave trade
Enwezor, Okwui, 179
epistemologies, 72, 77, 92, 161, 164, 225n61, 226n6, 227n15, 244–45n25; eighteenth-century, 233n73; figural, 153, 154, 155, 162, 164, 178; onto-epistemology, 61, 156, 174; scientific, 71, 92; Western, 167
Equiano, Olaudah/Vassa, Gustauvus, 113
equilibrium, 28, 37, 46, 66, 155, 213n10; affect, 156, 158; analogy establishes, 228n21; curated, 152; environmental and social, 56; of habit, 48; natural, 27; physiological, 102; relational, 43; self-regulating, 45; social, 38, 56; between subject and world, 187; supply-and-demand, 64
equivalence, 18, 27, 46, 61, 65, 67, 77, 114, 136. *See also* nonequivalence; convention, 49, 50; measure of, 22, 64, 66; relations of, 55, 76, 93, 132, 201, 212n10; standardization and, 93, 228n22; universal, 22, 48, 120, 126, 138, 202, 212n10, 228n25; value form of, 17
Eshun, Kodwo, 146, 151, 161
Eurocentrism, 6, 18, 213n14
Europe, 89, 104, 114, 119, 120, 124, 170, 237n35
Europeans, 98, 100, 113, 119, 202

exchange value, 93; accumulation and, 65; economy ordered by, 59; organizes multiple vectors of life, 58; productive forces produce, 18; subsistence and, 55, 62, 67, 68; vs. use values, 23; workers consumption of, 169
exclusion, constitutive, 194, 198, 204
expropriation, 55, 61, 71, 91, 94, 196; classic form of, 24; of identity, 204; poetics of, 85; primitive accumulation and, 93
exteriority, 146, 147, 151, 161, 162, 174, 176; racial as a signifier of, 140; stage of, 163

Fancy, 15, 86, 87, 230n50, 232n70
Federici, Silvia, 90, 100, 201; accumulations of differences, 3, 77; on enclosure and criminalization, 91; exhausted body of, 203; on human body as machine, 35; Nigerian diaries, 185; on primitive accumulation, 89, 212n7, 217n1; on witch hunts, 14, 99, 108, 112, 124, 200
feudalism, 2, 51, 82, 92, 194, 218n4, 232n68
figuration, 44–45, 47, 82, 171, 181, 191, 227n9; of accumulations of gendered reproduction, 203; ambivalent, 8, 92; apostrophic, 61; capital accumulation and, 64–67, 72, 160, 188; contested, 62; crystallized, 103; de Man on, 212n10; of distinct and adjacent bodies, 85; of food rioters, 15; "half-congeal'd," 83; of heterogeneous labors, 26; of the imagination, 142; initial, 9; of nature, 58; of riots, 51; self-figuration, 81; of subsistence, 15

figures, simultaneous, 147–64
food riots, 15, 27, 46, 51, 53, 68, 194, 199, 218n8. *See also* riots of 1795
form, 58, 116, 171, 242n4; affectable, 175; apostrophic, 51; classic, 24; coralline, 58; exchange, 67, 232n63; figural, 62, 66; heterogeneous, 29, 101; of labor, 17, 25; materiality of, 143; mixed, 21; money, 17, 19, 20, 76–77, 120, 121, 137; originary, 25, 42; residual, 87, 88; wage, 28, 29, 36, 63, 65, 169
form, commodity, 19, 132, 136, 137, 150, 170, 180, 228n22; Marx's analysis of, 16, 17, 18, 22
formal subsumption, 168, 218n4, 248–49n67
fortune-tellers, 88, 89, 91, 97, 101
Foucault, Michel, 196, 248n63
free market, 27, 51, 72, 148, 150
French Revolution, 150, 190, 225n61
froth, 39, 41, 42, 43, 47, 48
Fulford, Tim, 152

Garver, Newton, 215n30
gendered divisions of labor. *See* labor, gendered
Gilbert's Act, 220n22
global Romanticism, 163, 206
Goldstein, Amanda Jo, 52, 84
Goodman, Kevin, 59
Gordon Riots, 52, 222n40
gossip, 109, 122, 125, 129, 190; dreams and, 7; in "The Thorn," 124; village, 14, 105, 108, 110, 123
Green, Georgiana, 224n61
Griffiths, Devin, 72, 73, 76, 80, 226n6
Groce, Dorothy "Cherry," 241n1
gross body of life, 36, 86, 230n50

growth-by-death, 62
guerillas, 68, 198, 199, 203, 210
Guyana, 206
Guyer, Sara, 36, 95, 181

Haiti, 120, 121
Hall, Stuart, 58–59, 61, 225n2
Handsworth Songs, 139–47, 151, 161, 178; capitalism's emergence and, 31; constellation of, 175; making of, 217n68; organizing schema of, 143; race in, 162, 179; stills, *144, 145*
Haraway, Donna, 227n9
Hartley, David, 10, 41–42, 49, 52, 53, 56, 225n69; associationist principles, 152; on dreams, 73, 74, 80, 91; enclosure, 76, 232n68; materialism, 55, 59; mechanical expression of need, 44; mechanistic materialism, 45; *Observations on Man*, 245n35, 346n42; principle of vibration, 85, 86; progressive divisions, 50; regulated motions, 75; secondary automation, 222–23n45; spatial and temporal anachronisms, 75; theory of association, 40
Hartman, Saidiya, 52, 66, 89, 90, 91, 190, 232n65
Hawhee, Debra, 228n21
hearsay, 30, 104, 105, 107, 109, 115, 122, 123; superstitious, 111; transformation to weapon of enforced scarcity, 124
hedges, 116, 117, *117*, 118
Hegel, G. W. F., 100, 102, 103, 105, 107, 112, 136, 235n19; concept of totality, 213n13; self-conscious subjects, 115
Hethel Thorn, The, 107
historical origins, 4, 16, 22, 25, 170, 204

history, collective, 75, 232n70
history, universal, 140, 164, 165, 179; abstraction and, 171, 174; simultaneous figures and, 147–64
homogeneity, 2, 31, 64, 78, 95, 227n9. *See also* sameness
homogenization, 7, 73, 153, 173, 180; capitalism and, 151, 167; capitalist drivers of, 2; of the thorn, 118; of tree species, 117
Humboldt, Alexander von, 147, 175, 176, 177, 178, 179, 180, 181
Hunter, John, 28, 74, 75, 80
Husserl, Edmund, 214n24
hysteria, 90, 134, 234n5

Igbo ethnicity, 113
Imagination, 86, 230n50
inactivity, 3, 7, 8
incarceration, 91, 92, 232n65. *See also* criminalization
India, 105, 206, 238n58
Indigenous peoples, 126, 146, 165, 170, 175, 197
indirections, direct, 44, 45, 46, 47, 50, 63, 66, 146
indirections, rhetorical, 39, 40, 43, 45
Industrial Revolution, 140, 147, 242n5
industrialism, 4, 31, 61
industrialization, 64, 76, 148, 170; capitalism identified with, 36; Darwin on, 147; of England, 136, 170; in *Handsworth Songs*, 139, 140; of labor, 1, 37; of logic, 32, 142; Lunar Society's investments in, 146; Priestley is proponent of, 9; of production, 78; telos of, 171, 179
infinite circulation, 76, 77
invisible hand, 50, 72, 73, 78

Ireland, 190, 192, 201, 206, 254n50
Islamic State, 198, 252n29
Israel, 204, 205, 208, 253n39, 253n44
Italy, 176, 201

Jamaica, 119, 122, 171, 236n23; Moseley's plantocratic, 102, 121; Obeah in, 30, 98, 134; slavery in, 68, 104, 207, 235n22; sugar production in, 113; supernatural in, 99; witch hunts in, 138; witchcraft in, 31, 114, 234n4
Jarrett, Cynthia, 242n1
Johnson, Barbara, 36, 81, 85

Kant, Immanuel, 12, 127, 161, 213n10
Keller, Yacobi, 253n39
Kelley, Theresa M., 223n52
Khalip, Jacques, 213n13
King, Walker, 218n8
Küçük, Bülent, 198, 252n29
Kurdistan, 198, 199, 252n29

La Mettrie, Julian Offray de, 39, 142, 219n10
labor, divisions of, 109, 151; modern capitalist, 89, 99; organizational nature of, 221n33; in Romanticism, 202; social potential for, 112; in value form of equivalence, 17
labor, gendered, 14, 28, 29, 71, 88, 92, 93, 131, 191
labor, industrialized, 37
labor, reproductive, 65, 92, 197; devalued, 24; in Marx's Eurocentric model of history, 18; as subsistence, 25, 132; unpaid, 90, 231n53; as unproductive, 26, 87, 91; witch hunts and, 89, 109
labor, unmeasured, 36, 52, 63, 66

labor, unpaid, 123, 131, 132, 133, 136; deferral of commodification through, 66; dispossessions of, 38; of enslaved people, women, and nature, 18; reproductive labor becomes, 89, 90; subsistence ways of living associated with, 3; surplus of need distributed as, 27; women's labor became, 29
labor, unproductive, 26, 29, 89, 91, 131
labor, waged, 46, 50, 66, 122, 169, 170, 172; plantation, 239n65; resistance to, 181
labor market, 27, 46, 65, 201
labor power, 16, 18, 65, 66, 67, 82, 131, 171
Langan, Celeste, 76, 82, 92
language, 5, 93, 204, 216n51; of associationism, 210; Coleridge and, 9, 14, 15; figural, 7, 23, 52; figurative, 2, 10, 81; of magic, 136; materiality of, 20, 111; origins, 9, 10, 12, 13; poetic, 2, 6; Priestley on, 10–13, 240n84; rhetorical, 2, 6, 12, 22; simultaneity and spatiality, 179; of superstition, 114, 126; thingliness of, 110; translation, 21–22; use of, 7, 12, 13, 15, 16, 20, 21, 32; use value of, 7–8, 11, 20; Wordsworth on, 13, 15
language, rhetorical, 8
Laurence, French, 218n8
levers, 44, 45, 46, 65
Levine, Caroline, 226n6
Lévi-Strauss, Claude, 100
Lichfield, England, 53, 56, 58, 61
linearity, 147, 152, 187, 189, 242n4, 244n25; of time, 149
Linebaugh, Peter, 38, 54, 209, 254n50
Lloyd, David, 102, 138, 235n19, 250n83, 250n87

Locke, John, 9, 228n21
London, UK, 48, 54, 207, 208, 242n5, 243n5, 251n13. *See also* England
Lorrington, Meribah, 192
ludicrous anachronism, 28, 29, 74, 92
Lunar Society, 31, 55, 56, 171, 172, 177; industrial and scientific endeavors of, 169; role in Industrial Revolution, 146, 242n5; science of, 147; utopianism, technology, and capitalism of, 148
Luxemburg, Rosa, 23–24, 26, 28, 138
Lynch, Samuel, 60

Macbeth, 100, 108, 116
Mackey, Charles, 236n29
Makdisi, Saree, 30, 123, 171
Mandeville, Bernard, 54
maroons, 121, 135, 170, 199, 210, 239n64. *See also* enslaved
Marxism and Marxists, 185, 248n67; on enclosure, 169; feminists, 27, 28; on historical modes of production, 52; on modernity, 25; treatments of capitalism, 2, 6
materialism, 7, 43, 86, 247n52; account of translation, 22; Benjamin's historical work in, 189; conception of life and health in, 245n40; Darwin and, 55, 56, 59, 101, 222n45; economy of reciprocal relations, 40–41; empiricism, 247n52; Hartleyan, 45, 55, 59, 86; historical, 5, 37; historical materialist process, 167; history of, 113; horizontal ontologies and, 31; Humboldt and, 125, 175; irreducibly relational reproduction and, 52; poetic, 84; Priestley and, 4; product of associated differences,

245n35; in Romanticism, 7, 44, 171, 188
materiality, 21, 52, 140, 242n4; of association, 187; of bodies, 173; of everyday lives, 201; of form, 143; of language, 20, 111; metonymic, 102; Shelley's language of, 33; of time and space, 86
McLane, Maureen, 160, 219n16, 241n92
McNeil, Maureen, 56, 59, 172
means of reproduction, 39, 46, 67, 169, 194, 233n79; dispossession through, 4; noncommodified, 55; unwaged, 172
Memory, 86, 230n50
meter, 80, 82, 110, 230n41, 237n41
Mexico, 156, 175, 176
Mezzadra, Sandro, 250n87
Middle East, 252n29
Mill, John Stuart, 120–21
Mintz, Sidney, 236n26
Modern Language Association (MLA), 204, 205, 209
modernity, capitalist, 2, 99, 112, 114, 150, 151, 164
money form, 17, 19, 20, 76–77, 120, 121, 137. See also form
moral economy, 26, 27, 40, 221n34
Moseley, Benjamin, 99, 102, 112, 118–24, 133–36, 236n23, 238n58, 239n70; on Obeah, 101, 103, 104, 112, 114, 122, 134, 135; *Treatise on Sugar*, 30, 100, 104–5, 106
Moten, Fred, 7, 8, 94, 95, 118, 171, 172, 203
mutuality, 24, 94, 110

Naples, 176
nature, reverting to, *173*

needs, material, 43, 65, 66, 68, 142, 180, 187
Nemser, Daniel, 175
New Chart of History, A, 147, 150–56. See also Priestley, Joseph; blank spaces on, 158; color version of, *149*; *Handsworth Songs* and, 140; history and race, 250n87; linear concept, 246n41; linearity and uniformity, 244n25; linearity of time and uniformity of space, 149; as racial, 168; racial capitalism and, 171; sections from, *157*, *159*; self-regulation and universal history, 164–65; stagist theory of race, 167; subsistence-style living and, 172; subsumption of modern history, 31; understood within single visual frame, 180–81; uniform time flow, 148; vacant spaces of past and future on, 173; working class and, 174
New Historicism, 5, 213n13
New Kingdom of Spain, 163
New Spain, 175
New York, 201
New Zealand, 206
Newgate Prison, 49, 52
Nigeria, 185, 197, 200, 201, 203
Ninham, Henry, *107*
noncapitalist formations, 23
nonequivalence, 27, 50, 61, 92, 128, 136. See also equivalence
nonidentity, 73, 84, 92, 175
North America, 205. See also Canada; United States
Norwood forest, 97, 98

Obeah, 101, 103, 104, 112, 122, 234n3, 234n4, 235n10. See also Obi; in

Obeah (cont.)
    Jamaica, 30, 98, 134; Moseley on, 101, 103, 104, 112, 114, 122, 134, 135; objects, 100; originates from Africa, 98, 114, 134, 135; practices, 25, 30
Obi, 106, 127, 217n66, 234n2, 239n70. See also Obeah; objects, 30, 100, 114, 133, 135
"Oppressed, the," 39–41, 47, 48
origin scene, 10, 12, 14, 15
origins, historical, 4, 16, 22, 25, 170, 204
ornament, 9, 11, 14, 16
Osborne, Thomas, 166
overaccumulation, 172. See also accumulation
ownership, 94
Özselçuk, Ceren, 198, 252n29

Palestine, 185, 197, 204–9, 253n44, 254n51
Palmieri, Frank, 158, 160
palmistry, 89, 97. See also fortune-tellers
Pappe, Ilan, 253n44
Paris Commune, 221n35
Pasolini, Pier Paolo, 254n51
Paton, Diana, 98, 99, 122, 234n2, 234n4, 235n10
Perloff, Marjorie, 242n4
personification, 81, 82
Peru, 156
phenomenology, 103, 137, 214n24, 235n22
Picchio, Antonella, 64, 66, 67, 91, 221n33, 221n34, 224n59, 233n79
Pitt, William, 220n22
plantation economy, 120–21, 123, 131, 132, 236n23
Playfair, William, 244n25

poetics, 85, 86, 123; enclosure, 71–78; Romantic, 227n9, 229n30, 254n49
poetry, lyric, 5, 8, 11, 36, 95
poetry, Romantic, 1, 76, 92, 226n6, 227n9, 228n22
poets, Romantic, 13, 28, 94, 152
political economy, 8, 38, 59, 66, 78, 91, 228n21, 230n43, 232n68
Poor Laws, 168, 172. See also vagrancy laws
populations, surplus, 36, 44, 45, 46, 67, 194, 219n17
possession, 26, 82, 88, 132, 203
poverty, 67, 83, 190, 195, 196, 201, 239n70
Priestley, Joseph, 18, 20, 160. See also New Chart of History, A; axis of succession and simultaneity, 177; British empiricism and, 55; on commonality of the human species, 247n59; on costs of production and reproduction, 249n68; on dispossession, 180; distribution of space, 246n44; on figure, 245n35; Handsworth Songs and, 146; on history, 175, 178; history of, 32; on history of empire, 163; in the Industrial Revolution, 140; on industrialization, 9; on language, 10–13; language of simultaneity and spatiality, 179; narrative of subsistence, 174; nonidentitarian ontology of, 175; on process of reverting to nature, 173; science of language, 240n84; sense of history, 246n42; statue of, 141; on subsistence, 4–5, 172, 173, 176; on "The Thorn," 14–15; on universal history, 161, 162; on waged work, 169
primitive accumulation. See accumulation, primitive

Prince, Mary, 207
Prince of Wales, 71, 83, 193
production, mode of, 16, 95, 114, 120, 131, 209; agrarian, 1; capitalist, 17, 87, 91, 217n1, 249n67; mechanized, 59; slave, 103
profit, 23, 65, 66, 91, 120, 170, 221n34, 239n63; antiprofiteering, 51; capitalist, 44; loss of, 64
property, 3, 54, 90, 193, 202, 240n79; bourgeois, 189; communal, 2; to defy appropriation, 235n19; possession and, 88; private, 4, 55
proprietorship, 94

racialization, 142, 230n48; accumulation and, 77, 164, 169, 171, 174; capitalism, 137; civilization, 214n22; difference, 131; empathy, 190; of enclosure of subsistence ways of life, 32; of gender, 132; global capital accumulation through, 248n63; in *Handsworth Songs*, 146; of labor, 132; reproduction, 130; of subsistence, 3, 8, 25, 147, 163, 164–81; violence, 124; violence of dispossession as, 33
racism, 142, 167, 172, 232n65, 242n1, 250n88; scientific modes of, 32
reading, rhetorical, 2, 3, 4, 8, 164, 185, 190, 202, 209
Red Round Globe Burning Hot, 8, 209
regular irregularity, 80, 94
relation, indirect, 47, 58, 61, 62, 63, 65, 82, 83, 92
relationality, 67, 72, 77, 92, 162, 167, 226n6, 248n63; of emergent scientific epistemologies, 71
relations, rhetorical, 18, 19, 40, 43, 131, 153

repetition and tautology, 14, 138, 237n41
reproduction, indirect, 45–53, 62
rhetoric, Romantic, 2, 49, 52, 68
Ricardo, David, 45, 64, 224n58
Richter-Devroe, Sophie, 207
riot of 1981, 139
riot of 1985, 139
riots, food, 15, 27, 46, 51, 53, 68, 194, 199, 218n8
Riots, Gordon, 52, 222n40
riots of 1795, 15, 26, 27, 38, 45, 53, 66, 69, 220n22
Robinson, Cedric, 61, 137, 170
Robinson, Mary, 196, 197, 200, 201, 203, 207, 232n70; biography of, 191–92; Coleridge on, 229n31, 230n41; dream economies, 79–85; dreams and enclosure, 95; ludicrous anachronism of, 92; "The Maniac," 28, 29, 71, 73, 77, 78, 82, 87; memory and imagination, 86; mother-daughter-witch and, 190; primitive accumulation and, 193; Prince of Wales and, 71, 83; regular irregularity of poem, 94; spatial and temporal anachronisms, 75; on writing "The Maniac," 72
Rojava, Syria, 184, 197, 198, 200, 203, 252n29
Romantic period, 206, 210, 242n5; "biopoetics" of, 95; British, 168; capital accumulation in, 78; disciplinary knowledge and palliative poetics of, 229n30; early, 38, 147, 222n44; emergence of capitalism during, 31; figural vs. historical mode of subsistence, 16; habits of working poor in, 4; models of life and

284 INDEX

Romantic period (*cont.*)
history, 77; poetry of, 51; quasi-universal Woman in, 191; relevance to capitalism, 35; subsistence in, 67; subsistence ways of living in, 3, 36, 37, 63; ways of life and systems of knowledge, 114
Romantic rhetoric, 2, 49, 52, 68
Romantic science, 53, 72, 226n6
Romanticism, global, 163, 206
Rosenberg, Daniel, 149, 150, 152, 153, 156, 158, 246n41, 246n48; on historiography, 243n16
Rosenberg, Jordy, 54, 221n32, 222n42, 228n21, 232n68
Ross, Kristin, 51, 221–22n35
Ross, Marlon B., 167, 248n62
Rousseau, 9, 10, 13

Sachs, Jonathan, 150, 152, 181, 244n25
Sacks, Jeffrey, 204, 205
Said, Edward, 205
Salih, Ruba, 207
salt, 102–3, 112, 115, 116, 119, 125, 236n22, 238n58
sameness, 2, 9, 10, 25, 92, 127, 128, 138, 203. *See also* homogenization; abstract, 17; vs. difference, 226n6; historical, 114; of meaning, 21; production of, 153, 237n43; referential, 216n51; of repetition, 111; repetition of, 136
Sanyal, Kalyan, 24
schema, 23, 26, 143, 202; associative, 147; of histories of science, 175; organizing, 162; of primitive accumulation, 197; of representation, 194
Schey, Taylor, 77, 81, 84, 226n6
Schiebinger, Londa, 222n44

Schiller, Friedrich, 213n10
Schofield, Robert, 169
Schuller, Kyla, 214n22
self-regulation, 41, 45, 165, 167, 192, 237n41; of habits, 49, 124
self-representation, 82, 193, 197
sensation histories, 85–96, 232n70
sense experience, 100, 101, 102, 103, 110, 115, 135, 137
separation-with-equivalence, 67
Sha, Richard, 226n6
Shaw, Rosalind, 112–13, 114
Sheehan, Jonathan, 72, 76, 78, 85, 92, 226n6, 232n68
Shelley, Percy, 33, 84
Sierra Leone, 206. *See also* Africa
signification, 10, 11, 105, 135, 138, 227n9
Simmel, Georg, 223n47
simple elements, 110, 111, 177, 178
simultaneity, 3, 19, 32, 102, 186, 197, 199, 200, 201; axis of succession and, 177, 178; of back-stories, 85; capital accumulation ordered by, 75; of capitalism, 164, 168, 170, 171; of capital's traumatic origins, 188; contradictions of, 8; of "elsewhere," 165; enclosure and, 93; of impressions, 73; of industrialization, 147; language of, 5, 179; of opposing conditions, 74; preserves difference, 92; in Priestley's *A New Chart of History*, 177, 246n48; of subsistence, 11; of subsistence-style living and modernity, 147
simultaneous figures, 147–64
slave trade, 112–13, 114, 121, 130, 146, 170, 228n21. *See also* enslaved; enslavement
Sloane, Hans, 57

Smith, Adam, 22, 45, 64, 72, 150
social relations, 12, 16, 19, 112, 130, 133, 137, 185, 208; hierarchical, 99; open-ended, 73; of sense, 10
social reproduction, 19, 47, 49, 64, 65, 93, 130, 201, 221n33; accumulation and, 132, 184; antiracist labors of, 33; labors of, 197
societalization, 223n47
Sohn-Rethel, Alfred, 17
solidarity, 2, 28, 30, 85
solidity, 102, 153, 154
South Africa, 204, 206, 253n39. *See also* Africa
South America, 24, *106*. *See also* America
sovereignty, 94, 209, 224n61, 233n73
space-time, 29, 73, 74, 158, *159*, 180, 181, 252n23
Spanish America, 175
Spanish Empire, 146
spatiotemporality, 147, 150, 179, 248n63
speech, 31, 36, 48, 105, 111, 119, 122, 223n49, 241n92; acts, 9, 12, 222n35; direct, 38, 39, 40; figures of, 7, 39, 40; indirect, 38, 40, 42, 44, 219n15; tautological, 14
Speenhamland system, 220n22
Spence, Thomas, 48, 207
Spielrein, Sabina, 183, 184, 185, 186, 190, 191, 193, 195, 197
Spillers, Hortense, 131, 135, 137, 240n79
stagism, 160, 164, 165, 167, 174, 247n59
standardization, 17, 20, 21, 78, 147, 170, 173, 227n9, 228n25; epistemologies and technologies of, 244n25; equivalences and, 93, 228n22; of labor, 28; modern history and, 31; repetition of events and, 150, 152

stimulation, 42, 43, 152, 155; absence of external, 80–81; external, 148, 223n45; imbalance in, 79; of phenomena, 163; physiological, 39; of subsistence, 40; subsistence-style, 44
Stoler, Ann Laura, 207, 233n73
sublime, 213n10
subsistence, 33, 51, 209; affectability of, 248n62; apostrophic, 35–45; contingency and, 63; divisions of, 3; economy of, 46, 50, 55, 64; exchange value and, 55, 62, 67, 68; figuration of, 15; figuring, 9–19; nature of, 51, 52, 63, 64–67; racializing, 3, 8, 25, 147, 163, 164–81; reproductive labor as, 25, 132; simultaneity of, 11; temporal location of, *173*; thingliness, 118, 122
subsistence ways of living, 22, 36, 98, 99, 118, 142, 169, 179. *See also* ways of living, noncapitalist; criminalization of, 27; dependency of capital accumulation on, 8; destroyed in primitive accumulation, 17; dispossession and, 2, 4; in England, 37, 163, 170; in Romantic period, 37; unpaid labor and, 3; use value and, 19
substitution, 43, 193, 197, 202, 205, 240n79; historicizing, 9–19; Marx's tracking of, 212n10; reduction of figure to, 4; subsumption by, 26
succession, 74, 75, 93, 178, 197, 212n10; confines of, 186; figures become, 246n42; spatial and temporal conditions of, 73; of time, 177
sufficient commons, 14, 30, 115–26, 132
sugar, history of, 30, 104–5, 112. *See also* Treatise on Sugar: Medical Tracts, A

sugar production, 113, 119, 136
supernatural, 112, 129, 134; among the enslaved, 113; beliefs in England, 98–99; Coleridge, Wordsworth, and Moseley on, 136; conduits of, 135; depictions, 103; enacted in witching hour, 89; in "Goody Blake and Harry Gill," 230n43; Kant on, 127; Moseley on, 30; Robinson's use of, 81, 83; Shaw and Brown on, 114; in "The Thorn," 107; Witchcraft Act and, 111
supply-and-demand, 61, 64, 65
sympathy, 80, 83, 101, 110, 111, 124; economy of, 84; industry of, 190; with riotous dispositions, 69

Table of Excitement and Excitability, 60
Tacky's Rebellion, 98
Taussig, Michael, 24, 26
tautological gatherings, 97–115
tautology, 3, 4, 19, 109, 110, 128, 237n43; clustering effect of, 114; disorderly gathering of, 125; mode of, 111, 118; physiognomic, 129; reading situates, 138; and repetition, 14, 138, 237n41; repetition vs., 14, 29; of superstition, 124; in "The Three Graves," 126; Wordsworth on, 112, 237n40, 241n92; teleology, 19, 24, 164, 175, 203
temporalities, 32, 66, 110, 128, 150, 158, 168, 179; anachronistic, 87; developmental, 163; heterogeneous, 153; of immediacy, 28; of mature commodity capitalism, 19; multiple, 195; simultaneous, 233n73
Terada, Rei, 245n39
Thelwall, John, 69
thingliness, 19, 30, 110, 114, 116, 128, 136; arrangements, 136; bodies, 31, 109;

inextricability, 117; of language, 110; relations, 138; subsistence, 118, 122; tautological, 30
Thompson, E. P., 27, 46, 51, 54, 68, 221n34, 224n59, 243n5; moral economy of the past of, 26; parody of the riot, 215n38; rebellions of the belly of, 40; on riots, 38
thorn, 97, 107, 115–18, *117*, 123–26, 134; *Hethel Thorn, The*, *107*; tree, *108*, 117
"Three Graves, The," 30, 97, 126, 127, 128, 133, 239n68
translation, language, 21–22
Treatise on Sugar: Medical Tracts, A, 106
tropes, 30, 39, 52, 98, 138, 213n10; of analogy, 72, 228n21; apostrophe as, 36; as medium of exchange, 212n10; of metaphor, 73; of the stage, 193
Turkey, 198
Turtle Island, 170

ungendering, 131–32, 133, 240n79
uniformity, 152, 154, 174, 244n25, 247n52; of abstraction, 167; capitalism and, 161, 168, 170, 173; of space, 149, 150; temporal, 155, 163–64, 180
United States, 89, 95, 170, 206. *See also* North America
universal equivalence, 22, 48, 120, 126, 138, 202, 228n25; figure as, 212n10
universality, 28, 121, 127, 137, 161, 202
use value, 16, 17, 19, 21, 23, 24, 132; of language, 7–8, 9, 11, 20
Üstündağ, Nazan, 198–200, 203

Vagabond Act of 1597, 98
vagrancy laws, 26, 55, 71, 88–89, 98. *See also* Bloody Laws

Vassa, Gustauvus/Equiano, Olaudah, 113
Victorian period, 171
violences, state, 139, 170, 195, 197, 198
vulnerability, 28, 83, 89, 91, 94, 186, 192–93, 194; gendered, 191, 201; shared, 84

wage form, 28, 29, 36, 63, 65, 169. *See also* form
Wahrman, Dror, 72, 76, 78, 85, 92, 226n6, 232n68
Wales, 201, 206. *See also* British Empire
Walker, Gavin, 76
wanderings, 3, 7, 36, 72, 88, 89, 94, 192, 215n32; bodies, 92, 135; poor, 37; potential ways of, 199
Wang, Jackie, 27, 53, 93
Wang, Orrin, 227n15
Watt, James, 140, *141*, 146, 148, 169; flour mill of, 242–43n5; and Industrial Revolution, 147
way of meaning, 27, 28, 216n51
ways of being, 1, 6, 213n14, 243n13
ways of living, criminalized, 27
ways of living, noncapitalist, 3, 13, 22, 24, 98, 114, 126, 180, 189; accumulation of, 202; destruction of, 170, 195; reproduction of, 2
ways of living, subsistence. *See* subsistence ways of living
ways of meaning, 8, 21, 26, 32
Wedderburn, Robert, 4, 5, 48, 68, 122, 207, 236n23
Weheliye, Alexander G., 133, 137, 138
West Africa, 112–14, 138. *See also* Africa
West Indies, 100, 104, 119, 120, 121, 127, 165, 206. *See also* Caribbean; prisons for slaves in, 208; Romanticism in, 254n50; women in, 130
Wheeler, Roxanne, 164
Whitener, Brian, 195
Wilson Gilmore, Ruth, 170, 174, 250n88
Wimsatt, W. K., Jr., 86, 230n50
witch hunts, 26, 95, 114, 129, 132; in England and Jamaica, 138; Federici on, 14, 99, 108, 112, 124, 200; importance to capital accumulation, 112; modern violence of, 14; primitive accumulation of, 137; reproductive labor and, 89, 109
witchcraft, 7, 25, 101, 108, 124, 137, 138, 187; accusations of, 109, 114, 122; in the Americas, 234n4; criminalization of, 30–31, 97–98; Federici on, 89; historical revisioning of, 113; hysteria and, 234n5; Mackey on, 236n29; Moseley on, 239n70; Obi, 127; *On Obi, or African Witchcraft*, 106; in "The Thorn," 126; in West Africa, 112; in Wordsworth and Coleridge, 132
Witchcraft Act of 1736, 98, 107, 111, 128, 130
witching hours, 81, 82, 83, 85–96
Wordsworth, William, 35, 114, 127, 128, 130, 138, 225n67, 230n41; "Goody Blake and Harry Gill," 193, 230n43; on language, 13, 15; as liberal mediator, 122; orientation to a modern market, 1; on personification, 81; poetry of, 13, 30, 107, 112; poetry's recessive action, 52; remediating writing, 241n92; repetitive phrasing in, 117; science and poetry of regulation, 229n30; sense of tautology, 112; sobriety of, 80; sublime in,

Wordsworth, William (*cont.*) 213n10; on subsistence, 32; on the supernatural, 136; on supernatural with subsistence ways of living in, 99; on superstition, 111; superstition in work of, 123, 124; on tautology, 29, 112, 237n40, 241n92; theory of meter, 237n41; "The Thorn," 14, 97, 105, 107, 109, 110; "The Three Graves," 126; witchcraft in works of, 30, 132

working class, 46, 64, 66, 89, 133, 137, 212n7, 220n21, 241n91; English, 169–71, 174, 175; hatred of, 199; home of, 210

working poor, 4, 46, 48, 133, 137, 168, 169, 172, 175

wretched thing, 115–26, 132

Wynter, Silvia, 137

Xin, Wendy, 242n4

The authorized representative in the EU for product safety and compliance is:
Mare Nostrum Group
B.V Doelen 72
4831 GR Breda
The Netherlands

www.ingramcontent.com/pod-product-compliance
Lightning Source LLC
Chambersburg PA
CBHW021959220426
43663CB00007B/885